ASIAN DUMPLINGS

Asian Dumplings

Mastering Gyōza, Spring Rolls, Samosas, and More

ANDREA QUYNHGIAO NGUYEN

Photography by Penny De Los Santos

Ten Speed Press
Berkeley

All rights reserved.
Published in the United States by Ten Speed Press, an imprint of the Crown Publishing Group,
a division of Random House, Inc., New York.
www.crownpublishing.com
www.tenspeed.com

Ten Speed Press and the Ten Speed Press colophon are registered trademarks of Random House, Inc.

Library of Congress Cataloging-in-Publication Data on file with publisher.

ISBN: 978-1-58008-975-3

Printed in China

Design by Betsy Stromberg
Illustrations by Ann Miya

11

First Edition

Contents

Introduction

Dumplings make people smile. At their core, they are fun, uncomplicated, wonderfully satisfying foods that can be enjoyed with a crowd or savored in solitude. They're reminders of good times—preparing them for family, noshing on them with friends, or queuing up for them with great anticipation. The individual dough morsels, diminutive pouches, and leaf-wrapped packages contain treasures that never fail to please the palate.

I've enjoyed a dumpling-filled life since my youth. One of the first cooking assignments my mother gave me (after cooking rice) was folding wontons. After all, we ate rice daily and frequently ate fried wontons and wontons in soup. My mother was smart to figure out that a precocious ten-year-old was perfect for these elementary but crucial family kitchen duties.

Making batches of 150 to 200 wontons became part of my life, and I rarely thought of it as drudgery. I rather liked folding different shapes and devising new methods to make the work go faster and better. I didn't always work alone; sometimes my siblings and I challenged one another to see who could fold the prettiest wontons or pleated pot stickers.

We used premade wrappers for Chinese-style dumplings because they were readily available, but there was no such convenience for Vietnamese dumplings. Those were my mother's specialty, and she prepared hers from scratch to ensure that our family had the tastes of our homeland. Treats such as *bánh ít* (Steamed Sticky Rice Dumplings with Shrimp and Pork, page 168) were part of my options for both breakfast and afternoon snacks. We also exchanged gifts of homemade Vietnamese dumplings with family and friends—we all knew they were hard to come by in the United States.

I've probably eaten as many Asian dumplings "out" as I have at home. My father regularly piled us into our Buick Estate Wagon and drove over an hour to Chinatown in Los Angeles for Saturday morning dim sum. In the restaurants' din, I listened carefully for the dumpling ladies' melodious calls as they made their rounds of the tables: *har gow, siu mai, char siu bao*—the Cantonese names of perennial favorites (shrimp dumplings, cook-and-sell dumplings, and roasted pork buns, respectively).

During a yearlong fellowship in Hong Kong in the early 1990s, I explored first-rate

1

dim sum houses, experienced for the first time wondrous translucent Chiu Chow Dumplings (page 137) filled with a nutty surf-and-turf mixture, and nibbled on magnificent tiny steamed buns on a trip to Yunnan province in China. I observed professional dumpling cooks whenever possible, and upon returning to the United States, not only did I continue to seek out more Asian dumplings, I also began experimenting with making Chinese and other styles of wrappers from scratch. I asked my mother about Vietnamese dumplings, their fillings, dough, and cooking techniques. It wasn't long before I realized that there were many similarities among the dumplings enjoyed in Asia.

I studied cookbooks for tips and keys to unlock the world of Asian dumplings. My skills improved through lots of trial-and-error, as there was no publication dedicated to Asian dumplings and cooking classes on the subject were extremely rare. The dough and rolling techniques were hard to figure out at first, and

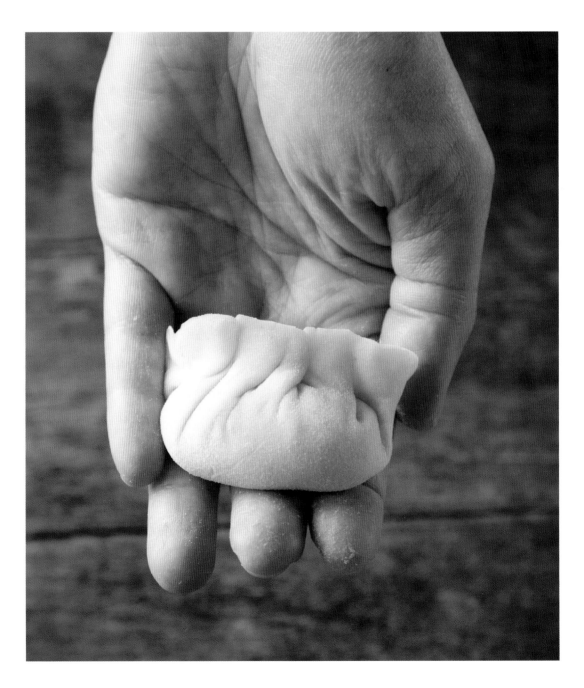

I made plenty of blunders, but my clumsy-looking results always at least tasted good. In fact, over my years of eating and cooking, and especially through the process of polishing the recipes for this book, the most important insights I've gained are these:

- Asian dumplings don't have to look pretty to taste fabulous.

- With few exceptions, there are numerous ways to fold and shape a dumpling.

- Practice is the way to mastery, but you really don't have to lead a dumpling-obsessed life to learn to make them well.

- You get to eat your mistakes! Enjoy them as much as you do your successes.

Defining Asia and Asian Dumplings

Asia is either huge or humongous, depending on where you draw the defining boundaries. Though the Middle East, Turkey, the Central Asian republics, and most of Russia are, geographically speaking, part of Asia, the recipes in this book come from the three subregions of East Asia, Southeast Asia, and South Asia. A good number of the dumplings from this vast swathe of territory have Chinese roots, as the Middle Kingdom's preparations begot many others throughout Asia, and because Cantonese dim sum is popular all over Asia and abroad wherever there are large Asian populations.

But what exactly is a dumpling in the Asian context? Many English speakers categorize Asian-filled pastas, such as pot stickers and wontons, as dumplings, but in actuality the concept of the dumpling does not exist in the Asian culinary framework.

Writing in the third century c.e., Chinese poet Shu Xi, considered one of the most learned men of his day, described a number of Chinese foods made from wheat as being members of the *bǐng* family of doughy concoctions. In "Rhapsody on Bǐng," Shu Xi lumped filled dumplings, stuffed buns, baked and fried breads, and noodles in that one category of food, without discriminating among their differences. Wheat-milling technology had been introduced to China from western Asia (now the Middle East), and at the time of Shu Xi's composition, meat-filled morsels were prepared in other parts of Asia, so the Chinese were adopters, not inventors. The point here is that there has long been a huge variety of foods that may be called Asian dumplings.

In the same vein as Shu Xi (if many hundreds of years later), acclaimed Chinese cookbook author Irene Kuo described pot stickers, *siu mai*, wontons, egg rolls, buns, and the like as "dough stuffs" in her classic 1977 work *The Key to Chinese Cooking*. In the Vietnamese repertoire, such foods belong in the immense category of *bánh*. Similarly, *kuih* is the Malay term attached to a large category of savory and sweet cakes, pastries, and dumplings. An Indian *vada* can be described as a fritter, doughnut, cake, or dumpling.

Ambiguity aside, all dumplings share certain characteristics. They are simple foods with few social pretensions. On occasion they feature meat or seafood, but for the most part, they involve dough made from staple grains, legumes, or vegetables, along with water, salt, and, sometimes, leaven. It is the humble nature of dumplings that steals people's hearts.

After spending much time pondering, researching, and preparing these foods, I can conclude that for the purposes of this book, Asian dumplings include savory and sweet dishes that are made from balls of dough, or are small parcels of food encased in pastry, dough, batter, or leaves. As you can imagine, there are endless possibilities, and the recipes herein offer a broad sampling to hone your skills and whet your appetite for more.

Why Make Wrappers from Scratch?

Commercially made wonton, pot sticker, egg roll, and spring roll skins are readily available in the refrigerated section of most supermarkets, but there is a marked difference in the end results when you make the wrappers from scratch. Many cooks cannot fathom preparing Asian dumplings without the store-bought skins; but in fact, there are Asian cooks who could not imagine dumplings without homemade ones.

I could not present a pan-Asian collection of dumplings if the focus was on premade wrappers because that would narrowly limit recipes to certain Chinese or Chinese-inspired preparations. The world of Asian dumplings is vast, and you can only begin to taste and experience the multitude of dumplings if you venture beyond the skins available on grocery store shelves. Asian dumpling masters, whether professionals or home cooks, take pride in making their own skins and dough. With a little guidance, you can too. Additionally, after you've made dumplings from scratch, you will become a more informed dumpling diner, as you'll have a deeper understanding of what goes into making stupendous ones.

Fresh wrappers are easier to prepare and to work with than people think, as they do not need to be moistened to seal. They also stretch and are very forgiving, yielding to your pulling, pleating, and pinching. Surprisingly, many dough ingredients are available at regular supermarkets, while specialty flours and starches are standard items at Asian markets. You may not always have time to make dumpling wrappers from scratch, which is why there are "Lazy Day Tips" scattered in this book to guide you when you want to substitute store-bought skins.

A Cook's Guide to This Book

To direct you toward success, the recipes in this book are arranged in a progressive manner. Chapters are organized by dough types to help you focus and develop your skills. A master dough or batter recipe often leads, and recipes with different fillings and cooking methods follow.

The collection begins with dumplings encased in a basic wrapper made of all-purpose flour and water. If you then add egg, leaven or fat, you can create more complex doughs for knockout thin wonton skins, pillowy stuffed buns, and flaky pastries. After the section on dumplings based on wheat-flour dough, subsequent chapters focus on dumplings that employ less familiar ingredients, such as wheat starch, tapioca starch, and legumes and tubers. Interspersed among those recipes are a few that use banana leaf as an inedible wrapper that imparts special fragrance and flavor. See "Tips for Success" on page 19 for specific hints on using the recipes.

Use the drawings in this book to help you shape dumplings, but also look online at Asiandumplingtips.com for additional assistance in the form of photos and video. You'll be able to obtain extra information, pose questions, and share knowledge.

Essential and Handy Equipment

You will need basic kitchen equipment and a few modestly priced additions to prepare the recipes in this book. Sharp knives make fast work of prepping filling ingredients; the Japanese-style *santoku* and *usuba* knives are great for producing thin slices and fine cuts. A food processor, an electric mini-chopper, and a spice grinder (or electric coffee grinder reserved for spices) are all great time-savers for making dumplings.

To this battery of equipment, I encourage you to add three essential tools for preparing Asian dumplings: a wooden-dowel rolling pin, a Chinese steamer, and a scale.

Wooden-Dowel Rolling Pin Producing delicate round wrappers for dumplings is faster and much easier with a skinny, lightweight wooden rolling pin. One hand works the pin in short downward strokes while the other hand rotates the dough to create a thin, delicate wrapper. You can't do this quickly and efficiently with the standard Western rolling pin. Look for the Asian rolling pins at housewares and restaurant supply shops in Asian enclaves. They come in different widths, but one that is about 3/4 inch thick is standard. Or, go to a home improvement or hardware store and have a 12-inch section cut from a 3/4-inch-thick dowel. Before using it, lightly sand the dowel to ensure a smooth surface.

Chinese Steamer There are various ways to improvise the Chinese steaming process—ranging from crisscrossing chopsticks in a wok and balancing a plate of food on top to using recycled tin cans and a Western collapsible metal vegetable steaming basket—but the best tool for cooking dumplings is an actual Chinese steamer. It is an ingenious, well-thought-out piece of equipment that has been indispensable to Asian cooks for eons.

A metal Chinese steamer costs about $50; a bamboo steamer set costs roughly half as much. Years ago, these pieces of equipment were hard to find; but nowadays, they are widely available at Asian markets and cookware shops and online.

Made of aluminum or stainless steel, a multitiered metal steamer comprises a large bottom pan; two sturdy, stackable trays for holding the food to be cooked; and a domed lid. The bottom is lightweight, allowing you to bring lots of water to a boil quickly and keep it going without having to replenish the water often. The trays are perforated, usually with holes the size of peas or smaller, to allow steam to jet upward to cook the food. The lid's shape allows steam to circulate and condensation to drip down the sides of the steamer, not onto the food cooking on the trays.

I grew up cooking with a metal steamer, and I like them because they are durable and easy to clean. However, they are not as attractive as old-fashioned bamboo steamers, which can be taken directly from stovetop to table. Bamboo steamers are prone to mildew, burning, and falling apart, but those disadvantages can mostly be overcome if you wash and dry them carefully. During steaming, the bamboo absorbs excess moisture so there is no worry about condensation dripping down onto the food. When a bamboo steamer is new, it lends a subtle fragrance to dumplings, too.

Traditionally, one cooks with a bamboo steamer by placing it directly in a wok filled with water, but that method robs the wok of its hard-earned patina. I prefer to use a large (5 or 6-quart) pot or stockpot and place a round, perforated pizza pan or Chinese steamer rack atop. The width of the pot should be the same or a bit bigger than the steamer, and some overhang of the pan or rack is fine so long as the steamer tray covers all the holes. Then I stack the bamboo steamer trays atop for cooking. If you own both metal and bamboo steamers, combine the two: put the bamboo trays directly on top of the bottom pan of water, if they fit; or put the bamboo trays inside or on top of the metal ones.

In purchasing a metal steamer, select one with 12-inch-wide trays. I prefer stainless steel to aluminum. Ten-inch-wide bamboo steamers work best with most pots; if your setup for boiling water (whether a wok, a stockpot, or the bottom of a metal steamer) is wide enough, go for one with 12-inch-wide steamer trays. If you can individually select the bam-

boo steamer trays and lid, stack them together to ensure they fit together snugly before purchasing them. The trays should feel weighty, and the lid should be tightly woven. See the Resources section (page 226) for online vendors if you can't find one nearby.

Scale You may consider weighing ingredients to be restrictive and fussy, but weighing flours and starches will enable you to more consistently produce good dumpling dough. Methods of measuring by volume can yield significant variance, but a scale never lies. Digital scales are highly accurate, affordable, and easy to find at housewares shops. For the dry ingredient weights provided in the recipes, I used the scoop-and-level method to determine the volume equivalents.

Handy Tools and Helpful Gadgets Traditionally, rolling out the wrappers was done entirely by hand with wooden-dowel rolling pins, with old and young pitching in as a group to move things along. But a number of Asian home cooks have recently taken to using a Mexican **tortilla press** to make round dumpling wrappers. Made from cast aluminum, plastic, or wood, and reasonably priced, tortilla presses can be found at Latino grocers and online. For the thin signature skins of wontons, *siu mai*, and egg rolls, a **pasta machine** yields remarkable results. With minimal skill, you can produce thin, supple skins that best store-bought ones. All that's required is repeatedly passing the dough through the machine's smooth metal rollers.

Restaurant supply and housewares shops in Chinatown are among my favorite places to visit. You can find all kinds of nifty, inexpensive tools there. If you venture to one, look for a bamboo dumpling spatula, a terrific gadget for scooping up dumpling fillings and depositing them onto wrappers without sticking. Admittedly, you can use a dinner knife or fork, but the little spatula (about $3) is a neat, old-fashioned tool.

Ingredients

Dumplings are prepared from everyday ingredients—that is their nature and genius. Most ingredients for recipes in this book are available at regular supermarkets, where ethnic food aisles are better stocked than ever. However, some ingredients will require a trip to an Asian grocer. This section will help you select ingredients for preparing the dumplings in this book.

Bamboo Shoots The earthy quality of bamboo shoots grounds many Asian foods, dumplings included. They come fresh, dried, frozen, and canned; for dumpling making, widely available canned bamboo shoots are fine. Presliced bamboo shoots are versatile as they can be cut into whatever size and shape is needed. Before using canned bamboo shoots, drain them of their canning liquid and boil them in water for a minute, then drain well and rinse with lots of cold water afterwards. This rids the shoots of their tinny flavor and any mustiness. If you purchase fresh bamboo shoots, they should be husked to reveal the creamy-white core and then boiled for 10 to 30 minutes to remove their natural toxins and render them tender crisp.

Banana Leaves Dumplings wrapped in banana leaves absorb their pale green color and mild tealike flavor and fragrance. Fresh leaves are increasingly available, but frozen ones are much easier to find. I always keep a one-pound package in the freezer. Look for packages of frozen banana leaves in Chinese, Southeast Asian, and Latin markets. Fresh banana leaves are sold in some markets in the United States.

When working with frozen banana leaves, partially thaw the package until you can gently pry the leaves open. Use scissors to cut off a tear-free section that meets your needs (torn leaves are hard to work with), then refold and refreeze the unused portion. As you trim thawed or fresh leaves to size, don't let the stiff ribs dictate your cut (or you will get a misshapen piece of leaf) and always remove any dark brown edge. Before using the leaf in cooking, rinse it and then wipe it dry with a paper towel to remove the white residue. If a leaf is particularly stiff, pass it over the flame of a gas stove or a hot electric burner to soften it.

Chiles The spicy heat of **fresh and dried chiles** adds excitement to many dumplings, either in the filling or as an accompaniment served at the table. Fresh chiles are typically enjoyed seeds and all for maximum flavor, though you may remove the seeds and inner membranes, the source of most of the heat. When an ample amount of heat is needed, use potent fresh Thai chiles or serranos. For moderately hot heat, look to cayenne, Fresno (sometimes mislabeled as red jalapeño), Holland (also known as Dutch and finger chiles), or jalapeño chiles. I love the red color of ripe chiles, but some recipes, such as Green Chutney (page 221), are best prepared with verdant green chiles. Stock up during the late summer and early fall when chiles are extra zippy; you can keep a stash frozen in zip-top plastic bags for up to a year.

ASIAN DUMPLING PANTRY

Keep these ingredients on hand, and you will be ready to make most Asian dumplings:

Flours and Starches
- All-purpose flour, bleached and unbleached
- Rice flour
- Glutinous (sweet) rice flour
- Cornstarch
- Tapioca starch
- Wheat starch

Seasonings
- Soy sauce (light and dark)
- Oyster sauce
- Shaoxing rice wine or dry sherry
- Chinkiang vinegar
- Unseasoned rice vinegar
- Sesame oil

Fresh Aromatics
- Scallions
- Ginger
- Garlic

When working with chiles, I do not don gloves to protect my hands from their fiery oils. I minimize contact by using the stem of the chile to scoot cut-up pieces and seeds onto my knife blade, and then use the stem to usher the chile bits off the blade and into wherever they are needed. If I do touch the chile, I wash my hands immediately. To work efficiently, I cut up chiles after the other ingredients have already been prepped on the cutting board.

Dried red chile flakes are widely available and offer a deep, weighty heat. You can experience that effect through homemade Chile Oil (page 216), a common sight at Chinese dumpling restaurants. When flakes aren't available, stem whole dried chiles (*chiles de árbol* are good) and then coarsely grind in a clean, dry spice grinder or electric coffee grinder reserved for spices.

Chinese Chives Resembling dark green, flat blades of grass, Chinese chives are significantly larger than Western chives. They have a delicate garlic, rather than onion, flavor. Many Asian cooks treat the chives like a leafy green vegetable, not a garnish, and judiciously use them in dumpling fillings for subtle flavor as well as color. Chinese Chive Dumplings (page 145) encased in translucent wheat-starch dough showcase this vegetable magnificently.

Despite their name, Chinese chives are not exclusive to Chinese cooking but are enjoyed throughout East and Southeast Asia. They are typically sold in one-pound bundles at Asian markets; pricier flowering chives are the plant's stiffer stems and are not typically used for dumplings. With few exceptions, Chinese chives can be replaced with scallions. The chives are known by many names, including garlic chives, *gow choy* and *jiǔcài* (China), *kucai* (Indonesia, Malaysia, and Singapore), *nira* (Japan), *buchu* (Korea), *gui chai* (Thailand), and *hẹ* (Vietnam).

Coconut Milk The sweet, creamy liquid pressed from the grated flesh of mature, brown coconuts enriches many Asian dumplings, particularly those prepared in the more tropical southern regions, where coconut palms flourish. Though you can certainly render fresh coconut milk, there is terrific coconut milk sold in cans and aseptically packaged boxes. Canned Chaokoh and Mae Ploy brands from Thailand offer excellent flavor and creaminess; both are sold at Asian markets and the former is stocked at some supermarkets. Aroy-D from Thailand comes in boxes and is harder to find but offers super fresh flavor. Always shake or whisk the contents well before measuring the amount needed.

For Asian recipes, use *unsweetened* coconut milk, not the stuff that goes into a piña colada. Insipid "light" coconut milk is not worth using. And the saturated fat in coconut milk is a good one. It is not hydrogenated (that is, it is not an unhealthy trans fatty acid); its chief fatty acid, lauric acid, is easily metabolized, which means it doesn't hang around to become bad cholesterol. So go for the full fat and enjoy.

Cornstarch In Asian dumpling making, cornstarch is used to bind fillings and to make dough. The silky fine starch contributes resiliency to superthin wonton and egg roll skins and prevents them from sticking. Cornstarch and tapioca starch (page 16) have similar thickening powers, but when used in rice-flour batters, they show subtle differences. Cornstarch adds a firm-but-chewy quality, and tapioca provides elasticity. Thus, when I made the batter for steamed rice sheets (page 155) with either of the starches used alone, the result was either too dry and firm or too wet and stretchy. But when I combined the two starches for the batter, I produced rice sheets that were perfectly tender, yet chewy and slightly firm.

Dried Shrimp Tiny and orange in color, dried shrimp are an often-used stealth ingredient in Asian dumplings. They contribute an alluring sweet brininess and savory depth to foods. Sold in plastic packages labeled small, medium, or large, they are usually in the cold-food section at Asian markets. Buy whole shrimp (not shrimp powder) that are pinkish-orange. Medium or large shrimp have more flavor than small ones. Refrigerate the package to prevent the shrimp from developing an off odor.

Fish Sauce Used like soy sauce in many Southeast Asian kitchens, fish sauce lends an unmistakable flavor to foods that it touches. I have a personal love for this condiment—*nước mắm* is the national seasoning of Vietnam, my native country. If you are unfamiliar with using fish sauce, purchase one that is made in a more delicate, so-called Vietnamese style. Excellent brands are Viet Huong's Three Crabs and Flying Lion.

When shopping for good fish sauce, select a premium one that is reddish brown and clear. Avoid dark, inky liquids, which are overly salty and flat tasting. Good fish sauce is fragrant and pleasant tasting; it typically comes in glass bottles, rather than plastic, and costs a little more than other brands. Look for clues on the label, such as *cốt, nhĩ,* or *thượng hạng,* which signal a premium product made with the first extraction of liquid from the salted fish. Phu Quoc and Phan Thiet are two places famous for the production of fish sauce in Vietnam. *Cá cơm* are anchovies native to the waters surrounding the island of Phu Quoc, and fish sauce made from these light-fleshed fish is considered prime. If you are at a complete loss, select a mid- to high-priced bottle. Fish sauce bottles are rarely well sealed, so transport and store them upright.

Flour (Wheat) Wheat flour in Asia is very similar to all-purpose flour in the United States.

In general, both have moderate protein levels (10 to 11 percent) and render dough that is tender-chewy. However, Asian wheat flour tends to be bright white, since light-colored dumplings are perceived positively, as a sign of modern progress.

For recipes in this book calling for **all-purpose flour**, I used Gold Medal brand, which is widely available and yields terrific results. Both bleached and unbleached all-purpose flours are employed, and I indicate which is preferred. In general, savory dumplings have a more pleasant chewiness when the dough is prepared with unbleached flour. Sweet dumplings, on the other hand, are a touch more tender when bleached flour is employed rather than unbleached. For Shanghai Soup Dumplings (page 59), however, Gold Medal unbleached all-purpose flour is combined with bread flour to produce well-balanced dough that is elastic and tender. High-protein flours, such as King Arthur all-purpose, are great for many Western preparations, but are overly tough and chewy for Asian dumplings. See the Rice Flour entry for details on flour milled from rice.

Ginger Fresh ginger root is an indispensable ingredient for many Asian dumplings, so keep a healthy supply on hand. Select heavy, hard rhizomes with taut skin. Wrinkly ones are over the hill. Fibrous, more mature ginger (check where the knobs are broken) is hotter and more flavorful but may be hard to finely cut or mince. Store ginger in a typical thin produce-section plastic bag in the vegetable crisper, where it will stay fresh for weeks.

Hoisin Sauce This sweet-garlicky-spicy Chinese sauce made from soybeans is widely available at Asian and mainstream grocery stores. Lee Kum Kee and Koon Chun are my preferred brands. Once opened, hoisin sauce will keep indefinitely in the refrigerator.

Mushrooms The musty fragrance, meaty texture, and deep flavor of **dried shiitake mushrooms** contribute unrivaled sumptuousness to dumplings. Buy whole mushrooms, not presliced ones, which are of questionable quality. Look for thick mushrooms with deep white fissures on the caps. They may be labeled *hana*, or "flower" mushroom, a term Japanese packagers use to signal the highest grade. Second-grade mushrooms, labeled superior, are also thick but have fewer fissures.

Asian markets and herbalist shops are the best places to look for these mushrooms. I keep dried shiitake mushrooms, also known as Chinese black mushrooms, in a plastic container at room temperature; others prefer to freeze them.

Dried shiitake mushrooms need to be reconstituted before being used. I typically soak them for 8 hours (or overnight) in water to cover; the temperature of the water doesn't matter. This yields deeply flavored mushrooms that are amazingly firm and velvety when cut; a rushed soaking in hot water won't produce the same results. Before using the mushrooms, rinse out any particles of sand or dirt trapped under the gills, give each a gentle squeeze to expel excess water, and slice off the knobby stem. Reconstituted shiitake mushrooms, drained of their soaking water, can be refrigerated for several days.

Black-gray, crunchy, and flavorless, **dried wood ear mushrooms** add terrific texture to foods. Also called black fungus, these mushrooms are mostly sold dried. They are available fresh, too; but I don't use them since they are not easily found. If you should happen upon fresh ones, store them as you would any fresh mushroom, and trim and cut them up for cooking. The dried mushrooms range from tiny ones that must be measured in a spoon to huge, tough ones. I buy them small to midsized because they are tender yet crunchy, can be cut into strips or finely chopped, and

neither disappear nor overwhelm. Dried wood ear mushrooms are sold at Asian markets in plastic packages. They keep indefinitely in the cupboard.

Reconstitute dried wood ear mushrooms in hot water to cover for about 15 minutes, or until they are pliable. If the tough "eye" remains at the center of the mushroom, remove it before cutting up the mushroom for a recipe. Because these mushrooms vary in size, gauge how much to use for a recipe by looking at the count and corresponding measurement.

Oyster Sauce At dim sum restaurants, oyster sauce appears in many guises, most notably poured on blanched leafy greens as a simple side dish. Cantonese dumpling cooks also like to add oyster sauce to dumpling fillings whenever a little rich, briny, salty-sweet flavor is needed. Lee Kum Kee's basic oyster sauce is good, but try to step up to their premium sauce, which has the woman and boy on the label; it has more oyster extractives and a richer flavor. Refrigerate oyster sauce after opening to keep it indefinitely. Before using, let it stand at room temperature for several minutes, so it is easier to pour and measure.

Rice Flour Milled from long-grain rice, **rice flour** is an essential ingredient in a number of Asian dumplings, mostly those that employ steamed rice sheets as wrappers (see page 154). For those applications, rice flour from Thailand works best. Sold in one-pound plastic bags at Asian markets, it is fine and soft and cooks up light, without the graininess found in other rice flours. All Thai rice flours are generally of good quality; Erawan (Elephant) brand is most popular. Don't mistakenly select glutinous rice flour (see below) when shopping for regular rice flour. Most manufacturers produce both kinds and use different-colored lettering to distinguish the

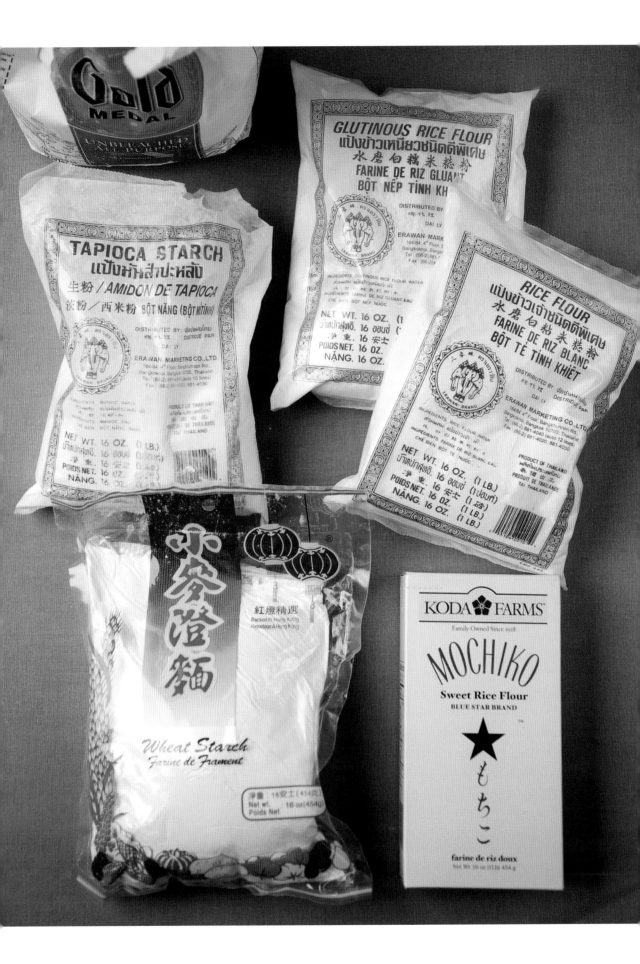

two flours—red is for regular rice flour and green is for glutinous rice flour. Mix up the two, and your recipe will not turn out right.

Glutinous rice flour, also known as **sweet rice flour**, is used to make dough for many savory and sweet dumplings. Domestic glutinous rice flour produced by Koda Farms under the Mochiko Blue Star label is ground straight from the grain, whereas glutinous rice flour from Thailand is soaked first and then ground, rendering it just slightly finer in texture and lighter in weight. Both flours are milled from sticky rice grains, which is why dumplings made with glutinous rice flour are generally described as sticky rice dumplings. Depending on a dumpling's cooking method and ideal texture, I may use Thai glutinous rice flour alone or in combination with its domestic counterpart or with wheat starch (see page 17). At Asian markets, look for all types of rice flour near the starches and spices. Mochiko Blue Star flour is sold at some regular supermarkets in the Asian food aisle.

Rice Though both regular and sticky rice are used for making Asian dumplings, **sticky rice** (also known as glutinous or sweet rice) is used more often. Because sticky rice is nearly all amylopectin starch molecules, it has a wonderful natural chewy sweetness.

Sticky rice is sold alongside regular rice (such as jasmine) at Asian markets, but don't confuse them. Uncooked sticky rice is opaque, while regular rice is translucent. Sticky rice comes in long-grain and short-grain varieties, the former preferred by Chinese and Southeast Asian cooks and the latter by Japanese and Korean cooks. For the recipes in this book, long-grain and short-grain varieties of sticky rice are used interchangeably.

Rice Wine Aromatic and pleasantly nutty-tasting **Shaoxing rice wine** is the standard spirit used in many Chinese preparations, including dump-ling fillings. I exclusively use Pagoda brand, which is actually made in Shaoxing, in Zhejiang Province. The tall 750-milliliter bottles are sold at Chinese markets. Pay a little more for the aged version, which tastes like a good dry sherry (a fine substitute when Shaoxing rice wine is unavailable). Avoid Shaoxing "cooking wine" and "cooking sherry," which are salted.

Sesame Oil Rich, nutty, amber-colored oil made from toasted sesame seeds is often used to enrich and perfume fillings for Chinese dumplings. Japanese sesame oils are excellent, particularly Kadoya brand. Asian markets have the best prices. Store the oil at room temperature in a dark, cool spot for up to 6 months or refrigerate for longer. Light-colored sesame oil made from untoasted seeds is used in Indian cooking, but only the dark toasted sesame oil is used in this book. Toasted black sesame oil can be used, though it has a slight bitter edge.

Sesame Seeds Sesame seeds, thought to be native to Africa or perhaps to Iran or India, were probably introduced to China by Persian traders in the earliest part of the Christian era, making them a Chinese food ingredient for about two thousand years. Though black sesame seeds are used for certain dumpling fillings, the recipes in this book employ hulled (white) sesame seeds.

To toast sesame seeds, put them in a skillet over medium heat, stirring frequently until they are lightly golden (about 8 minutes for 1 cup toasted in a 12-inch skillet); let the seeds cool before using. Freeze to keep them for several months.

Sichuan Peppercorns These dried dark-red berries are not related to familiar black peppercorns and have an appealing, distinctive pungency that is spicy and tingly on the tongue. Beloved in Sichuan cuisine, the scintillating aromatic is also enjoyed in Tibet and Nepal.

Sichuan peppercorns (*Zanthoxylum simulans*) are typically toasted in a dry skillet and then ground before they're used in cooking. Use medium heat and stir or shake the skillet frequently for about 3 minutes, until the peppercorns are very fragrant and slightly darker than original. Then render them into a fine texture with a spice grinder or mortar and pestle. Look for them in plastic bags at Chinese markets and specialty grocers. They are also called Chinese prickly-ash.

Soy Sauce The many types of soy sauces all taste different. Chinese soy sauces, the light (regular) and dark kinds, are used in most of the recipes here. **Light soy sauce**, sometimes called thin soy sauce, is not low in sodium. It is merely light in color. By comparison, **dark (black) soy sauce** is slightly sweet, and deeper in flavor and color.

Pearl River Bridge makes excellent soy sauces. The superior is good, but the golden label superior, which is fermented longer, is more complex and nuanced and costs pennies more. You can always find it at Chinese and Southeast Asian markets; in your supermarket, choose Kikkoman. Japanese and Korean soy sauces (called *shoyu* and *ganjang*, respectively) are similar to Chinese light soy sauce, but they are a touch sweeter and less salty; in a pinch substitute light (regular) soy sauce. Japanese and Korean markets have the best selection of soy sauces for those cuisines.

Pay attention to the sodium content when buying soy sauces. The brands I use have around 900 milligrams per tablespoon, so if you prefer saltier soy sauces, use a little less or lower the amount of salt, if it is part of the seasonings.

Tapioca Starch Also called tapioca flour, this is the starch of the cassava root (also known as yuca or manioc), a native of South America. In Asian kitchens, tapioca starch, like cornstarch, is used to bind ingredients, thicken foods, and create crisp fried crusts. Tapioca starch is also frequently used in dumpling dough, either alone or combined with other flours or starches, to lend translucency and elasticity. Compared with cornstarch, tapioca starch is finer and denser.

Tapioca starch is sold at Asian, Latin, African, Caribbean, and specialty grocers. Tapioca pearls (tapioca starch rolled into small balls) are available in various sizes at Asian markets. Thai Tapioca Pearl Dumplings (page 149) employ small ones, about 1/8 inch in diameter, to make the dough.

Tofu When squeezed of its liquid and mashed, **firm tofu** becomes a great binding ingredient for Korean *mandu* (pages 44 and 46). The velvety tofu absorbs strong flavors, such as those of kimchi, thus helping to harmonize all the dumpling filling ingredients.

When firm tofu is pressed to expel its water, it becomes almost meatlike. Called *dòufu gān* (dry bean curd) in Mandarin, **pressed tofu** is often featured in vegetarian dumplings because its texture lends substance

to the filling. Pressed tofu can be white and unseasoned or brown and flavored by seasonings such as soy sauce and Chinese five-spice powder. I prefer the more flavorful brown variety for dumpling fillings. Brown pressed tofu (often labeled as baked tofu) is sold at Chinese markets, as well as health food stores and specialty grocers. Check the refrigerated foods section for cryovac packages or bulk boxes of the 3/4-inch-thick, 3-inch squares or 6-inch rectangles.

Vinegar Inky, a little smoky, and slightly bitter **Chinkiang vinegar** is named after an area in China renowned for vinegar production. It is wonderful when used for dipping sauces to accompany tasty morsels like Shanghai Soup Dumplings (page 59). Italian balsamic vinegar and unseasoned rice vinegar are worthy stand-ins. Chinkiang vinegar is sold at Chinese markets, where you may also see Zhejiang vinegar, another good black vinegar. The Golden Plum brand of Chinkiang vinegar is excellent.

Wheat Starch Despite its name, wheat starch is not starchy in an elastic, glutinous way, but rather firm and dry. The snowy white starch is the byproduct of making wheat gluten (*seitan*), a popular Asian vegetarian ingredient. Dumpling dough prepared from wheat starch is beautifully translucent and white, the signature look for favorite dim sum treats like Cantonese Har Gow Shrimp Dumplings (page 135). Wheat starch is sold in one-pound plastic bags at Chinese markets near other starches and flours, and at some Middle Eastern grocers. When wheat starch is not clearly labeled as so, ask for *tang* flour, or *tang mien fun* in Cantonese and *chéng miàn fěn* in Mandarin. It is sometimes confusingly labeled as "wheaten cornflour" or "nonglutinous flour."

Cooking Techniques

Boiling, poaching, panfrying, and baking are relatively straightforward means of cooking dumplings, but steaming and deep-frying can be unfamiliar and thus daunting. This section offers insights to facilitate your success.

Steaming

As noted on page 6, the tools used for steaming and how you set them up can vary. However, there are certain consistent parameters to keep in mind when steaming food:

- Get the steamer going 10 to 15 minutes before you want to steam. The timing is like that for preheating an oven. When the steamer is ready, lower the heat to keep the water hot, then raise the heat and return to a boil before steaming.

- Achieve a steady, rolling boil before putting the steamer trays full of dumplings in place. If you use a superhot power burner and the boiling seems out of control, lower the heat slightly to steady the boil.

- Stacking multiple steamer trays to simultaneously cook a bunch of dumplings is fine if the burner is strong enough to send shots of steam to the uppermost tray. If puffs of steam come out of the lid, then your creations are cooking evenly. You can always switch the tray positions midway, lowering the heat and carefully lifting the lid to avoid injuring yourself with steam heat. If you are unsure, steam one tray of dumplings at a time.

- When called for in the recipe, line your steamer trays with parchment paper, keeping some space uncovered to allow steam to come through. Asian cooks use numerous things, including pine needles, cabbage leaves, banana leaves, and woven mats, to line the trays in order to prevent sticking and facilitate easy cleanup. Parchment paper is readily available and is virtually nonstick. Perforated parchment paper steamer liners are super convenient.

- In a metal steamer, condensation gathers and drips down the sides of the trays. When using that type of steamer, remember to arrange dumplings at least 1 inch away from the edge of the steamer so they don't get wet. Bamboo steamers do not have this problem.

- Remove a hot steamer lid with caution, turning it away from you to avoid getting a burst of very hot steam. Always lower or turn off the heat before lifting the lid.

Deep-Frying

The key to deep-frying is getting the oil to the proper temperature and keeping it there. Over time, you'll develop a sense of when the oil is hot enough to add the food, but to begin with, using a deep-frying thermometer (same as a candy thermometer) will set you on the right path. Use a straight-sided pan so you can clip the thermometer on. Position the tip of thermometer just above the bottom of the pan so you are measuring the heat of the oil and not the metal. When you feel more comfortable with deep-frying, try using the bamboo chopstick test described in the recipes to gauge the temperature. Hone your skills and then progress to deep-frying in a wok.

Other tips for successful deep-frying are:

- Make sure you have a sufficient depth of oil. If you are short of oil, fry in a medium saucepan rather than a larger pot. It will take more time but use less oil.

- Get organized before you begin frying. Put the food on one side of the stove and the setup for draining the crispy results on the other side. Keep utensils such as a wire skimmer or tongs nearby. Open windows and run the exhaust fan if frying odors are a concern.

- Put a few sheets of newspaper on the floor if you are worried about dirtying the kitchen. During or after frying, quickly wipe the stove and counter clean to prevent grease buildup.

- Never let the oil get so hot that it smokes. If it does, carefully move the pan to another burner. After the smoke dissipates, reheat the oil and continue frying.

- Test fry one or two dumplings when trying out a new recipe. A practice run is great for testing the oil temperature and getting used to the frying process.

- Fry in batches to avoid lowering the oil temperature. Always return the oil to the appropriate temperature, regulating the heat as needed, before adding the next batch.

- Fry a second time to refresh and restore a fresh-from-the-fryer crispness. When planning to fry again right before serving, slightly underfry the first time to avoid overbrowning on the second frying.

- Recycle the oil used for deep-frying. After frying, let the oil cool completely, then strain it through a fine-mesh sieve. If the oil is cloudy or contains lots of unsavory bits, line the strainer with paper towel or cheesecloth. Transfer the oil to a clean, dry jar or plastic bottle, cap tightly, and store in a cool, dry place. Don't reuse oil once it has turned brown (oil is golden when new) or if it has picked up funky odors from frying foods such as fish.

Tips for Success

If preparing dumplings is new to you, the process can seem overwhelming. But it really need not be. Here are tips to help you succeed:

- Read instructions carefully before trying a new recipe to get a sense of how the ingredients come together and to acquaint yourself with unfamiliar instructions and methods.

- Weigh flour and starches for dough. People have different approaches to measuring ingredients and those differences affect outcomes considerably. Dumpling dough requires the extra precision and consistency that weighing flour and starches provides.

- Pace yourself and spread the work out. Check recipes for advance preparation tips, from reconstituting ingredients to prepping dipping sauces or other components. For example, if you make the filling in advance you can focus on making the dough, rolling out wrappers, and assembling the dumplings in a single session. Most dumpling fillings and doughs can be readied ahead of time.

- Freeze dumplings for future use, when you can. Freezing tips are included in many recipes. If dumplings crack during freezing, partially thaw them and try to smooth over the cracks with your finger before cooking.

- Look online at Asiandumplingtips.com for additional support, such as instructional videos and photos.

- Practice and have fun. Asian dumplings do not have to look perfect to taste good. You can work and eat your way toward making good-looking ones.

1 Filled Pastas

Since ancient times, Asian cooks have mixed wheat flour and water into dough for remarkably tender, chewy wrappers that are stuffed and cooked into home-style, street-food, and restaurant favorites. I recommend that you begin your dumpling adventure here, by making some basic wrappers from a dough of flour and water. This dough will serve you for a pan-Asian selection of boiled, panfried, deep-fried, and steamed dumplings—all essentially filled pastas. These kinds of dumplings are an ideal place to start because getting the dough right isn't difficult, many of the tasty fillings employ few ingredients, artistry isn't required to shape the dumplings nicely, and there are many cooking methods. In fact, with the exception of Shanghai Soup Dumplings (page 59), the fillings here are interchangeable.

The techniques I present in this chapter, such as how to roll out wrappers, are used elsewhere in the book. This collection of recipes will allow you to experience several time-honored Asian culinary traditions and will show you that dumplings are a pleasure to make and not as difficult as you may think.

Basic Dumpling Dough

Makes about 1 pound, enough for 32 medium or 24 large dumplings

This dough is the foundation of many excellent dumplings, including Chinese *jiǎozi*, Korean *mandu*, and Nepali *momo*. The process of making the dough is easy to master, especially with a little help from modern tools such as a food processor (though you can mix the dough by hand).

Asian wheat flour wrappers may be made with cold or hot water—the temperature is traditionally dictated by the cooking method. Boiled dumplings are said to require thicker skins made from cold-water dough in order to withstand the pressures of boiling, whereas panfried and steamed dumplings require thinner skins made from hot-water dough for their gentler cooking processes. Over the years, I've found that homemade wrappers of medium thickness, a scant 1/8 inch thick in the center and about 1/16 inch thick at the rim, work well for all cooking methods. If dumplings are gently boiled as described for *shuǐjiǎo* on page 31, there is no need for thicker wrappers. Producing medium-thick wrappers is easier with hot-water dough as it is more yielding than its cold-water counterpart. The resulting wrappers taste superior to store-bought ones, and they need no water to seal. Grocery store all-purpose flour with a moderate amount of gluten, such as Gold Medal brand, works exceptionally well.

10 ounces (2 cups) unbleached all-purpose flour
About 3/4 cup just-boiled water (see Note)

1. To prepare the dough in a food processor, put the flour in the work bowl. With the machine running, add 3/4 cup of water in a steady stream through the feed tube. As soon as all the water has been added, stop the machine and check the dough. It should look rough and feel soft but firm enough to hold its shape when pinched. If necessary, add water by the teaspoon or flour by the tablespoon. When satisfied, run the machine for another 5 to 10 seconds to further knead and form a ball around the blade. Avoid overworking the dough.

2. Alternatively, make the dough by hand. Put a bowl atop a kitchen towel to prevent it from slipping while you work. Put the flour in the bowl and make a well in the center. Use a wooden spoon or bamboo rice paddle to stir the flour while you add 3/4 cup water in a

steady stream. Aim to evenly moisten the flour. It is okay to pause to stir or add water—it is hard to simultaneously do both actions. When all the water has been added, you will have lots of lumpy bits. Knead the dough in the bowl (it is not terribly hot) to bring all the lumps into one mass; if the dough does not come together easily, add water by the teaspoon.

3. Regardless of the mixing method, transfer the dough and any bits to a work surface; flour your work surface only if necessary, and then sparingly. Knead the dough (it is not hot) with the heel of your hand for about 30 seconds for machine-made dough, or about 2 minutes for handmade dough. The result should be nearly smooth and somewhat elastic; press on the dough; it should slowly bounce back, with a light impression of your finger remaining. Place the dough in a zip-top plastic bag and seal tightly closed, expelling excess air. Set aside to rest at room temperature for at least 15 minutes and up to 2 hours. The dough will

steam up the plastic bag and become earlobe soft, which makes wrappers easy to work with.

4. **After resting,** the dough can be used right away to form the wrappers. Or, refrigerate it overnight and returned it to room temperature before using.

Note: Recipes for hot-water dough often call for boiling water to hydrate the dry ingredients, but I find that practice too dangerous and prefer to let the water rest first. For the just-boiled water, half-fill a kettle or saucepan with water and bring it to a boil. Turn off the heat and after the bubbling action subsides, 30 to 90 seconds (depending on the heating vessel), pour the amount needed into a glass measuring cup and use for making the dough. I typically wait no more than 2 minutes after boiling to use the water.

LAZY DAY TIP

You can substitute purchased wrappers for homemade ones. Medium-thick pot sticker wrappers are good for boiled, panfried, and steamed dumplings; however, they do not deep-fry well. *Sui gow* wrappers are typically made relatively thick for boiled dumplings. If your wrappers are soft and fresh but on the thick side, try rolling them to create thinner ones. A commercially made wrapper holds less filling than a homemade one, so your yield will be higher for the filling recipes here. When using store-bought wrappers, moisten the edge with water to seal them. Purchased wheat flour wrappers are best used for shaping half-moons, pea pods, pleated crescents, and big hugs but *not* closed satchels.

PLAY WITH THE DOUGH

Once you've got the hang of making and using the basic dumpling dough, try coloring it with vegetable juice or ground spices or altering its texture with glutinous rice flour.

Jade Dough Liquefy 2 lightly packed cups of coarsely chopped spinach leaves (about 3 ounces) with a generous $1/2$ cup of water in a blender for about 90 seconds, or until there is an intensely green, smooth mixture. If needed, pause the blender to scrape down the sides. Transfer to a small saucepan and heat over medium heat. When the spinach comes to a near boil (look for foam all around the rim), turn off the heat. Stir to blend in the foam, measure out $3/4$ cup, then use it for the dough. You may have to add an extra teaspoon of spinach water to arrive at a nice softness. The extra bulk from the spinach produces more dough than usual, so the wrappers will be larger.

Orange Dough Use 100 percent carrot juice, available at many specialty grocers. Bring 1 cup to a boil in a small saucepan, turn off the heat, and then measure out the $3/4$ cup needed. Use as you would water to mix into the flour.

Golden Dough Mix $3/4$ teaspoon ground turmeric into the flour before adding the water. The dough will develop its color as it sits.

Extra-Chewy Dough For extra elasticity and natural sweetness, a quality favored by Korean and Japanese cooks, combine $71/2$ ounces ($11/2$ cups) unbleached all-purpose flour with $27/8$ ounces (ample $1/2$ cup) Mochiko Blue Star brand glutinous (sweet) rice flour. Use $3/4$ cup just-boiled water and proceed as usual. This dough is firmer than the basic dumpling dough, so you may find that the rice flour also makes the dough a bit easier to manipulate.

Forming Wrappers from Basic Dumpling Dough

Wrappers formed from basic dumpling dough are traditionally rolled out individually by hand with a skinny wooden rolling pin. I like to cut down the work by employing a Mexican tortilla press to first quickly flatten the dough into a thin disk and then finishing the job with the skinny rolling pin. You can use some other kind of heavy, flat-bottomed object, such as a 4-cup glass measuring cup, but it will require a little more energy than the press. Regardless, have on hand two 6 to 7-inch squares of medium-heavy plastic (I cut them from a zip-top freezer bag) for the pressing. Make sure to use a spacious work surface (for example, a large cutting board), lightly dusted with flour and with about 1/4 cup of additional flour in one corner for dusting. And regardless of how you initially flatten the dough, you'll definitely need the small rolling pin (see page 6) to finish the wrappers. Have your filling ready to go before you start rolling, as you'll want to fill the wrappers fairly promptly after they are rolled.

1. **Remove the dough** from the bag, turning the bag inside out if the dough is sticky. Put the dough on a lightly floured work surface and cut it in half. Put half back in the bag, squeezing out the air and sealing it closed to prevent drying.

2. **Roll the dough** into a 1-inch-thick log, and then cut it into the number of pieces required by the recipe. To cut even pieces, quarter the log first; the tapered end pieces should be cut a little longer than the rest. Weigh each piece of dough to be super precise, if you like. If your dough pieces are oval shaped, stand each one on a cut end and use your fingers to gently squeeze it into a round (see drawing 1). The resulting squat cylinder resembles a scallop. This bit of advance work makes it easier to form a nice circle in the remaining steps.

3. **To prevent the dough** from sticking and to flatten it a bit, take each piece of dough and press one of the cut ends in flour, then flip it over and do the same on the other end; the dough can be sticky. You should end up with a disk roughly 1/4 inch thick. As you work, set the floured disks to one side of your work area.

4. **Next, flatten each dough** disk into a thin circle that is about 1/8 inch thick, either with a tortilla press or with a heavy, flat-bottomed object. If you are using the tortilla press, open the press and lay a plastic square on the bottom plate. Center a disk of floured dough and cover with the other plastic square. Close the top plate, then fold the pressure handle over the top plate and press down. Use moderate pressure and press only once, or the resulting wrapper will stick to the plastic and be hard to remove.

Fold back the pressure handle, open the top plate, and peel off the top plastic square. Then gently peel the wrapper off the bottom plastic square (see drawing 2). Should the wrapper feel tacky, lightly swipe both sides on some flour before placing on the work surface.

Without the tortilla press, put the floured disk between the plastic squares and press down with a heavy object to produce a circle about 1/8 inch thick. You may have to press more than once. Gently peel back the plastic from the wrapper.

Regardless of method, repeat with the remaining dough pieces, setting them to one side of the work area as you finish them. It is okay to overlap the wrappers slightly.

5. **To finish the wrappers,** take a wrapper and place it on the work surface, flouring the surface only as needed to keep the dough from sticking. Imagine a quarter-size circle in the center. This is what the Chinese call the "belly" of the wrapper. You want to create a wrapper that is larger than its current size but retains a thick belly. This ensures an even distribution

of dough after the wrapper's edge has been gathered and closed around the filling.

To keep a thick belly, use the rolling pin to apply pressure on the outer 1/2 to 3/4-inch border of the wrapper, as follows. Try to roll the rolling pin with the flat palm of one hand while using the other hand to turn the wrapper in the opposite direction. For example, as your right palm works the rolling pin in short, downward strokes from the center toward your body, the fingers of your left hand turn the disk counterclockwise about one-quarter of a turn between each stroke (see drawing 3 and photo on page 7). Keep the thumb of the rotating hand near the center of the wrapper to guide the rolling pin and turn the wrapper.

If the wrapper sticks to the work surface or rolling pin, pause to dust the wrapper with flour and then continue. If you cannot get a wrapper thin enough on the first try, set it aside to relax for about 1 minute, and then roll again. Should the wrapper tear or be hopelessly misshapen, roll up the dough, let it rest for a few minutes, then press it again and roll it out. Resembling a flat fried egg, the finished wrapper does not need to be a perfect circle. Frilly edges are fine. The finished diameter of the wrapper depends on the dumpling, and each recipe provides an ideal size. Wrappers made from the Basic Dumpling Dough are moderately thick and suitable for boiled, steamed, panfried, and deep-fried morsels.

As you work, line up the finished wrappers on your work surface; if you need extra space, use a baking sheet lined with parchment paper and dusted with flour. A bit of overlapping is fine, but avoid stacking the wrappers. When a batch of wrappers is formed, fill them before making wrappers out of the other portion of dough, or the wrappers may stick together as they wait for you. Use the instructions in the recipe to fill, shape, and cook the dumplings.

Shaping Wrappers

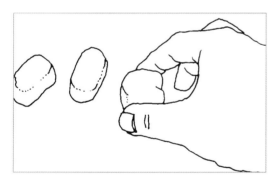

1. Shape cut dough pieces into squat cylinders.

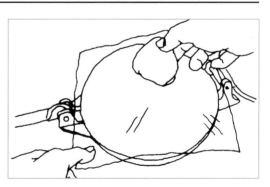

2. Peel the flattened dough from the plastic wrap in the tortilla press.

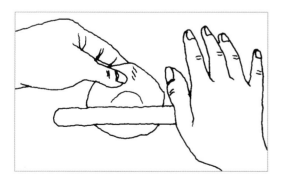

3. Roll out wrapper edges while rotating.

Master Shapes: Half-Moon, Pea Pod, Big Hug, and Pleated Crescent

Dumplings come in many shapes, and while aesthetics and tradition do matter, what is most important is getting the filling sealed up in its wrapper. Here are some basic shapes used in this book. Before you start, for some crucial tips read Keys to Filling and Shaping Nice Dumplings (page 28).

Half-Moon

This is the easiest shape and great for beginners. Half-moons are the foundation for a number of the other shapes (such as pea pod and big hug). It's also my default whenever I mistakenly put too much filling onto the wrapper and there isn't enough dough left to neatly pleat and press. After positioning the filling on the wrapper (see below), fold up the edge of the wrapper that's closest to you to meet the top edge and pinch together to seal well or press on the rim with your thumb and index finger (keep the index finger bent to provide a flat surface that supports from the bottom). Holding the ends, put the dumpling straight side down on your work surface and gently push down to steady the dumpling and make it sit flat.

Pea Pod

Pea pods are a tiny baby step above half-moons. Put a half-moon dumpling on your work surface and, using your fingers, fold the sealed edges of the dumpling to make a pleat on either side of the center or a series of pleats from one end to the other. When pleated, the dumpling not only resembles a fat pea pod

Shaping Half-Moons

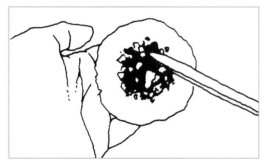

1. Place wrapper in palm and add filling.

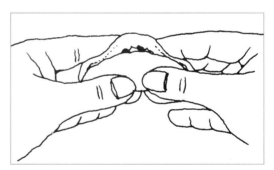

2. Fold the wrapper so the edges meet.

3. Press the edges to seal.

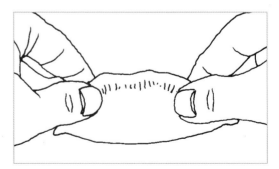

4. Gently push the dumpling down on the work surface to steady and flatten.

but also sits extra nice and flat for panfrying and steaming; this shape works beautifully for boiled dumplings, too.

Big Hug

For this charming, plump shape, first make a half-moon. Holding the dumpling by its two sealed ends, fold the sealed edge upward toward your body. Then bring the two ends together as if they're arms and overlap their hands (pointy ends), pressing them firmly flat together. To help the dumpling sit upright on its flat, filled edge, place the dumpling on the work surface, push the folded back up slightly, and if necessary fold over the sealed edge.

BEGINNER'S TIPS

If you're new to rolling out these wrappers by hand, review the instructions, drawings, and online video (visit Asiandumplingtips.com) in advance to understand the hand motions. This will help lessen your stress. Work on a quarter of the dough at a time to pace yourself. Also invite others to help out. Those with some muscle power can form the wrappers, while others who have manual dexterity can fill and shape the dumplings. Make it a group activity.

Shaping Pea Pods

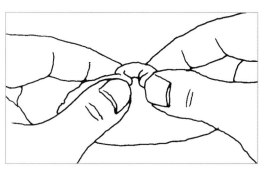

1. Forming a pea pod with a pleat on either side of the center.

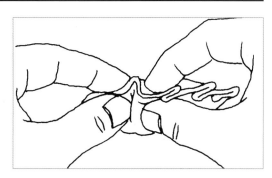

2. Pea pod being pleated from one side to the other.

Shaping Big Hugs

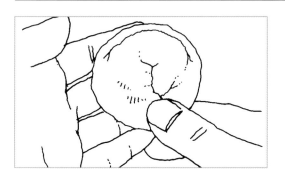

1. Bring the two ends of a half-moon together and press them to seal.

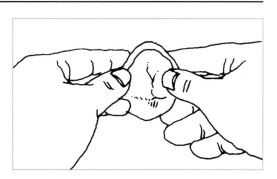

2. Push and fold the dumpling to make it stand up.

Pleated Crescent

This graceful, slightly curved shape is produced by folding pleats along one portion of the wrapper and pressing them against the unpleated edge of the wrapper to seal the dumpling closed. If you are right-handed, hold the wrapper in the left hand with the filling in place and imagine the wrapper as the face of a clock (if you are left handed, hold the wrapper in your right hand and use your left hand to start the shaping, reversing the following directions). Use the thumb and index finger of your right hand to pinch the dough together at the two o'clock position (ten o'clock if you are a lefty); this will serve as the edge of the wrapper top. The left hand will naturally close a bit, bringing up the front edge for pleating. Now use your right fingers to fold the front edge of the wrap-per over on itself to form the first pleat. Bring that pleat up to meet the first pinch, pressing them together and against the back edge, thus beginning to seal the dumpling.

Holding the pinch you just made steady with the right fingers, use the left thumb and index finger to make the remaining pleats along the front edge, one about every 1/4 inch or so. The left fingers pass a pleat to the right fingers, which then press it against the finished pleats and against the unpleated back edge of the wrapper to seal the edges. Work this way across the dumpling to pleat and close it up; there should be 8 or 9 pleats when done. Finish by pressing the edges together to seal well. If the ends of the dumpling poke out like classic car tail fins, and the dumpling doesn't sit up straight, fold them inward and press into place.

KEYS TO FILLING AND SHAPING NICE DUMPLINGS

- To more easily maneuver the wrapper as you fill and shape, position it in your hand with an edge close to your fingertips.

- Fold, pleat, and press with your thumbs and index fingers while your remaining fingers cradle the dumpling and keep it in place. This is especially key when you are making pleated crescents and closed satchels (see pages 29 and 52).

- The recipes in this book usually tell you to use a measuring spoon to portion out the filling to the wrappers. Start with that method to develop a good visual sense of how much filling is needed. To eyeball filling portions, level out the filling in the bowl or on a plate and then use a knife or spatula to divide it into 2 or 4 roughly equal wedges. Then portion out the filling from the wedges according to the number of wrappers you have. For example, if you have 16 wrappers and 4 wedges, use about one fourth of each wedge to fill each wrapper. It's a rough and ready method, but it helps ensure that, even if you have odd amounts of filling or wrappers, you won't end up with extras of either.

- Use a moderate amount of filling—it is hard to fold an overstuffed wrapper. There should be a 1/2 to 3/4-inch border of wrapper showing after you've placed the filling.

- Flatten and shape the filling after you've positioned it by lightly tapping it down and smoothing it out with the spoon or spatula. A heaped mound of filling is hard to encase.

- If you have put too much filling in the wrapper, poke it down into the wrapper or gingerly remove bits of it with your fingers as you work.

- Stretch the dough a bit by gently pulling it when you need extra wrapper to seal in the filling.

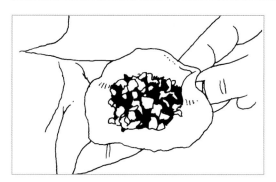

1. Make the first pinch between index finger and thumb.

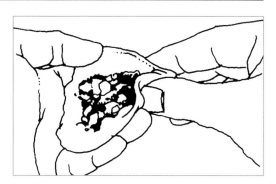

2. Fold over the front edge to form the first pleat and press it against the first pinch and the back edge.

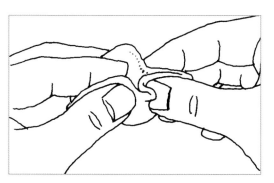

3. Pass the second pleat to the right hand as you form it.

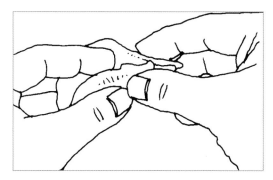

4. With the right fingers, press the second pleat to the back edge and the first pleat.

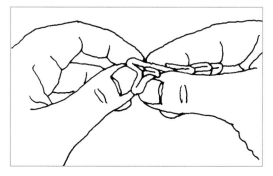

5. Making the last pleat.

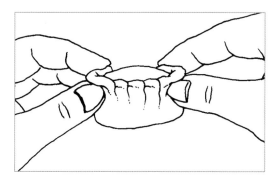

6. Settle the dumpling on the work surface and fold in the ends if they stick out.

Pork and Napa Cabbage Water Dumplings
Shuǐjiǎo

Makes 32 dumplings, serving 4 as a main course, 6 to 8 as a snack or starter

Bursting with flavor, these northern Chinese dumplings are a specialty of Beijing. Dating as far back as the late Han Dynasty (25 to 220 C.E.), plump boiled morsels such as these are members of the *jiǎozi* family of dumplings, which include panfried *guōtiē* (page 30) and steamed *zhēngjiǎo* (page 35).

Jiǎozi are not just for a modest snack or meal, they are a must-have for northern Chinese Lunar New Year celebrations. Their shape resembles gold ingots, harbingers of good fortune. Easy to make for a crowd, *shuǐjiǎo* (which means "water dumpling") are especially good hot from the pot and tumbled in a soy-vinegar dipping sauce spiked with chile oil. Pork and napa cabbage comprise the classic *jiǎozi* filling, but you can use one of the lamb, beef, vegetable, or fish fillings on the following pages. Or substitute chopped shrimp or reconstituted dried shiitake mushrooms for half of the pork.

FILLING

2 cups lightly packed finely chopped napa cabbage, cut from whole leaves (about 7 ounces)

1/2 teaspoon plus scant 1/2 teaspoon salt

1 tablespoon finely minced fresh ginger

1/4 cup chopped Chinese chives or scallions (white and green parts)

2/3 pound ground pork, fattier kind preferred, coarsely chopped to loosen

1/8 teaspoon ground white pepper

1/4 cup Chicken Stock (page 222) or water

1 1/2 tablespoons light (regular) soy sauce

1 tablespoon Shaoxing rice wine or dry sherry

1 tablespoon canola oil

1 1/2 tablespoons sesame oil

1 pound Basic Dumpling Dough (page 22)

2/3 cup Tangy Soy Dipping Sauce (page 215)

1. To make the filling, put the cabbage in a bowl and toss with the 1/2 teaspoon salt. Set aside for about 15 minutes to draw excess moisture from the cabbage. Drain in a mesh strainer (the cabbage could fall through the large holes of a colander), flush with water, and drain again. To remove more moisture, squeeze the cabbage in your hands over the sink, or put on a cotton kitchen towel (not terry cloth) and wring out the moisture over the sink. You should have about 1/2 cup firmly packed cabbage.

2. Transfer the cabbage to a bowl and add the ginger, Chinese chives, and pork. Use a fork or spatula to stir and lightly mash the ingredients so that they start coming together.

3. In a small bowl, stir together the remaining scant 1/2 teaspoon salt, the white pepper, chicken stock, soy sauce, rice wine, canola oil, and sesame oil. Pour these seasonings over the pork and cabbage mixture, then stir and fold the ingredients together. Once the pork has broken up, briskly stir to blend the ingredients into a cohesive, thick mixture. There should not be any visible large chunks of pork. To develop the flavors, cover and set aside at room temperature for 30 minutes. You should have about 2 cups of filling. (The filling can be prepared 1 day ahead and refrigerated. Bring

continued

it to room temperature before assembling the dumplings.)

4. In the meantime, make 16 wrappers from half of the dough. Aim for 3¹/4-inch-diameter wrappers (see page 24).

5. Before assembling the dumplings, line a baking sheet with parchment paper. (If you plan to refrigerate the dumplings for several hours, or freeze them, lightly dust the paper with flour to avoid sticking.) For each dumpling, hold a wrapper in a slightly cupped hand. Scoop up about 1 tablespoon of filling with a bamboo dumpling spatula, dinner knife, or fork and position it slightly off-center toward the upper half of the wrapper, pressing and shaping it into a flat mound and keeping about ¹/2 to ³/4 inch of wrapper clear on all sides. Then fold, pleat, and press to enclose the filling and create half-moons, pea pods, big hugs, or pleated crescents (see pages 26 to 29).

Place the finished dumpling on the prepared baking sheet. Repeat with the other wrappers, assembling the dumplings and spacing them a good ¹/2 inch apart on the baking sheet. Keeping the finished dumplings covered with a dry kitchen towel, form and fill the wrappers from the remaining dough.

6. Once all the dumplings are assembled, they can be covered with plastic wrap and refrigerated for several hours; they can be cooked straight from the refrigerator. (For longer storage, freeze them on the baking sheet until hard (about 1 hour), transfer them to a zip-top freezer bag, pressing out excess air before sealing, and keep them frozen for up to 1 month; partially thaw, using your finger to smooth over any cracks that may have formed during freezing, before cooking.)

7. To cook the dumplings, half-fill a large pot with water and bring to a boil over high heat. Add half the dumplings, gently dropping each one into the water. Nudge the dumplings apart with a wooden spoon to keep them from sticking together and/or to the bottom of the pot. Return the water to a simmer and then lower the heat to maintain the simmer and gently cook: a hard boil can make a dumpling burst. Cook the dumplings for about 8 minutes, or until they float to the surface, look glossy, and are puffed up and a tad translucent. Use a slotted spoon or skimmer to scoop up the dumplings from the pot, a few at a time, pausing the spoon's motion over the pot to allow excess water to drip back down before putting the dumplings on a serving plate. Cover the plate with a large inverted bowl to keep the dumplings warm.

Return the water to a boil and cook the remaining dumplings. When done, return the first batch to the hot water to reheat for a minute or two. There is no need to reboil.

8. Serve the hot dumplings immediately, placing the serving plate in the middle of the table for people to reach to or pass along. Serve the soy dipping sauce either in a communal bowl with a spoon for people to help themselves or divided up among individual rice bowls or large dipping sauce dishes. To eat, pick up a dumpling with chopsticks (you can stab it if you like) and dip or roll it in the dipping sauce. Getting an assist from a soupspoon or the rice bowl, deliver the dumpling to your mouth with the chopsticks. If there are juices inside, they'll spill out into the spoon or bowl when you bite into the dumpling.

Meat and Chinese Chive Pot Stickers
Guōtiē

Makes 32 dumplings, serving 4 as a main course, 6 to 8 as a snack or starter

I first tasted pot stickers in the late 1980s at the tiny Mandarin Deli in Los Angeles's Chinatown. Behind the glass window, a dumpling maker steadily worked, rolling out thin wrappers, filling them, and creating large pea pod–shaped dumplings. I watched intently, distracted only when my fragrant pot stickers arrived. The hearty dumplings were so hot that I burned my mouth, but they were well worth the minor injury.

Pot stickers supposedly started out as boiled dumplings that a chef forgot about in the wok (*guō*) and they stuck (*tiē*) after the water had cooked away. His guests loved the contrasts between succulent filling, tender-chewy skin, and crusty bottom, and thus the pot sticker was born. The modern way to mimic the chef's delicious accident is to cook pot stickers in a skillet with water and oil, which steams the dumplings and fries their bottoms to a golden, toasty finish. They are technically called *jiānjiǎo* in Chinese, which means shallow-fried dumplings; but in the West, we commonly know them as pot stickers and panfried dumplings. "Fried" dumplings can be panfried or deep-fried.

FILLING

2/3 pound ground beef (preferably chuck) or lamb, coarsely chopped to loosen

2/3 cup chopped Chinese chives or scallions (white and green parts)

1 1/2 to 2 tablespoons finely minced fresh ginger (use 2 tablespoons for lamb)

1/2 teaspoon salt

1/8 teaspoon ground white pepper

1/3 cup Chicken Stock (page 222) or water

2 tablespoons light (regular) soy sauce

1 tablespoon Shaoxing rice wine or dry sherry

1 1/2 tablespoons canola oil

1 1/2 tablespoons sesame oil

1 pound Basic Dumpling Dough (page 22)

Canola or peanut oil, for panfrying

2/3 cup Tangy Soy Dipping Sauce (page 215)

1. **To make the filling,** combine the beef, Chinese chives, and ginger in a bowl. Use a fork or spatula to stir and lightly mash the ingredients so that they start commingling.

2. **In a small bowl,** stir together the salt, white pepper, chicken stock, soy sauce, rice wine, canola oil, and sesame oil. Pour these seasonings over the beef mixture, then stir and fold the ingredients together. Once you have broken up the large chunks of beef, briskly stir to blend the ingredients into a cohesive, thick mixture. To develop the flavors, cover with plastic wrap and set aside at room temperature for 30 minutes. You should have about 2 cups of filling. (The filling can be prepared 1 day ahead and refrigerated. Bring it to room temperature before assembling the dumplings.)

3. **Meanwhile, form** 16 wrappers from half of the dough. Aim for wrappers that are about 3 1/4 inches in diameter. (For guidance, see page 24.)

4. **Before assembling** the dumplings, line a baking sheet with parchment paper. (If you plan to refrigerate the dumplings for several hours

continued

or freeze them, lightly dust the paper with flour to avoid sticking.)

5. **For each dumpling,** hold a wrapper in a slightly cupped hand. Scoop up about 1 tablespoon of filling with a bamboo dumpling spatula, dinner knife, or fork and position it slightly off-center toward the upper half of the wrapper, pressing and shaping it into a flat mound and keeping about $1/2$ to $3/4$ inch of wrapper clear on all sides. Fold, pleat, and press to enclose the filling and create half-moon, pea pod, or pleated crescent shapes (see pages 26 to 29 for instructions).

Place the finished dumpling on the prepared baking sheet. Repeat with the other wrappers, assembling the dumplings and spacing them a good $1/2$ inch apart on the baking sheet. Keeping the finished dumplings covered with a dry kitchen towel, form and fill the wrappers from the remaining dough.

6. **Once all the dumplings** are assembled, they can be covered with plastic wrap and refrigerated for several hours; they can be cooked straight from the refrigerator. For longer storage, freeze them on their baking sheet until hard (about 1 hour), transfer them to a zip-top freezer bag, pressing out excess air before sealing, and keep them frozen for up to 1 month; partially thaw, using your finger to smooth over any cracks that may have formed during freezing, before cooking.

7. **To panfry the dumplings,** use a medium or large nonstick skillet; if both sizes are handy, cook two batches at the same time. Heat the skillet over medium-high heat and add $11/2$ tablespoons oil for a medium skillet and 2 tablespoons for a large one. Place the dump-

lings 1 at a time, sealed edges up, in a winding circle pattern. The dumplings can touch. (In general, medium skillets will fit 12 to 14 dumplings, large skillets will fit 16 to 18 dumplings.) Fry the dumplings for 1 to 2 minutes, until they are golden or light brown on the bottom.

8. **Holding the lid** close to the skillet to lessen the dramatic effect of water hitting hot oil, use a kettle or measuring cup to add water to a depth of roughly $1/4$ inch; expect to use about $1/3$ cup of water. The water will immediately sputter and boil vigorously. Cover with a lid or aluminum foil, lower the heat to medium, and let the water bubble away for 8 to 10 minutes, until it is mostly gone. After 6 to 8 minutes, move the lid or foil so that it is slightly ajar to allow steam to shoot out from underneath. This lessens the drama of condensation dripping down onto to the hot oil when you remove the lid. When you hear sizzling noises (a sign that most of the water is gone), remove the lid. Let the dumplings fry for another 1 to 2 minutes, until the bottoms are brown and crisp.

Turn off the heat and wait until the sizzling stops before using a spatula to transfer the dumplings to a serving plate. Display them with their bottoms facing up so that they remain crisp.

9. **Serve with the** dipping sauce in a communal bowl for people to help themselves or divided up among individual rice bowls or large dipping sauce dishes. Eat these with chopsticks in one hand and a spoon or rice bowl in the other to catch any drips of dipping sauce or juices that spill out when you bite into the pot sticker.

Steamed Vegetable Dumplings
Zhēngjiǎo

Makes 32 dumplings, serving 4 as a main course, 6 to 8 as a snack or starter

Whereas boiled dumplings have crinkly skins that are tender from having been immersed in hot water, and panfried dumplings have skins that are a combination of crisp bottom and chewy top, steamed dumplings are texturally in between—the skins are slightly chewy and soft. Gentle steam heat also protects the filling flavor and you taste it more, a bonus for delicate combinations such as this one.

Unlike many other Chinese dumpling fillings, this vegetarian filling is cooked first to allow the cornstarch to work its cohesive magic, binding the vegetables and pressed tofu together so that they are easier to control when you are assembling the dumplings. I like to use some of the liquid from soaking the mushrooms to season the filling with an earthy savor; if you do too, remember to strain the heady liquid through cheesecloth or paper towel to remove any bits of grit. For details on brown, meatlike pressed tofu, see page 17.

FILLING

4 cups lightly packed, coarsely chopped spinach (7 to 8 ounces)

4 large dried shiitake mushrooms, reconstituted and liquid reserved (see page 13), stemmed, and chopped (1/2 cup)

1/4 teaspoon salt

1/4 teaspoon ground white pepper

3/4 teaspoon sugar

1 1/2 tablespoons light (regular) soy sauce

2 tablespoons sesame oil

2 tablespoons canola oil

1 tablespoon finely minced fresh ginger

1/3 cup finely chopped carrot

3 ounces brown pressed tofu, finely chopped (2/3 cup total)

2 teaspoons cornstarch dissolved in 1 tablespoon water

1/2 cup chopped Chinese chives or scallions (white and green parts)

1 pound Basic Dumpling Dough (page 22)

2/3 cup Tangy Soy Dipping Sauce (page 215)

1. To make the filling, put the spinach in a large bowl. Bring a kettle of water to a boil and pour a generous amount over the spinach. Let the spinach wilt for about 30 seconds, drain, rinse with cold water, and drain again. To remove excess moisture, squeeze the spinach in your hands over the sink. When you are done, there should be about 1/2 cup firmly packed spinach.

2. In a bowl, combine 1/4 cup of the reserved mushroom soaking liquid, salt, white pepper, sugar, soy sauce, and sesame oil. Stir to dissolve the sugar. Set this flavoring sauce aside.

3. In a wok or large skillet, heat the canola oil over medium heat. Add the ginger and stir-fry for about 30 seconds, until aromatic. Add the spinach, carrot, mushrooms, and pressed tofu. Stir to combine and then pour in the flavoring sauce. At first all the liquid will seem to have been absorbed, but after 2 minutes, there will be a little bubbling liquid in the skillet. At that point, give the cornstarch mixture a final stir and stir it into the filling. When the mixture

continued

thickens, turn off the heat and add the Chinese chives. Transfer to a bowl and set aside to cool completely before assembling the dumplings. You should have about 2 cups of filling. (The filling can be prepared 1 day in advance and refrigerated. Bring it to room temperature before assembling the dumplings.)

4. **Form 16 wrappers** from half of the dough. Aim for wrappers that are about 3¹/4 inches in diameter (see page 24).

5. **Before assembling** the dumplings, line steamer trays or a baking sheet with parchment paper and set aside (see page 17 for more on preparing steamers). (If you are making the dumplings in advance, or freezing them, lightly dust the parchment paper–lined tray with flour to avoid sticking.)

6. **To assemble the dumplings,** hold a wrapper in a slightly cupped hand. Scoop up about 1 tablespoon of filling with a bamboo dumpling spatula, dinner knife, or fork and position it slightly off-center toward the upper half of the wrapper, pressing and shaping it into a flat mound and keeping about 1/2 to 3/4 inch of wrapper clear on all sides. Then fold, pleat, and press to enclose the filling to create a half-moon, pea pod, big hug, or pleated crescent shape (see pages 26 to 29).

If you are steaming right away, place the finished dumpling in a steamer tray, sealed side up and 1 inch away from the edge if you are using a metal steamer. Repeat with the other wrappers before forming and filling

wrappers from the remaining dough, keeping the finished dumplings covered with a dry kitchen towel as you make the rest. If you don't have enough space on your steamer trays to steam all the dumplings at once, or if you are not steaming them right away, place the waiting ones on the prepared baking sheet spaced a good 1/2 inch apart.

7. **Once all the dumplings** are assembled, they can be covered with plastic wrap and refrigerated for several hours; they can be cooked straight from the refrigerator. For longer storage, freeze them on the baking sheet until hard (about 1 hour), transfer them to a zip-top freezer bag, pressing out excess air before sealing, and keep them frozen for up to 1 month; thaw completely on lined steamer trays, using your finger to smooth over any cracks that may have formed during freezing, before steaming.

8. **To cook, steam** the dumplings (see page 17 for guidance) over boiling water for about 8 minutes, or until slightly puffed and somewhat translucent. Remove the trays and place each atop a serving plate.

9. **Serve immediately** with the dipping sauce, either in a communal bowl with a spoon or portioned into individual bowls or dipping sauce dishes. As with all *jiǎozi*, it is easiest to eat these with chopsticks in one hand and soupspoon or rice bowl in the other, angling the bowl or spoon to catch any drips.

Fish and Chinese Chive Dumplings
Yújiǎo

Makes 32 dumplings, serving 4 as a main course, 6 to 8 as a snack or starter

If your preference is for seafood, substitute this fish filling for the ones given for boiled Pork and Napa Cabbage Water Dumplings (page 31), the panfried Meat and Chinese Chive Pot Stickers (page 33), or the Steamed Vegetable Dumplings (page 35). Regardless of cooking method, you'll produce dumplings filled with the elements of classic Chinese steamed fish. For the best results, select the freshest fish possible—it should have a bit of sheen and be devoid of any off odors.

Because this dough filling is light in color, I often encase it in jade green dough made with spinach for a pretty presentation (see page 23).

FILLING

2/3 pound mild-tasting white fish fillet, such as cod or sole

Scant 1/2 teaspoon salt

1/8 teaspoon ground white pepper

1/4 cup Chicken Stock (page 222) or water

1 1/2 tablespoons light (regular) soy sauce

1 tablespoon Shaoxing rice wine or dry sherry

2 tablespoons canola oil

1 1/2 tablespoons sesame oil

1 1/2 tablespoons finely minced fresh ginger

3/4 cup chopped Chinese chives or scallions (white and green parts)

1 pound Basic Dumpling Dough (page 22)

Canola or peanut oil (if panfrying)

2/3 cup Tangy Soy Dipping Sauce (page 215)

1. **To make the filling,** cut the fish into 1-inch chunks, discarding any bones you discover along the way (bevel-tipped tweezers will help, if you have them). Put the fish in a food processor.

2. **In a small bowl,** combine the salt, white pepper, chicken stock, soy sauce, wine, canola oil, and sesame oil. Mix well to create a seasoning liquid, and then pour about 2 tablespoons of the liquid into the food processor. Run the food processor, pouring the remaining sea-soning liquid through the feed tube. Grind to a coarse paste, stopping occasionally to scrape down the sides.

3. **Return the paste** to the bowl and mix in the ginger and Chinese chives. To develop the flavors, cover with plastic wrap and set aside at room temperature for 30 minutes. You should have about 2 cups of filling. (The filling can be prepared 1 day ahead and refrigerated. Return it to room temperature for dumpling assembly.)

4. **Form 16 wrappers** from half of the dough. Aim for wrappers that are about 3 1/4 inches in diameter (see page 24).

5. **Before assembling** the dumplings, line a baking sheet with parchment paper. (If you plan to refrigerate the dumplings for several hours, or freeze them, lightly dust the paper with flour to avoid sticking.)

6. **For each dumpling,** hold a wrapper in a slightly cupped hand. Scoop up about 1 tablespoon of filling with a bamboo dumpling spatula, dinner knife, or fork and position it slightly off-center toward the upper half of

continued

the wrapper, pressing and shaping it into a flat mound and keeping about 1/2 to 3/4 inch of wrapper clear on all sides. Fold, pleat, and press to enclose the filling and create a half-moon, pea pod, big hug, or pleated crescent shape (see pages 26 to 29).

Place the finished dumpling on the prepared baking sheet. Repeat with the other wrappers, spacing the finished dumplings a good 1/2 inch apart on the baking sheet. Keep the finished dumplings covered with a dry kitchen towel as you form wrappers from the remaining dough and fill them with the remaining filling.

7. **Once assembled,** the dumplings can be covered with plastic wrap and refrigerated for several hours; they can be cooked straight from the refrigerator. For longer storage, freeze them on their baking sheet until hard (about 1 hour), transfer them to a zip-top freezer bag, seal well, and keep them frozen for up to 1 month; partially thaw, using your finger to smooth over any cracks that may have formed during freezing, before cooking.

8. **Depending on** your desired cooking method, follow the instructions in the preceding recipes for poached water dumplings (page 31), pan-fried pot stickers (page 33), or steamed dumplings (page 35). Serve with the dipping sauce.

WONDERFUL WAYS WITH WHEAT

Many people associate Asian cuisines with rice, but for those who live in the northern parts of Asia, wheat is a staple grain. It's hard to grow rice in that region's extreme climates, which tend to be cold and dry. In fact, with regard to Chinese food, wheat has traditionally been more commonly used in northern fare than in southern fare, which is defined by rice; the geographic demarcation between the two is the Yangtze River.

One of the world's oldest grains, wheat is believed to have originated in southwest Asia, in the Fertile Crescent region of the Middle East. Its cultivation spread in all directions to wherever the grass may be grown, reaching India and China during prehistoric times. By about 1000 B.C.E., it was an established crop in Korea.

Today, China and India are among the world's biggest wheat producers, accounting for over a quarter of the global production for the 2005 to 2006 season. The Chinese consume so much of the grain that they are also a leading importer of it.

Given the important role of wheat at the Asian table, it's understandable that many dumplings are encased by wheat-flour wrappers. For example, the very familiar pot stickers, wontons, and spring rolls (also known as egg rolls) are all made with wheat-flour skins. But those are just the tip of the iceberg. Other favorite wheat-based dumplings include soul-satisfying Chinese water dumplings (*shuǐjiǎo*), Japanese panfried dumplings (*gyōza*), and hearty Mongolian *khuushuur* and Tibetan *momo*—comfort foods that define their respective cuisines. There are also leavened buns with pillowy dough and sumptuous fillings. Wheat is absolutely necessary for the rich and flaky pastries that envelop Indian samosas, Filipino empanadas, and Malay curry puffs.

As you can see, a vast array of Asian dumplings relies on wheat flour, and the first four chapters of this book illuminate some of the major ones. Most of the recipes here call for readily available ingredients from your neighborhood grocery store, so dive in and enjoy.

Japanese Pork and Shrimp Pot Stickers
Gyōza

Makes 32 dumplings, serving 4 as a main course, 6 to 8 as a snack or starter

"If I can't have sushi, I must have *gyōza*," says my friend Makiko Tsuzuki, a self-described *gyōza otaku* (dumpling fanatic). The Japanese love pot stickers, ordering them at ramen noodle shops, patronizing *gyōza* restaurants, and visiting the Gyōza Stadium food theme park in Tokyo. They consider the dumplings essential to their cuisine, despite the fact that *gyōza* were popularized only after World War II, when Japanese soldiers returning from China brought back their taste and knack for making Chinese dumplings. *Gyōza* is the Japanese pronunciation of *jiǎozi*.

Like their Chinese parent, *gyōza* can be boiled, steamed, fried, or served in soup (see Variation). Panfrying is the most popular cooking method, which is why *gyōza* are commonly known as pot stickers. The filling strays from Chinese tradition by including a kick of garlic, a touch of sugar, a dose of black pepper, and a smidgen of sake. Sesame oil has a lesser role in the filling but a bigger role in panfrying the dumplings. Sesame oil has the same smoking point as butter and thus cooking with it is fine. *Gyōza* may be dipped in vinegary soy dipping sauce or biting hot mustard.

FILLING

2 cups lightly packed, finely chopped napa cabbage, cut from whole leaves (about 7 ounces)

1/2 teaspoon plus 1/4 teaspoon salt

2 cloves garlic, minced and crushed into a paste

1 teaspoon grated fresh ginger, or 1 tablespoon finely minced fresh ginger

2 tablespoons chopped Chinese chives or scallions (white and green parts)

6 ounces ground pork, fattier kind preferred, coarsely chopped to loosen

1/3 pound medium shrimp, shelled, deveined, and chopped (41/2 ounces net weight)

Scant 1/4 teaspoon sugar

Generous 1/2 teaspoon black pepper

11/2 tablespoons Japanese soy sauce or light (regular) soy sauce

1 tablespoon sake

1 teaspoon sesame oil

1 pound Basic Dumpling Dough (page 22)

Canola oil or sesame oil or a combination of both, for panfrying

5 tablespoons Japanese soy sauce or light (regular) soy sauce

21/2 tablespoons unseasoned rice vinegar

1/2 to 1 teaspoon chile oil (page 216) (optional)

Japanese hot mustard (see Note)

1. To make the filling, in a large bowl, toss the cabbage with the 1/2 teaspoon salt. Set aside for about 15 minutes to draw excess moisture from the cabbage. Drain in a fine-mesh strainer (the cabbage may fall through the large holes of a colander), rinse with water, and drain again. To remove more moisture, squeeze the cabbage in your hands over the sink, or put into a cotton (not terry cloth) kitchen towel and wring out the moisture over the sink. You should have about 1/2 cup firmly packed cabbage.

2. Transfer the cabbage to a bowl and add the garlic, ginger, Chinese chives, pork, and shrimp. Stir and lightly mash the ingredients so that they start coming together.

continued

3. In a small bowl, stir together the remaining 1/4 teaspoon salt, the sugar, pepper, soy sauce, sake, and sesame oil. Pour these seasonings over the meat and cabbage mixture, and then stir and fold the ingredients together. Once you have broken up the large chunks of pork so none are visible, briskly stir to blend the ingredients into a cohesive, thick mixture. To develop the flavors, cover with plastic wrap and set aside at room temperature for 30 minutes. You should have about 2 cups of filling. (The filling can be prepared 1 day ahead and refrigerated. Bring it to room temperature before assembling the dumplings.)

4. Meanwhile, form 16 wrappers from half of the dough. Aim for wrappers that are about 3 1/4 inches in diameter (see page 24).

5. Before assembling the dumplings, line a baking sheet with parchment paper. (If you plan to refrigerate the dumplings for several hours, or freeze them, lightly dust the paper with flour to avoid sticking.) For each dumpling, hold a wrapper in a slightly cupped hand. Scoop up about 1 tablespoon of filling with a bamboo dumpling spatula, dinner knife, or fork and position it slightly off-center toward the upper half of the wrapper, pressing and shaping it into a flat mound and keeping about 1/2 to 3/4 inch of wrapper clear on all sides. Fold, pleat, and press to enclose the filling and create a half-moon, pea pod, or pleated crescent shape (see pages 26 to 29 for instructions). Place the finished dumpling on the prepared baking sheet. Repeat with the remaining wrappers, spacing them a good 1/2 inch apart. Keep the finished dumplings covered with a dry kitchen towel as you make wrappers with the remaining dough and fill with the remaining filling.

6. Once all the dumplings are assembled, they can be covered with plastic wrap and refrigerated for several hours; they can be cooked straight from the refrigerator. For longer storage, freeze them on their tray until hard (about 1 hour), transfer them to a zip-top freezer bag, seal well, and keep them frozen for up to 1 month; partially thaw, using your finger to smooth over any cracks that may have formed during freezing, before cooking.

7. To panfry the dumplings, use a medium or large nonstick skillet; if both sizes are handy, cook two batches at the same time. Heat the skillet over medium-high heat and add 1 1/2 tablespoons canola oil for a medium skillet and 2 tablespoons for a large one. (If you are combining oils, use 2 parts canola oil and 1 part sesame oil.) Add the dumplings one at a time, placing them sealed edges up in a winding circle pattern or several straight rows. The dumplings may touch. (In general, medium skillets will fit 12 to 14 dumplings, large skillets will fit 16 to 18 dumplings.) Fry the dumplings for 1 to 2 minutes, until they're golden or light brown at the bottom.

8. Holding the lid close to the skillet to lessen the dramatic effect of water hitting hot oil, use a kettle or measuring cup to add water to a depth of about 1/4 inch; expect to use about 1/3 cup water for each skillet. The water will immediately sputter and boil vigorously.

Cover each skillet with a lid or aluminum foil, lower the heat to medium, and let the water bubble away until it is mostly gone, 8 to 10 minutes. After 6 to 8 minutes, move the lid or foil so that it is slightly ajar to allow steam to shoot out from underneath. This lessens the drama of condensation dripping down onto the hot oil when you remove the lid.

9. While the dumplings cook, combine the soy sauce, rice vinegar, and chile oil in a small bowl to create a dipping sauce. Taste and make any flavor adjustments.

10. When the bubbling noise in the skillet turns into a gentle frying sound (a sign that most of the water is gone), remove the lid. Allow the dumplings to fry for another 1 to 2 minutes, or until the bottoms are brown and crisp. Turn off the heat and wait until the sizzling stops before transferring the dumplings to a serving plate, using a spatula to lift up a few of them at a time. Display them with their bottoms up so that they remain crisp.

11. Serve immediately with the dipping sauce in a communal bowl for people to help themselves or divided up among individual rice bowls or large dipping bowls. Pass the mustard at the table. Eat these with chopsticks in one hand and a spoon or rice bowl in the other.

Note: Punchy Japanese mustard (*karashi*) is sold in prepared and powdered forms at Japanese and sometimes Chinese markets. Chinese hot mustard and Colman's English mustard are fine substitutes. When using powdered mustard, add a few drops of cold water and stir to make a thick, smooth paste.

VARIATION: GYŌZA IN SMOKY CHICKEN SOUP

Instead of panfrying these dumplings, poach and serve them in smoky chicken broth for satisfying *sui gyōza* (Japanese dumplings in soup).

In a large pot, combine 4 cups of chicken stock (page 222), 1 tablespoon of sake, and 2 pieces of *kombu* (dried Japanese kelp), each the size of a playing card. Let the *kombu* soak for 15 minutes to develop flavor, then bring to a simmer, cover, and cook for 5 minutes. Remove from the heat and scatter in $1/2$ loosely packed cup of *katsuo-bushi* (Japanese dried bonito flakes, available along with the *kombu* at Asian markets and specialty grocers). Let sit for 3 to 4 minutes, then strain through a mesh strainer lined with cheesecloth or paper towel; save the *kombu* for another use, if you wish. Transfer the stock to a pot, cover, and reheat to a low simmer.

Parboil 16 uncooked *gyōza* dumplings in a large pot of water (see Pork and Napa Cabbage Water Dumplings, step 7, for guidance), until they float to the top, about 5 minutes. Meanwhile, cut $1 1/2$ to 2 inches of carrot into fine shreds and set aside. Use a slotted spoon or skimmer to scoop up dumplings from the pot, then add them to the hot stock; keep the water boiling. Add the carrot to the stock, and adjust the heat to maintain a simmer and finish cooking the dumplings, about 3 minutes.

Meanwhile, wilt 2 lightly packed cups of spinach leaves in the boiling water. Drain the spinach, rinse with cold water, and drain again. Divide among 4 individual bowls.

When the dumplings are puffy, glossy, and a bit translucent, scoop them from the stock and divide among the soup bowls. Taste and add salt as needed, then bring the stock to a boil. Ladle the stock and carrot into the bowls. Serve immediately.

Kimchi Dumplings
Kimchi Mandu

Makes 32 dumplings, serving 4 as a main course, 6 to 8 as a snack or starter

Nothing says "Korean dumpling" more than one filled with kimchi, the spicy pickled cabbage that's essential to the Korean table. *Mandu* are the Korean version of Chinese *jiǎozi* and Japanese *gyōza*. The fillings often incorporate firm tofu as a binder and protein substitute—tofu is used in these kimchi *mandu*. In addition, the ground Korean red chile pepper used for making kimchi turns the filling a pretty orange color, and there's plenty of garlic pungency to wake up the palate. Though these can be panfried, deep-fried, and steamed, I love them boiled. The dryish filling gets a boost of succulence from the hot water bath.

Purchased or homemade napa cabbage kimchi, especially older (stinkier) kimchi, works extra well. A side of shredded Korean or daikon radish tossed with a little salt and equal parts rice vinegar and sugar is a refreshing accompaniment.

FILLING

1¼ cups kimchi, coarsely chopped (remove scallions if present)

1 (5-ounce) zucchini, finely diced (about 1 cup)

½ teaspoon plus ¼ teaspoon salt

10 ounces firm tofu

2 large scallions (white and green parts), finely chopped

2 large cloves garlic, minced and crushed into a paste

½ teaspoon black pepper

¼ teaspoon sugar

1 tablespoon sesame oil

1 pound Basic Dumpling Dough (page 22) or Extra Chewy Dough (page 23)

⅔ cup Korean Dipping Sauce (page 215)

1. To make the filling, process the kimchi in a food processor or electric mini-chopper until finely chopped, pausing to scrape down the sides, as needed. To expel excess kimchi juices, transfer to a mesh strainer and firmly press with a spatula. Save the juices for another use or discard. Put the kimchi in a bowl.

2. Put the zucchini in a small bowl and toss with the ¼ teaspoon salt. Set aside for about 15 minutes to draw excess moisture from the zucchini. Drain in the mesh strainer, rinse with water, and drain again. To remove moisture, put the zucchini into a cotton (not terry cloth) kitchen towel and wring it out. Add the zucchini to the kimchi.

3. Put the tofu in the same towel. Gather the towel up and, standing over a sink, squeeze on the tofu. Unwrap the towel and add the crumbled tofu to the kimchi and zucchini, using the dull edge of a knife or plastic dough scraper, if needed, to remove the tofu from the towel. Add the scallions and garlic, and use a fork or spatula to combine the ingredients.

4. Add the remaining ½ teaspoon salt, the pepper, sugar, and sesame oil and mix well. Taste and adjust the seasonings for a savory-spicy balance. Cover with plastic wrap and set aside at room temperature for 30 minutes to develop the flavors. You should have about

2 cups of filling. (The filling can be prepared 1 day ahead and refrigerated. Bring it to room temperature for dumpling assembly.)

5. **In the meantime,** make 16 wrappers from half of the dough. Aim for wrappers 3¹/4 inches in diameter (see page 24).

6. **Before assembling** the dumplings, line a baking sheet with parchment paper. (If you plan to refrigerate the dumplings for several hours, or freeze them, lightly dust the paper with flour to avoid sticking.) Hold a wrapper in a slightly cupped hand. Scoop up about 1 tablespoon of filling with a bamboo dumpling spatula, dinner knife, or fork and position it slightly off-center toward the upper half of the wrapper, pressing and shaping it into a flat mound and keeping about ¹/2 to ³/4 inch of wrapper clear on all sides. Fold, pleat, and press to enclose the filling and create a big hug, half-moon, pea pod, or pleated crescent shape (see pages 26 to 29). Place the finished dumpling on the prepared baking sheet. Repeat with the other wrappers, placing them a good ¹/2 inch apart on the baking sheet. Keep the finished dumplings covered with a dry kitchen towel as you form wrappers from the remaining dough and fill with the remaining filling.

7. **Once all the** dumplings are assembled, they can be covered with plastic wrap and refrigerated for several hours; they can be cooked straight from the refrigerator. For longer storage, freeze them on their baking sheet until hard (about 1 hour), transfer them to a zip-top freezer bag, pressing out excess air before sealing, and keep them frozen for up to 1 month; partially thaw, using your finger to smooth over any cracks that may have formed during freezing, before cooking.

8. **To cook the** dumplings, half-fill a large pot with water, cover, and bring to a boil over high heat. Add half the dumplings, gently dropping each one into the water. Nudge the dumplings apart with a wooden spoon to prevent sticking. Return the water to a simmer and then lower the heat to maintain the simmer and gently cook: a hard boil can make a dumpling burst. Cook the dumplings for about 8 minutes, or until they float to the surface, look glossy, and are puffed up and somewhat translucent. Use a slotted spoon or skimmer to scoop out the dumplings from the pot, pausing above the pot to allow excess water to drip back down, and put the dumplings on a serving plate. Cover with a large inverted bowl to keep warm.

Return the water to a boil and cook the remaining dumplings. When they are done, return the first batch to the water to reheat them for a minute or two.

9. **Serve the hot** dumplings immediately with the sauce, either in a communal bowl for people to help themselves or divided up among individual rice bowls or large dipping sauce dishes. Eat these with chopsticks and a spoon or rice bowl to catch any drips.

Korean Meat and Vegetable Dumplings
Gun Mandu

Makes 32 dumplings, serving 4 as a main course, 6 to 8 as a snack or starter

Meat and vegetable dumplings such as these are a standard offering at Korean dumpling and noodle shops. A favorite way to enjoy them is poached in broth for a warming *mandu guk* soup (page 49), but they are equally fabulous when fried.

However, don't expect the standard Chinese pot sticker. Korean cooks like to panfry at least two sides of their dumplings for a greater amount of crispy-chewy goodness. When made with extra chewy dough comprised of wheat and sweet rice flour, the dumplings are even tastier. *Gun mandu* may also be quickly deep-fried in 1¼ inches of oil heated to 350°F for 2 to 3 minutes total; the resulting pebbled golden skin is a delightful reminder of American frozen egg roll snacks.

FILLING

1 cup bean sprouts (about 3 ounces)

6 ounces firm tofu

2 large scallions (white and pale green parts, reserve dark green part for dipping sauce), finely chopped

¼ cup finely chopped yellow onion

2 large cloves garlic, minced and crushed into a paste

1 teaspoon grated fresh ginger, or 1 tablespoon finely minced fresh ginger

½ pound ground beef (chuck preferred) or ground pork (fattier kind preferred), coarsely chopped to loosen

Scant ½ teaspoon salt

½ teaspoon black pepper

1½ tablespoons Korean, Japanese, or light (regular) soy sauce

2 teaspoons sesame oil

1 pound Basic Dumpling Dough (page 22) or Extra Chewy Dough (page 23)

Canola oil, for panfrying

⅔ cup Korean Dipping Sauce (page 215)

1. To make the filling, blanch the bean sprouts in a saucepan of boiling water for about 20 seconds, or until no longer stiff. Drain, rinse with cold water, and drain again. Use your hands to squeeze excess water from the sprouts. Chop the sprouts into ¼-inch lengths and put in a bowl.

2. To expel water from the tofu, put it in a cotton (not terry cloth) kitchen towel. Gather the towel up and, standing over a sink, firmly squeeze on the tofu. Unwrap the towel and add the crumbled tofu to the bean sprouts. Use the dull edge of a knife or plastic dough scraper, if needed, to remove the tofu from the towel. Use a fork or spatula to mash any remaining chunks of tofu. Add the scallions, onion, garlic, ginger, and meat to the bean sprouts and tofu. Stir and lightly mash the ingredients so that they start commingling.

3. In a small bowl, stir together the salt, pepper, soy sauce, and sesame oil. Pour the seasonings over the meat and vegetable mixture, then stir and fold the ingredients together. Break up any large chunks of beef and briskly stir to blend the ingredients into a cohesive, thick mixture. To develop the flavors, cover with plastic wrap and set aside at room temperature for 30 minutes, or refrigerate overnight and return to room temperature for dumpling assembly. Makes about 2 cups.

4. **Meanwhile, form** 16 wrappers from half of the dough. Aim for wrappers that are about $3^1/4$ inches in diameter (see page 24).

5. **Before assembling** the dumplings, line a baking sheet with parchment paper. (If you plan to refrigerate the dumplings for several hours, or freeze them, lightly dust the paper with flour to avoid sticking.) Hold a wrapper in a slightly cupped hand. Scoop up about 1 tablespoon of filling with a bamboo dumpling spatula, dinner knife, or fork and position it slightly off-center toward the upper half of the wrapper, pressing and shaping it into a flat mound and keeping about $1/2$ to $3/4$ inch of wrapper clear on all sides. Fold, pleat, and press to enclose the filling and create a half-moon, pea pod, or pleated crescent shape (see pages 26 to 29). Place the finished dumpling on the prepared baking sheet. Repeat with the other wrappers, placing the finished dumplings on the baking sheet at least $1/2$ inch apart. Cover the dumplings with a dry towel as you form wrappers from the remaining dough and fill them.

Assembled dumplings can be covered with plastic wrap, refrigerated for several hours, and cooked straight from the refrigerator. Or, freeze them on their baking sheet until hard (about 1 hour), transfer them to a zip-top freezer bag, pressing out excess air before sealing, and keep them frozen for up to 1 month; partially thaw, using your finger to smooth over any cracks that may have formed during freezing, before cooking.

6. **To panfry the dumplings,** use a medium or large nonstick skillet; if both sizes are handy, cook two batches at the same time. Heat the skillet over medium-high heat and add enough oil to film the bottom. Add the dumplings, one at a time, placing them on one of their sides. Don't let the dumplings touch. Fry the dumplings for 1 to 2 minutes, until they are golden or light brown on the one side. Using chopsticks, and maybe a spatula, too, turn each dumpling to brown another side, 1 to 2 minutes longer.

7. **Holding the lid close** to the skillet to lessen the dramatic effect of water hitting hot oil, use a kettle or measuring cup to add water to a depth of roughly $1/4$ inch; you will use about $1/3$ cup water for each skillet. The water will immediately sputter and boil vigorously. Cover the skillet with a lid or aluminum foil, lower the heat to medium, and let the water bubble away until it is mostly gone, 8 to 10 minutes. After 6 to 8 minutes, move the lid or foil so that it is slightly ajar to allow steam to shoot out from underneath. This lessens the drama of condensation dripping down onto the hot oil when you remove the lid.

8. **When you hear** sizzling noises, remove the lid. Let the dumplings fry for another 1 to 2 minutes, until the bottoms are brown and crisp. (At this point, you can also brown the third side, if you want.) Turn off the heat, wait for the cooking action to cease, and then use a spatula to transfer the dumplings to a serving plate. Display them with their crisp sides facing up.

9. **Serve with the** dipping sauce in a communal bowl for people to help themselves, or divided up among individual rice bowls or large dipping sauce dishes. Eat these with chopsticks in one hand and a spoon or rice bowl in the other to catch any drips.

Korean Dumpling Soup
Mandu Guk

Serves 4 to 6

One of the common ways to enjoy Korean dumplings is in a fragrant beef stock. A hot bowl of *mandu guk* is extra satisfying on a cold winter's day. It's easy to assemble if you've got frozen *mandu* and stock on hand.

Any dumpling filling will do, but meat dumplings are generally preferred. For fun, you could mix different kinds or even make them out of different colored doughs (see page 23). The shape of choice for Korean dumpling soup is the big hug, though you can shape your dumplings anyway you'd like. The stock imbues the wrapper with its flavors and also thickens a tiny bit from the starches in the dough. For Korean New Year celebrations, chewy slices of dense rice cakes called *duk* are added to the stock for bowls of *duk mandu guk*.

10 cups Korean Beef Stock (page 223)

32 uncooked Korean Meat and Vegetable Dumplings (page 46)

2 large eggs, beaten

1 or 2 pinches of salt

1 or 2 pinches of black pepper

1 teaspoon canola oil

1 large scallion (green part only), cut into thin rings

1 full-size sheet toasted nori (seaweed), cut into thin, 2 to 3-inch-long strips (use scissors)

1. Bring the beef stock to a boil in a large pot over high heat. Add half the dumplings, gently dropping each one into the stock. Use a wooden spoon to nudge the dumplings to prevent sticking. Return the stock to a simmer, then lower the heat to maintain the simmer and gently cook; a hard boil can make a dumpling burst. Cook the dumplings for about 8 minutes, or until they float to the surface, look glossy, and are puffed up and somewhat translucent. Use a slotted spoon or skimmer to scoop up the dumplings, pausing above the pot to allow excess stock to drip back down before putting the dumplings on a plate. Cover to keep warm.

Return the stock to a boil and cook the remaining dumplings. When they are done, return the first batch to the stock to reheat them for a minute or two.

2. While the dumplings cook, make an egg sheet. Season the egg with the salt and pepper. Heat the oil in a medium nonstick skillet over medium heat. Pour in the egg and swirl the hot skillet to cover the bottom with egg. Cook, undisturbed, for about 1 minute, or until the edges start curling away from the sides. Use your fingers to pick up the egg sheet (it won't be too hot) and flip it over. Cook for another 30 seconds, or until cooked through, and then slide onto a plate or cutting board. Allow the egg sheet to cool for a few minutes, then quarter it and cut it into thin strips to match the nori. Set aside.

3. Divide the dumplings among the soup bowls. Taste the stock and add extra salt, as needed. Return the stock to a boil and then ladle over the dumplings. Top each bowl with some egg, scallion, and nori. Add a little pepper and serve.

Mongolian Meat and Caraway Pockets

Khuushuur

Makes 24 pockets, serving 4 as a main course, 6 to 8 as a snack or starter

---

A traditionally nomadic people with little arable land, Mongolians have a small variety of vegetables and spices to enhance their cuisine and instead enjoy a hearty diet of mostly meat and dairy products. The creative use of a few ingredients is a hallmark of Mongolian cooking, and these very popular deep-fried stuffed pockets prove that less can be more.

Cultivated in Mongolia, caraway leaves its warm yet sharp imprint on the filling, which remarkably amplifies the natural sweetness of the wheat wrapper. (If you have whole caraway, lightly toast it, then grind it in a clean coffee grinder.) Fresh mutton or air-dried meat called *borts* is traditionally featured in the filling, but beef or lamb is a fine substitute. The wrapper fries up to a nubby, chewy-crispness that's hard to resist. In a pinch, stir together a spicy-sweet sauce of ketchup and Sriracha sauce or Chile Garlic Sauce (page 216), instead of the roasted tomato sauce. This filling can be used for boiled and steamed dumplings, which are called *bansh* and *buuz*, respectively.

FILLING

3/4 pound ground beef (preferably chuck) or lamb, coarsely chopped to loosen

3/4 cup finely chopped yellow onion

2 cloves garlic, minced and crushed into a paste

1 teaspoon salt

1 1/2 teaspoons ground caraway seeds

1/2 teaspoon black pepper

2 tablespoons canola oil

5 tablespoons water

1 pound Basic Dumpling Dough (page 22)

Canola or peanut oil, for deep-frying

1 1/2 cups Spicy Roasted Tomato Sauce (page 218)

1. **In a bowl,** combine the beef, onion, and garlic. Use a fork or spatula to stir and lightly mash the ingredients together.

2. **Stir together** the salt, caraway seeds, pepper, oil, and water in a small bowl. Pour over the meat mixture and stir with the fork or spatula to blend well. There should not be any visible large chunks of meat. To develop the flavors, cover with plastic wrap and set aside at room temperature for 30 minutes. You should have about 2 cups of filling. (The filling can be prepared 1 day ahead and refrigerated. Bring it to room temperature before assembling the dumplings.)

3. **Meanwhile,** form 12 wrappers from half of the dough. Aim for wrappers that are 3 3/4 to 4 inches in diameter. (For guidance, see "Forming Wrappers from Basic Dumpling Dough," page 24.)

4. **Before assembling** the dumplings, line a baking sheet with parchment paper. Hold a wrapper in a slightly cupped hand. Scoop up 4 teaspoons (a heaping tablespoon) of filling with a bamboo dumpling spatula, dinner knife, or fork and position it slightly off-center toward the upper half of the wrapper, pressing and shaping it into a flat mound and keeping about 1/2 to 3/4 inch of wrapper clear on all sides. As you work, your hand should naturally close a bit more to keep the dumpling in shape. Bring up the wrapper side closest to you and firmly press to enclose the filling and create a half-

moon (see page 26), sealing the edges well. To seal even more securely, use your thumb and index fingers to form a rope edge (see below) or press the edges together with the tines of a fork.

These dumplings have more filling than others, and the pockets can stick as they sit. Lightly dust one side with flour before placing each dumpling on the prepared baking sheet. Repeat with the other wrappers, placing them about 1/2 inch apart on the baking sheet. Cover the finished dumplings with a dry kitchen towel as you make wrappers from the remaining dough and fill them.

5. Line a platter with paper towels. To deep-fry, heat 1¼ inches of oil in a wok, saucepan, or deep skillet over medium-high heat to about 350°F on a deep-fry thermometer. (If you don't have a deep-fry thermometer, stick a dry bamboo chopstick into the oil; if bubbles rise immediately to the surface and encircle the chopstick, the oil is ready.) Fry the pockets in batches, as many as can fit without crowding, for 2 to 3 minutes total, turning as needed, until richly golden and crisp with little bubbles all over. Remove from the oil and drain on the paper towels. Allow the oil to return to 350°F between batches as you fry the remaining pockets. If you like, increase the oil temperature slightly and quickly refry the earlier ones, in batches, for about 30 seconds, to restore their crispiness.

6. Serve immediately with the sauce. I like to eat these by picking one up with my fingers, biting off a corner, pouring out the juices into a spoon and drinking that before dipping it into the sauce or spooning some sauce into it.

Refrigerate leftovers; to serve, return to room temperature, and reheat in a 375°F oven for about 6 minutes or until hot.

Master Shape: Rope Edge

Asian cooks like to make a lovely edge for turnover-shaped pastries, which not only seals the edges well but is decorative, too. After shaping a half-moon (see page 26), press the edges together well, pressing out any air bubbles if you will be frying the dumpling. Working incrementally from one end to the other, slightly pull on the dough edge and then fold it over, twisting forward with the index finger while twisting back with the thumb. When working with rich pastries (pages 111 to 129), don't stretch the dough. Just fold over the rim in a twisting motion.

Shaping Rope Edges

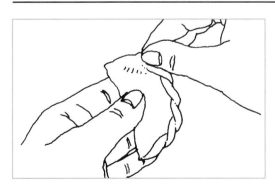

1. Pull on the sealed dough edge, then twist between index finger and thumb.

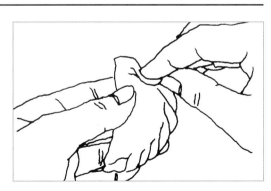

2. For rich pastries, don't pull on the dough, just fold the rim using a twisting motion.

Master Shape: Closed Satchel

This shape is used for *momos,* Shanghai soup dumplings, and stuffed buns.

If you are right handed, hold the wrapper in the left hand and use your right hand to center a mound of filling on the wrapper (lefties, reverse the following directions). Place the left thumb atop the filling to keep it down as you use the right thumb and index finger to make the first pleat by pulling up on the wrapper edge and folding it over itself, pressing it to seal. Keeping the right thumb and index finger in place to steady the pleat (both thumbs are now inside the dumpling), move the left index finger clockwise along the edge to fold the rim over itself to create the second pleat. With this small motion, the left index finger passes the new pleat to the right index finger, which will take it over and press it against the first pleat.

As you repeat this motion along the rim, the right index finger and thumb are pinching and holding the accumulating pleats together. The dumpling will rotate and an accordionlike spiral of pleats will form to gradually close the opening. When the opening is too small to fit both thumbs, move the left thumb to the wrapper edge or remove it and let it rest on the side of the dumpling to keep the dumpling in place. Finish by twisting and pinching shut the opening. If there's excess of dough, pinch the dough edge all around to form a thin lip that better distributes the dough.

Straighten up the sides by holding the dumpling in the crook of your hand and giving it a gentle squeeze, or setting it upright on the work surface and patting the sides. A closed satchel can be cooked and served with the pleats facing up or down. See the individual recipes for instructions.

Shaping Closed Satchels

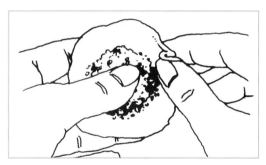

1. Make the first pleat with right thumb and index finger; keep left thumb atop filling.

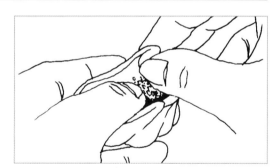

2. Move the left index finger along the wrapper edge, folding the rim over itself to form the second and subsequent pleats.

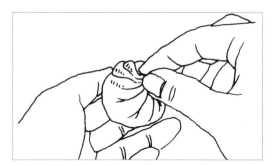

3. Finish by twisting and pinching shut the opening.

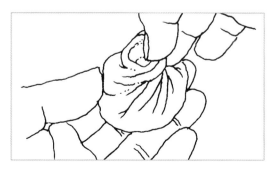

4. Pinch the edge all around to even out excess dough.

Nepalese Vegetable and Cheese Dumplings
Tarkari Momo

Makes 32 dumplings, serving 4 as a main course, 6 to 8 as a snack or starter

Tarkari momo are strikingly similar in concept to Italian ravioli with a ricotta-based filling, but the seasonings in these Nepalese dumplings reveal their Asian roots. Cumin, ginger, and Sichuan peppercorn commingle with *chenna*, or crumbly curds of Indian cheese (a precursor to paneer). Those ingredients combine with fresh chile, vegetables, and butter to make a wonderful vegetarian dumpling. The eye-poppingly spicy tomato sauce is a fabulous pairing with the delicate, rich filling.

The cheese is very easy to prepare, but you can substitute 1/3 pound paneer, crumbling or mincing it before using. For a pretty presentation, consider tinting the wrappers orange or gold by using some carrot juice or turmeric (see page 23).

FILLING

4 cups whole milk

2 tablespoons fresh lemon juice, or 1 1/2 tablespoons distilled white vinegar or cider vinegar

3 cups lightly packed chopped green cabbage

2 cups lightly packed coarsely chopped spinach

3 tablespoons ghee or unsalted butter

1/2 cup finely chopped yellow onion

1 large clove garlic, minced

1 1/2 teaspoons minced fresh ginger

1 large medium-hot red chile, such as Holland or Fresno, finely chopped

1/2 teaspoon Sichuan peppercorn, toasted in a dry skillet for 2 to 3 minutes, until fragrant, then crushed with a mortar and pestle

1/4 teaspoon ground cumin

2 large scallions (white and green parts), chopped

1/3 cup chopped fresh cilantro

1 teaspoon salt

2 teaspoons cornstarch dissolved in 1 tablespoon water

1 pound Basic Dumpling Dough (page 22)

1 1/2 cups Spicy Roasted Tomato Sauce (page 218)

1. Put the milk in a heavy-bottomed saucepan and heat over medium-high heat, stirring frequently. Meanwhile, line a colander with a flour-sack towel, a piece of muslin, or four layers of cheesecloth.

When the milk begins to boil, decrease the heat to prevent boiling over. Add the lemon juice, stirring gently for about 10 seconds, or until white curds start forming and separating from the clear green-yellow whey. Remove from the heat and strain through the fabric-lined colander. Rinse the curds under cold water at a medium flow for about 5 seconds, to cool slightly and remove residual tang.

Gather up the towel around the curds, gently twisting to extract excess water. (If the cheese is still too hot, try again after it has hung for 10 minutes.) Tie up the corners of the towel, then hang the cheese to drain (I use the sink faucet) for 30 to 45 minutes, or until cool.

Transfer the cheese to a bowl, then mash it into a crumble; there should be about 1 cup. Cover to prevent drying. The cheese can be made up to 4 days in advance and refrigerated.

2. Half-fill a pot with water and bring to a boil over high heat. Add the cabbage. When the water returns to a boil, add the spinach, stirring

continued

to wilt it. Remove from the heat, drain the cabbage and spinach, rinse with cold water, then drain again. Expel excess water by squeezing batches of the vegetables in a towel or the same cloth used for making the cheese. Transfer to a bowl and set aside. There should be about 1 1/2 packed cups.

3. **Melt the ghee** in a medium skillet over medium heat. Add the onion and cook for about 2 minutes, stirring occasionally, until soft and fragrantly sweet. Add the garlic, ginger, and chile, stirring for 30 seconds, or until aromatic. Sprinkle in the Sichuan peppercorn and cumin, stirring for another 30 seconds, or until fragrant. Add the cabbage and spinach, and continue cooking for 1 to 2 minutes, until heated through. Stir in the cheese, scallions, and cilantro to combine. Sprinkle in the salt and mix well. Cook for about 1 minute to heat through.

Give the cornstarch mixture a stir and add to the filling mixture. Gently stir and fold until the mixture coheres. Transfer to a bowl, partially cover, and set aside to cool completely before using. You should have about 2 cups. (Or, cover in plastic wrap, refrigerate overnight, and return to temperature before proceeding.)

4. **Meanwhile,** form 16 wrappers from half of the dough (see page 24). Aim for wrappers that are about 3 1/4 inches in diameter.

5. **Before assembling** the dumplings, line steamer trays and/or a baking sheet with parchment paper. (If you are making the dumplings in advance, or plan to freeze them, lightly dust the paper with flour to avoid sticking.) For each dumpling, hold a wrapper in a slightly cupped hand. Scoop up about 1 tablespoon of filling with a bamboo dumpling spatula, dinner knife, or fork and position it in the center of the wrapper, pressing and shaping it into

a mound and keeping about 1/2 to 3/4 inch of wrapper clear on all sides. Use your fingers to pleat and pinch the edge together to enclose the filling and form a closed satchel (see page 52). If that shape is too challenging, make the dumplings into half-moons, pea pods, big hugs, or pleated crescents (see pages 26 to 29 for instructions).

If you are steaming right away, place each finished dumpling in a steamer tray, sealed side up, and 1 inch away from the edge if you are using metal steamers. Repeat with the remaining wrappers, placing them in the steamer about 1/2 inch apart. If you don't have enough space on your steamer trays to steam all the dumplings at once, or if you are not steaming them right away, place the waiting ones on the prepared baking sheet, spaced a good 1/2 inch apart.

Keeping the finished dumplings covered with a dry kitchen towel, form wrappers from the remaining dough and fill them.

6. **Assembled dumplings** can be covered with plastic wrap, refrigerated for several hours, and cooked straight from the refrigerator. Or, freeze them on the baking sheet until hard (about 1 hour), transfer them to a zip-top plastic bag, pressing out excess air before sealing, and keep them frozen for up to 1 month; partially thaw, using your finger to smooth over any cracks that may have formed, before steaming.

7. **To cook,** steam the dumplings (see page 17 for guidance) over boiling water for about 8 minutes, or until they have puffed slightly and become somewhat translucent. Remove each tray and place it atop a serving plate.

8. **Serve immediately** with the sauce in a communal bowl for guests to help themselves. Enjoy with fork and spoon.

Spiced Lamb Dumplings
Khasi Momo

Makes 32 dumplings, serving 4 as a main course, 6 to 8 as a snack or starter

Nepalese cooking combines Indian and Tibetan cuisines, and these classic dumplings illuminate that wonderful marriage. In this filling, Indian garam masala is combined with Sichuan peppercorn, an important spice in Nepal and Tibet. Nepalese *momos* often feature water buffalo, but lamb pairs exceptionally well with the aromatics. You can opt to substitute ground beef, pork, or dark-meat chicken or turkey. Regardless of the meat, these dumplings are like their Tibetan brethren (page 57), full of flavor and delectable juices. If there are leftovers, panfry or deep-fry them the next day.

Note that these dumplings are eaten with fork and spoon. Chopsticks are the standard and prevailing utensils in only four Asian nations—China, Japan, Korea, and Vietnam.

FILLING

3/4 pound ground lamb, coarsely chopped to loosen

1/3 cup finely chopped yellow onion

2 large scallions (white and green parts), finely chopped

1/3 cup finely chopped fresh cilantro

1 large medium-hot chile, such as Holland or Fresno, finely chopped

1 1/2 teaspoons finely minced fresh ginger

1 clove garlic, minced and crushed into a paste

1/2 teaspoon ground coriander

1/2 teaspoon ground cumin

1 1/4 teaspoons garam masala (page 219)

1/4 teaspoon Sichuan peppercorn, toasted in a dry skillet for 2 to 3 minutes, until fragrant, then crushed with a mortar and pestle (optional)

1 generous teaspoon salt

2 tablespoons canola oil

6 tablespoons water

1 pound Basic Dumpling Dough (page 22)

1 1/2 cups Spicy Roasted Tomato Sauce (page 218)

1. To make the filling, combine the lamb, onion, scallions, cilantro, chile, ginger, and garlic in a bowl. Use a fork or spatula to stir and lightly mash the ingredients together. In a small bowl, stir together the coriander, cumin, garam masala, Sichuan peppercorn, salt, oil, and water. Pour these seasonings over the meat mixture, then stir and fold the ingredients together. Once you have broken up the large chunks of meat, briskly stir to blend the ingredients into a cohesive, thick mixture. To develop the flavors, cover with plastic wrap and set aside at room temperature for 30 minutes. You should have about 2 cups. (The filling can be prepared 1 day ahead and refrigerated. Bring it to room temperature before assembling the dumplings.)

2. Meanwhile, roll out 16 wrappers from half of the dough (see page 24). Aim for wrappers that are about 3 1/4 inches in diameter.

3. To assemble and steam the dumplings, follow steps 5 through 7 in the recipe for Nepalese Vegetable and Cheese Dumplings (page 54).

4. Serve immediately with the sauce on the side. Enjoy with fork and spoon.

Tibetan Beef and Sichuan Peppercorn Dumplings
Sha Momo

Makes 32 dumplings, serving 4 as a main course, 6 to 8 as a snack or starter

Practically the national food of Tibet, these hearty steamed dumplings are full of fragrant ginger, garlic, and Sichuan peppercorn. *Momos* are festive foods which are often prepared as a group activity for parties and special celebrations, particularly Losar, the Tibetan New Year.

To minimize the karmic damage of eating meat, Tibetans favor larger animals for food, since one can feed many people. Naturally juicy and rich-tasting yak meat is typically hand-chopped for *sha momo*, but ground beef, particularly chuck, works well. Fatty ground pork or lamb, or dark meat chicken are excellent too. If you have time, hand-chop or grind the meat (instructions are on page 158) yourself for a nice toothsome bite. Adding oil and water enriches and hydrates the filling, making it extra succulent.

FILLING

3/4 pound ground beef (preferably chuck), coarsely chopped to loosen

1/2 cup finely chopped yellow onion

1/3 cup chopped Chinese chives or scallions (white and green parts)

2 1/2 tablespoons minced fresh ginger

3 cloves garlic, minced and crushed into a paste

1 teaspoon salt

3/4 teaspoon Sichuan peppercorn, toasted in a dry skillet for 2 to 3 minutes, until fragrant, then crushed with a mortar and pestle

2 tablespoons canola oil

6 tablespoons water

1 pound Basic Dumpling Dough (page 22)

1 1/2 cups Spicy Roasted Tomato Sauce (page 218)

1. To make the filling, combine the beef, onion, Chinese chives, ginger, and garlic in a bowl. Use a fork or spatula to stir and lightly mash the ingredients together.

2. Stir together the salt, Sichuan peppercorn, oil, and water in a small bowl. Pour over the meat mixture and then stir with the fork or spatula to blend well. There should not be any

visible large chunks of meat. To develop the flavors, cover with plastic wrap and set aside at room temperature for 30 minutes. Makes about 2 cups. (The filling can be prepared 1 day ahead and refrigerated. Bring it to room temperature before assembling the dumplings.)

3. Meanwhile, to roll out 16 wrappers from half of the dough (see page 24). Aim for wrappers that are about 3 1/4 inches in diameter.

4. To assemble and steam the dumplings, follow steps 5 through 7 in the recipe for Nepalese Vegetable and Cheese Dumplings (page 54).

5. Serve immediately with the sauce in a communal bowl. Eat these with fork and spoon on a dish to catch all the juices. Put a little sauce inside the dumpling after you've taken a bite and sucked out the juices.

Note: Feel free to substitute this filling in Mongolian Meat and Caraway Pockets (page 50) to make the Tibetan version, called *sha paley*.

Shanghai Soup Dumplings
Xiǎolóngbāo

Makes 32 small dumplings, serving 3 to 4 as a main course, 6 to 8 as a snack or starter

These delicate dumplings bursting with flavor were invented in the late 1800s in Nanxiang village outside Shanghai. Despite their name, they are not served floating in soup. The soup is contained within the thin, chewy-soft wrapper, along with a rich pork mixture. A delectable culinary trick, these "little bamboo steamer buns" (the literal translation of the Chinese name) are the quintessential Shanghai snack served at dumpling restaurants as well as small food joints.

To get the soup into the dumplings, broth is gelled, chopped, and then mixed with the meat to produce a firm filling that can be stuffed efficiently into the wrapper. Under steam heat, the broth melts back into soup. Gelatinous pork skin is traditionally simmered for the broth, but many modern cooks employ agar-agar (see Note) or unflavored gelatin to insure proper gelling. For a robust soup, I infuse homemade chicken stock with smoky American country ham, which is often sold in slices at Chinese markets as "Virginia" or "Smithfield" ham; scrape and discard the black pepper coating, if present.

Combining bread flour (Gold Medal brand, which has 12 percent protein, is what I use) with all-purpose flour for hot-water dough produces thin and elastic wrappers that don't break during cooking or when picked up by chopsticks at the table. Fatty ground pork, the less expensive option at a Chinese market, or ground pork belly (cut it up into 1/2-inch cubes before processing), makes the most succulent filling. Prepare and gel the soup the day before to lessen your workload.

SOUP

Generous 1 1/3 cups Chicken Stock (page 222)

1 tablespoon packed chopped Virginia (Smithfield) ham or other salty, smoky ham

1 scallion (white and green parts), cut into 2-inch lengths and lightly smashed with the broad side of a knife

3 quarter-size slices ginger, smashed with the broad side of a knife

1/2 teaspoon agar-agar powder (see Note), or 1 1/2 teaspoons unflavored gelatin

DOUGH

3 3/4 ounces (3/4 cup) unbleached bread flour

2 ounces (6 tablespoons) unbleached all-purpose flour

About 7 tablespoons just-boiled water (see Note, page 23)

1 1/2 teaspoons canola oil

FILLING AND SAUCE

Chubby 2-inch piece fresh ginger, peeled

1 scallion (white and green parts), chopped

Scant 1/2 teaspoon salt

1/8 teaspoon ground white pepper

1 1/2 teaspoons sugar

1 teaspoon light (regular) soy sauce

1 tablespoon Shaoxing rice wine or dry sherry

1 1/2 teaspoons sesame oil

1/2 pound fatty ground pork, coarsely chopped to loosen

1/4 cup Chinkiang or balsamic vinegar

1. To prepare the soup, combine the stock, ham, scallion, and ginger in a small saucepan. Bring to a boil and cook, uncovered, for about

continued

8 minutes, or until the stock has reduced by half and you have a generous 2/3 cup. Strain the stock, discarding the solids, and set aside to cool for 15 minutes.

Return the stock to the saucepan and sprinkle in the agar-agar or gelatin; there is no need to soften the gelatin in the stock beforehand. Heat over medium-high heat, stirring until the agar-agar is dissolved. After the stock comes to a boil, turn off the heat. Pour it into an 8 by 8-inch baking pan or a shallow bowl to make a thin layer that will cool quickly and be easy to cut up. Refrigerate for 20 to 40 minutes, until the soup is completely cooled and hardened. Quarter it and then peel from the pan. Finely chop and set aside. Cover with plastic wrap and refrigerate if you are preparing the soup in advance.

2. **Make the dough** as you would for the Basic Dumpling Dough (page 22). Combine the two flours in the food processor or a bowl. Measure out the just-boiled water and add the oil. With the machine running, add the water and oil through the feed tube, or stir it in by hand, until you have a soft, warm dough. Add additional water by the 1/2 teaspoon, if needed. Gather the dough into a ball and transfer to a very lightly floured work surface. Knead processed dough for about 2 minutes and hand-made dough for about 5 minutes, or until the dough is smooth and a tad elastic. Press your finger into the dough and it should bounce back fairly fast, but with a shallow indentation remaining. Place in a zip-top plastic bag and seal well, expelling excess air as you seal the bag. Let rest at room temperature for 1 hour before using. (The dough can be refrigerated overnight and returned to room temperature before proceeding.)

3. **To make the filling,** thinly slice 1/2 inch of ginger and put it into an electric mini-chopper. Add the scallion, salt, white pepper, sugar, soy sauce, rice wine, and sesame oil. Process until creamy and fragrant. Transfer to a bowl, add the pork, and use a spatula to combine. Add the gelled stock and continue mixing until well blended and firm. Cover and set aside for 30 minutes to develop the flavors. Makes about 1 2/3 cups. (Unlike other fillings, this one can break down if it sits overnight. If you prepared the gelled soup a day ahead, combine it with the meat the day you make the dumplings.)

4. **To make the dipping sauce,** cut the remaining 1 1/2-inch piece of ginger into fine shreds. Divide the ginger and vinegar between two communal bowls. Taste, and if the vinegar is too tart, add a bit of water. Set aside.

5. **To make the wrappers,** remove the dough from the bag, turning the bag inside out if necessary; the dough will be sticky. On a very lightly floured surface, gently shape the dough into a ball. Cut it in half and replace one of the halves in the plastic bag, sealing well.

Roll the other half into a 10 to 12-inch log. Cut into 16 pieces and then roll them into balls, dusting them with flour afterward to prevent sticking. Work on 8 dough balls at a time, keeping the others covered by a dry kitchen towel or inverted bowl to prevent drying. Shape each ball into a circle 2 1/2 inches in diameter, with a 1-inch diameter "belly" in the center; this helps to prevent the soup from leaking out and to keep a consistent thickness throughout. The finished outer rim should be thin enough for you to see the shadow of your fingers when you hold up the wrapper. (For guidance on shaping and rolling, see pages 24 to 25.)

6. **Before assembling** the dumplings, line steamer trays and/or a baking sheet with parchment paper and set aside. (If you are making the dumplings in advance, or freezing them, lightly dust the parchment paper with flour to avoid sticking.) Hold a wrapper in a slightly cupped hand. Scoop up about 2^1/$_2$ teaspoons of filling with a bamboo dumpling spatula, dinner knife, or fork and position it in the center of the wrapper, pressing and shaping it into a mound and keeping about ^{1}/$_2$ to ^{3}/$_4$ inch of wrapper clear on all sides. This will seem like a lot of filling. Use the thumb of the hand cradling the dumpling to push down the filling and keep it in place while the fingers of the other hand pull up the dough edge and pleat and pinch the rim together to form a closed satchel (see page 52), the only shape for these dumplings. Make sure to pinch and twist the dough at the end to completely close. The finished dumpling will look very pregnant.

If you are steaming right away, place each finished dumpling in a steamer tray, sealed side up, spacing them ^{3}/$_4$ inch apart, and 1 inch away from the edge if you are using a metal steamer. If you are unable to steam all the dumplings at once, or if you are going to steam them later, place the waiting ones on the prepared baking sheet with a good ^{1}/$_2$ inch between them.

Loosely cover the finished dumplings with a dry kitchen towel or plastic wrap as you form and fill wrappers from the remaining dough.

7. **While these dumplings** can be prepared in advance and frozen like the other dumplings in this chapter, they are at their very best when steamed as soon as they are made. Freeze them on the baking sheet until hard (about 1 hour), transfer them to a zip-top plastic bag, pressing out excess air before sealing, and keep them frozen for up to 1 month; partially thaw, using your finger to smooth over any cracks that may have formed during freezing, before steaming.

8. **To cook the dumplings,** steam them over boiling water (see steaming guidelines on page 17) for 6 to 8 minutes. The dumplings should have puffed up and become somewhat translucent. Remove each tray and place it atop a serving plate.

9. **Serve the dumplings** immediately with the sauce. To eat, pick up a dumpling with chopsticks and place it in a soup spoon; think of the spoon as a tiny bowl. Either bite or poke a small hole at the top with a chopstick. Carefully slurp out the hot soup inside or pour it into the spoon and sip it from there. Finish off the dumpling by eating it straight or dunking it first in the dipping sauce; to be more graceful, spoon a bit of sauce onto the dumpling or into the hole.

Note: Agar-agar powder, a seaweed-based gelatin popular in Asia, is sold at Asian markets in 25-gram packages. Telephone brand from Thailand, sold at Chinese and Southeast Asian grocers, is the standard of excellence; I often ask the cashier for it because the small packages are easily missed on store shelves. Agar-agar flakes, sold at many health food markets, do not dissolve as quickly as agar-agar powder and unflavored gelatin. By the time the flakes dissolve, much of the soup has evaporated. The flakes do not work well for making the soup in this recipe.

2 Thin Skins

If you work extra elasticity into a wheat-flour dough, you can stretch it into thin, supple dumpling skins.

In this chapter, the first group of recipes is based on egg and flour dough that's quite similar to Italian pasta. Rolling it out involves a pasta machine, which I've seen used in Southeast Asia for fresh noodles. There is little skill involved in operating a pasta machine to produce wonton, *siu mai*, and Cantonese spring roll (also known as egg roll) skins that best most commercially prepared ones. Incorporating cornstarch into the dough is key to giving the dough its stretch.

Adventurous cooks should step up to making Shanghai spring roll skins, which require a tad more skill and practice to smear a thin film of dough on a skillet for each skin. Mastering these wrappers is fun and very rewarding.

Wonton, Siu Mai, and Cantonese Spring Roll Skins

Yúntūn Pí, Shāomài Pí, Guǎngdōng Chūnjuǎn Pí

Makes about 2/3 pound to yield 12 large square Cantonese spring roll skins,
48 small square wonton skins, or 48 small round *siu mai* skins

One of my favorite sources for fresh wonton skins is a market-cum-noodle shop in Oakland's Chinatown called Hop Yuen. A three-hour round-trip excursion to this shop is worth it to me because I can get pliant, thin skins that are made without coloring or other additives. Those are the benchmark for these homemade ones, which are just as nice, and they come together handily with just a few ingredients and a low-tech, hand-cranked pasta machine. The Chinese term for these wrappers is *pí*, which literally means skin, and they function as a light, supple casing that protects and contributes texture to a dumpling.

You may have a source for excellent Chinese skins, but do try making them yourself. You can control the thickness and cut them to whatever size you like, and it is a fun project. The dough can be made in a food processor or by hand, and a pasta machine makes rolling out the dough an easy and quick job. Moderate-gluten flour, such as Gold Medal all-purpose, produces terrific results that are neither overly chewy nor too soft.

6 3/4 ounces (generous 1 1/3 cups) unbleached all-purpose flour

3/4 teaspoon salt

1/4 cup water

1 large egg

1/4 cup cornstarch, for dusting

1. To make the dough in a food processor, combine the flour and salt in the work bowl and pulse two or three times to blend. Combine the water and egg in a measuring cup and lightly beat. With the machine running, pour the liquid mixture through the feed tube in a thin, steady stream. After all the liquid has been added and the mixture looks crumbly, run the machine for another 20 to 30 seconds, until a large, medium-soft, slightly sticky ball forms (a few crumbly side bits are okay). If the dough doesn't come together, add water by the 1/2 teaspoon. If the dough sticks to the side of the bowl, add flour by the teaspoon to absorb excess moisture.

Alternatively, to make the dough by hand, combine the flour and salt in a bowl and then make a well in the center. Lightly beat together the water and egg and then pour into the well. Use a wooden spoon or fork to slowly and steadily stir, moving out from the center toward the rim, to work all the flour into the liquid. Keep stirring as a ragged, slightly sticky mass forms. Then use your fingers to gather and pat the dough together. Add water by the 1/2 teaspoon if the dough feels too stiff or a sprinkling of flour if it is too wet.

Regardless of method, transfer the dough and all the bits to a work surface, gather into one ball, and then vigorously knead for about 2 minutes if you used a food processor, or 6 minutes if you made the dough by hand. Properly made dough should be just slightly tacky but not sticky. If the dough sticks to the work surface or your fingers, lightly dust the surface with flour and continue kneading. The finished dough should be fairly smooth and feel as firm as your fingertip. Press on processor dough with a finger, and it should spring back, with no indentation remaining. A faint indention remains on handmade dough, which is not as stiff as its machine-made counterpart.

Put the finished dough in a small zip-top bag and expel excess air as you seal it. Set aside at room temperature to rest for at least 1 and up to 3 hours. (The dough can be refrigerated overnight. Return it to room temperature before moving on.)

2. **To roll out the dough,** use a pasta machine. Remove the dough from the bag and cut into 3 equal pieces, replacing 2 of them in the bag and resealing to prevent drying. Flatten a piece of dough with your fingers or a rolling pin to a 1/4-inch-thick rectangle. Use your fingers to dust and then smooth some cornstarch on both sides. Run the dough through the machine at the widest setting (notch 1). Fold the dough into thirds like a letter with one end toward the middle and the other end on top to cover. Press to flatten the dough again so it will easily go through the machine, add another light coating of cornstarch to both sides, and then run it through the machine with one of the *unfolded* sides entering the rollers first. Repeat the folding, flattening, smoothing, and rolling 3 to 5 times more, until the dough is smooth and elastic. After this initial workout, there's no need to fold the dough again.

Set the machine to the next thinnest setting (notch 2). Lightly dust both sides of the dough with cornstarch and then run it through the rollers. Decrease the setting again to notch 3, and pass the dough through once more. Repeat this process 2 more times, reducing the width of the rollers each time and dusting the dough with cornstarch, until the dough is 1/32 inch thin. On an Atlas pasta machine, I pause after notch 4 to cut the sheet (now about 18 inches long) in half, lest it become too long and unwieldy. I'm satisfied after notch 5. You should be able to see the shadow of your fingers through the dough when held up in the light.

3. **The ideal width** for the dough sheets is about 6 inches wide. Most home pasta machines yield narrower results so simply put the finished dough sheets on a cornstarch-dusted work surface, smooth the top with more cornstarch, and then use a rolling pin to widen them. Do your best to come close to a 6-inch width. It is fine if the width is not optimal and edges are uneven. When the skins are made into dumplings, imperfections disappear.

Put the finished dough sheets on a dry kitchen towel for 8 to 10 minutes, flipping it midway so it dries and firms up enough to easily cut. (If widening the sheets earlier proved difficult, try it after this resting period.) Repeat with the other dough pieces. Cover the finished sheets with a dry kitchen towel.

4. **To cut the dough sheets,** smooth a thin layer of cornstarch over your work surface with your hand. Put the dough on the work surface and smooth a layer of cornstarch on top of it. For Cantonese spring rolls (also known as egg rolls), cut across the sheets at about 6-inch intervals to create large squares. For wontons, use a ruler and sharp knife to cut 3-inch squares. For *siu mai*, use a 3-inch-round cutter to stamp out as many wrappers as you can from the sheets, dipping the cutter in cornstarch as you work to prevent sticking.

Stack the finished skins, wrap them loosely in parchment paper, and put them in an airtight zip-top plastic bag, squeezing out any excess air before you seal the bag. Lay the bag flat on a plate or in a plastic container. Refrigerate for up to 3 days. You can freeze the wrappers, though they are best when fresh. These wrappers may turn grayish in the refrigerator, but their flavor and texture will remain excellent.

Master Shapes: Wontons

Wonton skins can be made into many shapes, and here are a few of the typical ones. These shapes are presented in rising levels of difficulty. Start with the triangle and work your way up.

A single chopstick makes a surprisingly great tool for grabbing just about 1 teaspoon of filling (the amount generally needed to fill a wonton) and depositing it on the skin, all while keeping your hands clean. It can also be used to wet the skin. Instead of a chopstick, you can use a small spoon or fork.

Triangle

Position a square-cut skin on one hand, with one of the corners near the tip of your middle finger. Use a chopstick, spoon, or fork to pick up and position the filling in the center of the skin. Dip the chopstick or a finger in water and lightly wet the two top edges of the skin; freshly made skins require very little water to moisten. Pick up the near corner of the skin and fold it over, enclosing the filling and forming a triangle. Press the edges of the triangle firmly with your finger to seal. Make sure that there are no air bubbles and that the edges are well sealed.

Nurse's Cap

Hold the skin with one of the edges lined up along your fingertips. Center the filling on the skin and then lightly wet 3 of the 4 edges with a touch of water, using your chopstick or finger. Bring the lower edge up to meet the upper

Shaping Nurse's Caps

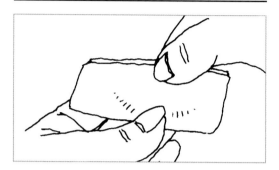

1. Bring the lower edge of the filled skin up to meet the upper edge, forming a rectangle.

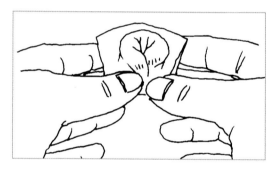

2. Bring together the two corners of the folded edge, overlapping slightly, and press to seal.

Shaping Triangles

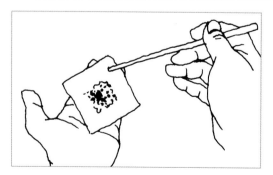

1. Fill the skin and wet the edges with a chopstick.

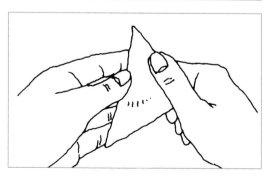

2. Fold the skin into a triangle, and press firmly with your fingers to seal.

one and to create a rectangle. Press firmly to seal well and eliminate air bubbles. Then bring the two corners of the folded edge together to cross over one another and press to seal; if it's easier, fold up the flat sealed edge of the skin before joining the corners. Add a dot of water, if needed. The result resembles a nurse's cap.

Flower Bud

There are two ways to make the dainty flower bud. The easy way is to first make a triangle (see above). Holding a finished triangle with the pointy center facing toward your wrist, roll the far edge over toward the pointy center so that it forms a sort of cylinder. Dab a bit of water on top of one of the long rolled ends and then bring the two rolled ends together like crossed forearms. Direct the motion away from you and the ends will naturally wrap around the wonton. Pinch the ends together.

The nifty way to make a flower bud is to hold the skin in one hand with one of the corners at the tip of your middle finger. Take a chopstick and scoop up the filling and position it at the uppermost corner. Keeping the chopstick in place, use it to roll the skin over (use your free thumb to fold over the skin, if needed) until the filling is completely encased. Pull the chopstick out and then press on either side of the filling to secure it in place and remove any air bubbles. Use the chopstick to wet one of the rolled ends and then bring the rolled ends together, pinching and sealing as described above.

Shaping Flower Buds

1. To form a flower bud with a finished triangle, roll the far end of the triangle over towards the point.

2. To form a flower bud using a chopstick, roll the wrapper over the chopstick until the filling is completely encased.

3. When done, one point of the triangle will be sticking out.

4. To seal a flower bud, dab a bit of water on the ends of the roll and bring the two rolled ends together like crossed forearms.

5. Pinch the ends together to seal the finished flower bud.

Fried Wontons
Zhá Yúntūn

Makes 48 wontons, serving 6 to 8 as a snack

I've met few people who dislike fried wontons. They are irresistible: they fry up to a wonderful light crispness, staying true to their Cantonese name, which literally means "swallowing clouds."

Wrapping the filling in a thin skin is the secret to generating such an ethereal quality. Most commercial wonton skins are, sadly, on the thick side and turn a bit chewy after frying. For better results, look for Hong Kong–style thin wonton skins at an Asian market or, better yet, make your own at home. Fried wontons are most often enjoyed dipped in sweet and sour sauce, but they can also be served in a bowl covered by hot broth; the skins turn chewy and contribute a delightful richness to the soup.

FILLING

1/3 pound medium shrimp, peeled, deveined, and cut into pea-size pieces (4 1/2 ounces net weight)

1/4 pound ground pork, fattier kind preferred, coarsely chopped to loosen

1 scallion (white and green parts), finely chopped

1/2 teaspoon plus 1/8 teaspoon cornstarch

1/4 teaspoon sugar

Scant 1/2 teaspoon salt

1 pinch of black or white pepper

48 small square wonton skins (page 64)
Canola or peanut oil, for deep-frying
1 cup Sweet and Sour Sauce (page 217)

1. To make the filling, combine the shrimp, pork, scallion, cornstarch, sugar, salt, and pepper in a bowl and use chopsticks or a fork to mix well. Cover and set aside for 30 minutes before using, or refrigerate for up to a day in advance. You should have about 1 cup.

2. Before assembling the wontons, line a baking sheet with parchment paper and lightly dust with cornstarch. Fill each wonton skin with about 1 teaspoon of the filling, creating triangles, flower buds, or nurse's caps (see pages 66 to 67). As you work, put the finished wontons on the prepared baking sheet. When all are made, loosely cover with a kitchen towel to prevent drying. The wontons also can be covered with plastic wrap and refrigerated for several hours; let them sit at room temperature to remove the chill before frying.

3. Put a wire rack on a baking sheet and place next to the stove. Pour oil to a depth of 1 1/2 inches into a wok, deep skillet, or 5-quart Dutch oven and heat over medium-high heat to about 325°F on a deep-fry thermometer. (If you don't have a deep-fry thermometer, stick a *dry* bamboo chopstick into the oil; if it takes about 2 seconds for bubbles to rise and encircle the chopstick, the oil is ready.)

4. Working in batches of 4 to 6, slide the wontons into the hot oil and fry for about 1 minute on each side, or until golden brown. Use a skimmer to transfer to the rack to drain.

5. Arrange the wontons on a platter and serve hot as finger food along with the sauce for dipping.

Shrimp Wonton Soup
Yúntūn Tāng

Serves 4 to 6 as a starter course

Soup marks the beginning of many Asian meals, and a little bowl of delicate wontons floating in fragrant broth is a fine way to kick things off. The clean flavors prepare the palate for anything that may follow.

Shrimp-laden dumplings star in this simple recipe, but you may want to adorn the finished soup with some blanched leafy greens, such as spinach, bok choy, or watercress, and perhaps even slices of roasted Cantonese Char Siu Pork (page 166). Instead of the shrimp filling, you can use a half batch of the pork and shrimp filling for the Fried Wontons on page 69.

FILLING
1/3 pound medium shrimp, peeled and deveined (41/2 ounces net weight)
Salt
1 scallion
1/2 teaspoon cornstarch
Black or white pepper
1/2 teaspoon sesame oil, plus extra for garnish

24 small square wonton skins (page 64)
4 cups Chicken Stock (page 222)

1. To make the filling, toss the shrimp with 2 generous pinches of salt, put them in a strainer, and rinse under cold water. Transfer the shrimp to a paper towel and blot dry. Finely chop the shrimp (they will form a sticky mass) and then put into a bowl.

2. Mince all the white part and some of the green part of the scallion to yield 1 tablespoon. Thinly slice the remaining green part and reserve for a garnish. Add the minced scallion and 1/4 teaspoon salt, the cornstarch, a pinch of pepper, and the sesame oil to the shrimp. Stir with chopsticks or a fork until the mixture is thoroughly blended and dense. Cover with plastic wrap and set aside for 30 minutes before using, or refrigerate for up to a day in advance. You should have about 1/2 cup.

3. Before assembling the wontons, line a baking sheet with parchment paper and lightly dust with cornstarch. Fill each wonton skin with about 1 teaspoon of the filling, creating triangles, flower buds, or nurse's caps (see pages 66 to 67). As you work, put the finished wontons on the prepared baking sheet. When all are made, loosely cover with a kitchen towel to prevent drying. If you are making the wontons several hours in advance of cooking, cover the wontons with plastic wrap and refrigerate; they can be cooked directly from the refrigerator. Or, freeze them on their baking sheet until hard (about 1 hour), transfer them to a plastic container, and keep them frozen for up to 1 month; partially thaw them before boiling.

4. To cook the wontons, half-fill a large pot with water and bring to a boil over high heat. At the same time, bring the stock to a boil in a separate pan, lower the heat to a gentle simmer, and cover to keep hot.

Add all the wontons to the boiling water, gently dropping them in one at a time. Use a wooden spoon to nudge them to prevent sticking. Return the water to a gentle boil and then lower the heat to medium to maintain it. After the wontons have floated to the top, let them cook for another 2 minutes, or until they are translucent. Use a slotted spoon or skimmer to scoop up the wontons, pausing above the pot to allow excess water to drip back down before putting them into the hot stock. Increase the heat on the stock slightly and let the wontons soak up some of the stock and finish cooking, about 1 minute.

5. **Transfer the wontons** to individual soup bowls or a large serving bowl. Taste the stock and add salt, if necessary. Ladle the stock over the wontons and add a dash of sesame oil and a sprinkling of pepper. Top with the remaining scallion and serve immediately.

LAZY DAY TIP

Good commercially made wonton and *siu mai* skins are sold at Chinese and Southeast Asian markets. Look for ones that are labeled "thin" or "Hong Kong style," or you'll end up with thick ones. Skins made with no food coloring are best, though they're harder to find. If round *siu mai* skins are unavailable, use scissors or a round cookie cutter to cut them from square wonton skins.

Commercially made Cantonese spring roll skins are often labeled "egg roll skins" and are shelved in the refrigerated or frozen section of an Asian market. These skins are a tad larger than homemade ones, so you'll be able to stuff a little more into them. They are drier, too, so you may have to wet them more to ensure a good seal.

Vegetable and Pork Wontons in Spicy Oil
Hóng Yóu Yúntūn

Serves 4 as a snack, 6 to 8 as a starter

Most people think of wontons as being fried and in soup broth, but they may also be served like Italian ravioli in a light coating of splendid sauce. Here, the sauce is nutty, spicy chile oil punctuated with fresh garlic and soy sauce. Feel free to dial the heat up or down by varying the amount of chile oil. The full amount is definitely not for the faint of heart. If you have semirefined, cold-pressed peanut oil on hand (the kind employed for making the chile oil on page 216), use it instead of the canola oil for an extra roasty dimension.

These wontons make a terrific snack or an elegant, eye-opening starter. If you can, substitute the greens below with 1/4 cup thawed and well-squeezed shepherd's purse, a mild vegetable that's sold frozen at Chinese-American markets.

1/4 pound tender leafy greens, such as mustard greens, baby bok choy, or spinach

2 ounces ground pork, fattier kind preferred, coarsely chopped to loosen

3/4 teaspoon minced fresh ginger

1 small scallion (white and green parts), finely chopped

Generous 1/8 teaspoon salt

1 pinch of white pepper

Scant 1/4 teaspoon sugar

1 tablespoon plus 11/4 teaspoons light (regular) soy sauce

Scant 1 teaspoon Shaoxing rice wine or dry sherry

Scant 1 teaspoon sesame oil, plus more for sauce

24 small square wonton skins (page 64)

1 to 2 tablespoons chile oil (page 216)

2 tablespoons canola oil

1 small clove garlic, minced and crushed into a paste

3 to 4 sprigs cilantro, coarsely chopped

1. **Fill a saucepan** with water and bring to a boil. Add the leafy greens and blanch for about 1 minute, or until tender. Drain immediately, rinse with cold water, and drain well. Finely chop and then put in a kitchen towel and squeeze to remove excess moisture. You should have about 1/4 firmly packed cup.

2. **Combine the chopped** greens, pork, ginger, and scallion in a bowl. Use a fork to stir and lightly mash the ingredients together.

3. **In another bowl,** combine the salt, pepper, sugar, the 11/4 teaspoons soy sauce, the rice wine, and sesame oil, stirring well. Pour over the vegetable and meat mixture, and vigorously stir to create a compact mixture. Cover the filling with plastic wrap and set aside for 30 minutes, or refrigerate overnight, returning it to room temperature before assembling the wontons. You should have about 1/2 cup.

4. **Before assembling** the wontons, line a baking sheet with parchment paper and lightly dust with cornstarch. Fill each wonton skin with about 1 teaspoon of the filling, creating triangles, flower buds, or nurse's caps (see pages 66 to 67). As you work, put the finished wontons on the prepared baking sheet. When all are made, loosely cover with plastic wrap or a dry kitchen towel to prevent drying.

5. To cook the wontons, half-fill a large pot with water and bring to a boil over high heat. Add all the wontons to the boiling water, gently dropping them in one at a time. Use a wooden spoon to nudge them apart and prevent sticking. Return the water to a gentle boil and then lower the heat to medium to maintain it. After the wontons have floated to the top, let them cook for another 3 minutes, or until they are translucent.

6. While the wontons cook, combine the remaining 1 tablespoon soy sauce, the chile oil, canola oil, and garlic on a serving plate or shallow bowl. Taste and make any flavor adjustments. Add a touch of sesame oil for extra nutty goodness. Set near the stove.

7. Use a slotted spoon or skimmer to scoop up the wontons, pausing above the pot to allow excess water to drip back down. Put the wontons in the dish with the sauce and toss gently to coat. Sprinkle with chopped cilantro and serve immediately.

PLANNING A DUMPLING PARTY

To impress your friends with your dumpling prowess—and to share your skills with them—build a dinner party around dumplings. Have a lively, hands-on gathering where guests participate in assembling and cooking the dumplings. Select a theme, such as dumplings made with basic dumpling dough (Chapter 1) or thin skins (Chapter 2). Prepare the filling(s) and dough in advance. Ditto for any broths involved. After your guests arrive, divide them to tackle different tasks, such as rolling out the wrappers, assembling dumplings, and making dipping sauces or chutneys. Use several cooking methods (boiling, panfrying, steaming, deep-frying, and/or baking) to efficiently use your stove and to offer a varied experience and meal. To whet your guests' appetites, serve a few premade dumplings, such as empanadas (page 125) or karipap (curry puffs, page 129), as snacks. Finish with a sweet dumpling that you've prepared or one that resulted from the group activity.

For a more formal affair with no guest participation, make dumplings in advance to the extent that the recipe allows. Some dumplings can be assembled and kept refrigerated. Others freeze beautifully either raw or cooked. Many can be precooked and then reheated. Check individual recipes for tips on advance preparation and reheating. Do not make all your dumplings fresh on the day of the event; this will only make you grumpy.

Master Shapes: Open Bag and Cigar

Shaping *siu mai* open-faced dumplings and spring rolls is not difficult—in fact, these are among the easier shapes to make.

Open Bag

For this shape, position the skin in one hand and use your other hand to center the filling atop the skin, gently pressing on it to seat the filling well. Use both sets of index fingers and thumbs to bring up the sides of the skin and gently press it into the filling at four equidistant places. The skin should stick easily. Then repeatedly gather, pinch, and rotate the dumpling to form the sides of the bag. There should be a slight waist near the top. Secure that waist by wrapping your index finger and thumb around it as if you're making a very loose fist. Sprinkle some garnish on top, if using, and gently press it into the filling. Hold the dumpling a few inches over the work surface, then drop it to flatten the bottom and ensure it sits upright.

Shaping Open Bags

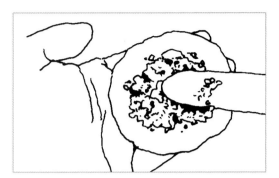

1. Gently press on the filling to seat it.

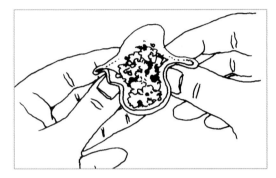

2. Bring up the sides of the skin and press.

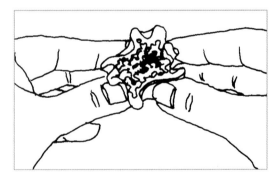

3. Gather and pinch the dumpling, rotating it as you work, to form the gathered sides of the "bag."

4. Wrap thumb and index finger around the bag's "waist" to secure it.

Cigar

Making this shape is a lot like making a burrito; it can be done with either square (Cantonese) or round (Shanghai) spring roll skins. Lay a skin on the work surface; if you are using a square skin, make sure one of the pointy corners is facing you. Put a mound of filling slightly below the center. Use your fingers to shape the mound into a log. Wipe your fingers clean, if needed, and then lift the bottom edge up and over the filling, tucking the point under it. If you are using square skins, fold in the sides, brush the upper edges with egg wash, and then roll from the bottom up to seal and finish. If you are using round skins, you need to ensure the seal by brushing all exposed edges with egg wash *before* folding in the sides and rolling up to finish. If the Shanghai skin seems dry at any spot, give it a dab of egg wash.

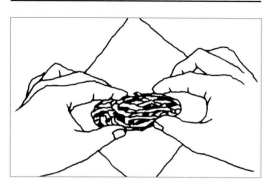

1. Form the filling into a log slightly below center in a square skin.

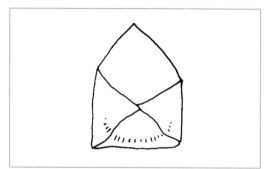

2. Fold in the sides of the square skin, brush the upper edges with egg wash, then roll from the bottom up to seal and finish.

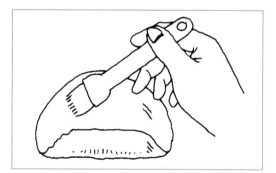

3. To make a cigar with a round spring roll skin, brush the exposed edges with egg wash before folding in the sides, rolling it up, and sealing it.

Siu Mai Open-Faced Dumplings
Shāomài

Makes 30 dumplings, serving 6 to 8 as a snack

These open-faced dumplings are a requisite part of the Cantonese dim sum reper-toire. In contrast to their dainty size and frilly edge, *shāomài* (*siu mai* in Cantonese) are packed with a pork filling that's typically punctuated by earthy mushrooms and crunchy water chestnuts. The dumplings here are made from thin wonton skins that have been cut into circles. Don't confuse them with the Jiangnan version from the area between Shanghai and Nanjing, which is made from hot-water dough wrappers and filled with a sticky rice mixture. Both go by the name *shāomài*, which literally means "cook and sell," reflecting their perennial popularity.

Feel free to add chopped raw shrimp to the filling (cut back on the vegetables) for variety. Any of the wonton fillings can be used, too; but do remember to double the pork and shrimp filling on page 41 or quadruple the shrimp filling on page 70, add-ing a beaten egg white in each case to insure a smoother texture. The shape of *siu mai* enables them to hold a lot more filling than other dumplings of the same size.

FILLING

2/3 pound coarsely ground pork, fattier kind preferred, coarsely chopped to loosen

4 large dried shiitake mushrooms, reconstituted (see page 13), stemmed, and chopped (1/2 cup)

Generous 1/4 cup finely diced water chestnuts (fresh preferred)

3 tablespoons finely chopped scallions (white and green parts)

1/4 teaspoon salt

Generous 1 teaspoon sugar

1/4 teaspoon white pepper

1 tablespoon cornstarch

1 tablespoon light (regular) soy sauce

1 tablespoon Shaoxing rice wine or dry sherry

1 1/2 teaspoons sesame oil

1 large egg white, beaten

30 small round siu mai skins (page 64)

1 1/2 tablespoons finely diced carrot, or 30 peas, for garnish

Light (regular) soy sauce

Chinese hot mustard or Colman's English mustard

1. **To make the filling,** in a bowl, combine the pork, mushrooms, water chestnuts, and scal-lions. Use a fork or spatula to stir and lightly mash the ingredients together so they begin to blend.

2. **Put the salt,** sugar, white pepper, cornstarch, soy sauce, rice wine, sesame oil, and egg white into a small bowl and stir to combine well. Pour over the meat mixture, and stir, fold, and mash everything together until they cohere into a compact mass. Cover the filling with plastic wrap and set aside for 30 minutes, or refrigerate overnight, returning it to room temperature before assembling the dumplings. You should have a generous 2 cups of filling.

3. **Before assembling** the dumplings, line steamer trays and/or a baking sheet with parch-ment paper. For the baking sheet, lightly dust the paper with cornstarch to prevent sticking. Set aside. Hold a skin in one hand. Scoop up

continued

about 1 tablespoon of filling with a bamboo dumpling spatula, dinner knife, or fork and position it in the center of the skin, pressing down gently. Pick up the skin and gather and pinch it together to form an open bag (see page 74). Crown the dumpling with some finely diced carrot or a pea.

If steaming right away, place each finished dumpling in a steamer tray open side up, spacing them 1/2 inch apart, and 1 inch away from the edge if you are using a metal steamer. Otherwise, place the waiting dumplings on the baking sheet a good 1/2 inch apart.

Keeping the finished dumplings covered with a dry kitchen towel to prevent drying, form and fill wrappers from the remaining dough. Dumplings made several hours in advance of cooking should be covered with plastic wrap and refrigerated. For longer storage, freeze them on their baking sheet until hard (about 1 hour), transfer them to a plastic container, and keep them frozen for up to 1 month; partially thaw them before steaming.

5. **To cook,** steam the dumplings over boiling water (steaming guidelines are on page 17) for 6 to 8 minutes, until the dumplings have puffed slightly and their skins have become translucent. Remove each tray and place it atop a serving plate.

6. **Serve immediately** with the soy sauce and hot mustard. Invite guests to mix up their own dipping sauce.

Cantonese Char Siu Pork and Vegetable Spring Rolls

Guǎngdōng Chūnjuǎn

Makes 12 rolls, serving 6 to 8 as a snack

The Chinese repertoire has many kinds of rolls—savory, sweet, thin, fat, fried, and unfried—and they're all hard to pass up. The Cantonese fried version is bigger than its Shanghai kin, and it is encased in a large version of a wonton skin. Cantonese spring rolls, also known as egg rolls, have gotten a bad rap in America because they're often greasy, overly doughy, and bland. However, when made from thin skins and a savory-sweet mixture of fresh vegetables and meat, Cantonese spring rolls reveal their worth as a splendid snack. Resembling gold bars and symbolizing wealth, prosperity, and good fortune, spring rolls are savored during the Lunar New Year, which is called the Spring Festival in Chinese.

Cantonese spring rolls often combine pork and shrimp, but I prefer to keep the focus on tasty roast pork, which is best when homemade. Finely chopping and shredding the ingredients is time consuming, but you want the filling to be compact so that it fills out the long shape of the roll. Lighten your workload by making the filling and skins in advance.

FILLING

3/4 teaspoon sugar

1/4 teaspoon salt

1/2 teaspoon white pepper

2 teaspoons light (regular) soy sauce

1 1/2 tablespoons oyster sauce

2 tablespoons water

2 tablespoons canola oil

2 scallions (white and green parts), chopped

2 cups lightly packed finely shredded cabbage (omit thick center spines)

1 cup finely chopped celery

1 carrot, cut into fine shreds (about 1 cup)

1/2 pound Char Siu Pork, homemade (page 224) or store-bought, cut into 1 1/2-inch-long matchsticks

1 tablespoon cornstarch dissolved in 1 1/2 tablespoons water

12 Cantonese spring roll skins (page 64)

1 large egg, lightly beaten

Canola or peanut oil, for deep-frying

1 cup Sweet and Sour Sauce (page 217), or 2 tablespoons unseasoned rice vinegar, Chinese black vinegar, or balsamic vinegar mixed with 1 teaspoon chile oil (page 216)

1. To make the filling, combine the sugar, salt, white pepper, soy sauce, oyster sauce, and water in a small bowl. Stir this flavoring sauce well and set aside.

Heat the oil in a large skillet over medium-high heat. Add the scallions and cook, stirring, for about 30 seconds until soft and aromatic. Add the cabbage, celery, and carrot, stirring to combine well. Cook, stirring frequently, for about 1 minute, until the vegetables have collapsed slightly. Add the flavoring sauce, stirring to combine, and continue cooking for about 2 minutes, until most of the liquid has disappeared and the vegetables have just cooked through. Add the pork and continue cooking, stirring to combine the flavors and

continued

heat through, about 1 minute. Give the cornstarch a final stir, and pour over the filling mixture. Cook for about 30 seconds, to bind the mixture nicely. Transfer to a platter and spread out. Set aside to cool completely before using. You should have about 3 cups. (The filling can be prepared 2 days in advance, covered, and refrigerated after cooling. Return to room temperature before wrapping.)

3. **Before assembling** the spring rolls, line a baking sheet with parchment paper and lightly dust with cornstarch. For each spring roll, use about 1/4 cup of filling, placing it slightly below the center of the skin. Follow the directions on page 75 to create the cigar shape, taking care to not wrap too tightly because you want just two layers of skin around the filling. Before rolling up the spring roll all the way to seal it, brush beaten egg on the upper two edges to ensure that the skin seals well. Set the finished rolls, seam side up, on the prepared baking sheet. Cover with a kitchen towel to prevent drying.

4. **Fry the rolls** in two stages. Heat 1 inch of oil in a wok, saucepan, or deep skillet over medium-high heat to about 350°F on a deep-fry thermometer. (If you don't have a deep-fry thermometer, stick a *dry* bamboo chopstick into the oil; if bubbles rise immediately to the surface and encircle the chopstick, the oil is ready.) Slide in few spring rolls and fry for about 1 1/2 minutes, turning as needed, until light golden. Remove from the oil and drain on paper towels. Repeat with the other rolls. These rolls soften as they sit, so after their first frying, refry them for 45 to 60 seconds in 350°F oil until crispy and golden brown.

5. **Serve hot,** whole or cut in half diagonally, with the dipping sauce of your choice.

Shanghai Spring Roll Skins
Shànghǎi Chūnjuǎn Pí

Makes about 20 (6 to 7-inch) round skins

Most American diners are familiar with the Cantonese spring roll skins made with an egg and flour pastalike skin, but there's another kind from Shanghai that is made without eggs and is cooked before it is stuffed and rolled. The resulting rolls are skinnier and fry up a little crisper than their Cantonese counterparts.

Shanghai spring roll skins can also be used, unfried, like a soft flour tortilla for *popiah* handrolls, a favorite food in Fujian, Chaozhou, Taiwan, Singapore, and Malaysia. In the Thai repertoire, *popiah tod* refers to fried spring rolls. Asian cooks have also used these skins for Vietnamese *chả giò* rolls and Burmese samosas.

Excellent commercial Shanghai spring roll skins are available at Chinese and Southeast Asian markets, and I didn't know if making them at home would be worth the trouble. They're a bit tricky to prepare, but once you understand and get the hang of the unusually sticky, elastic dough, the process becomes addictively fun as you aim for perfect round skins. I rarely achieve it, but the skins fry up beautifully every time. A moderate-gluten flour, such as all-purpose Gold Medal brand, works extremely well.

If you are a first-timer, visit Asiandumplingtips.com to watch the video demonstration and to observe the unique cooking process; double the recipe to ensure plenty of extra dough for practice.

10 ounces (2 cups) bleached all-purpose flour

1/2 teaspoon salt

2 tablespoons tapioca starch

1 cup water

1 tablespoon canola oil

1. **Combine the flour,** salt, and tapioca starch in a medium bowl. Make a well in the center and pour in the water and oil. Use a bamboo rice paddle or wooden spatula to stir and incorporate the flour with the water, working from the center to the rim of the bowl. Try to stir in one direction to develop the gluten in the dough.

After the ingredients have blended together into a rough, soft, sticky mass, start stirring in one direction. Within seconds, the dough should become fully hydrated and turn into a thick paste (resembling a starter for bread) and slightly glisten from moisture; it should *not* hold a mounded shape. If needed, add water by the teaspoon to loosen the dough.

Stir for 4 to 5 minutes, about 200 strokes. Strands of glutinous, pasty dough will form, attaching themselves to the rim of the bowl as you stir, and become longer as you progress. Slow down and/or pause if you get tired. When done, the thick pasty dough should be elastic enough for you to lift and stretch it 12 to 14 inches from the bottom of the bowl. If you are unsure, keep stirring for a little longer. Gather the finished dough together; it should hold a slightly mounded shape for a few minutes before spreading out to touch the walls of the bowl. Cover with plastic wrap and set aside at room temperature for 3 to 4 hours, or refrigerate overnight and return to room temperature before using.

continued

Alternatively, use a mixer fitted with the dough hook attachment. Put all the ingredients in the mixer bowl and stir by hand to combine well. Then run the machine at medium speed for 1 1/2 to 2 minutes. Keep the dough in the mixer bowl or transfer it to another bowl, cover with plastic wrap, and set aside at room temperature for 3 to 4 hours, or refrigerate overnight and return to room temperature before using.

2. **To prepare the skins,** slightly dampen a kitchen towel (I wet my hand up to my forearms and wipe them dry on the towel) and put it atop a large plate. Place next to the stove. Preheat a large, heavy-bottomed nonstick skillet to medium-low and then lower the heat slightly. The skillet should be hot enough for you to touch it with your finger without you flinching, but not cool enough for you to leave it there for any length of time. The dough won't stick to an overheated skillet but on an underheated skillet, it will stick too much and result in thick skins. Adjusting the flame is tricky, and I use a standard burner for these skins. If you have a high-output burner or stove, it may be necessary to use a flame tamer to diffuse the heat and/or to remove the skillet from the heat in between skins.

Because slightly chilled dough is firmer and easier to manipulate into a thin film, put the bowl containing the dough in a larger bowl in which you have put 8 ice cubes (without water). Set on or near the stove.

3. **Take a large handful** of dough, all of it if you can, and hold it with your palm facing upward. (When making a double batch, separate the dough into two bowls.) The gloppy dough will begin to drip, so control it by working it with your fingers while slowly rotating your wrist; your palm will naturally follow your wrist and go up and down. As this happens, the dough will form into a round sacklike shape. Finish with your wrist facing up with the dough in a manageable globular mass.

To make a skin, gently press the dough onto the skillet and slowly wipe it in a circular motion. Lift the dough upward as you complete the circle. The dough will naturally twist and come off the skillet. If excess white dough remains, smooth it out with a rubber spatula. You can quickly patch small holes this way too. Aim to create a thin 6 to 7-inch round film of dough on the skillet. It does not need to be perfect and a tiny hole now and then is forgivable. After forming the skin, you can keep the dough in your hand, but I like to let it drip back down into the chilled bowl to firm up; it takes seconds to retrieve and work it for the next one. Should the dough get cold,

LAZY DAY TIP

Shanghai spring roll skins, often labeled "spring roll skins" or "lumpia skins," are stocked in the frozen section at Chinese and Southeast Asian markets. They may be square or round and will be larger than homemade ones, so you can fill them with a bit more than what's specified in the recipes here. Thaw them before using and separate them one by one, restacking them and covering them with a damp kitchen towel to prevent drying, just as if you made them fresh. If they are dry, apply the steaming method outlined in step 4 to revitalize and soften them. When filling a square spring roll skin, position it as a diamond with a corner pointing toward you. You can moisten them with either beaten egg or water, whereas egg works best with homemade skins.

warm it up by working it with the rotating wrist motion before making another skin.

After about 15 seconds, part of the lacy edge should dry out and lift off the skillet, the sign of doneness. Use your fingers to peel the skin from the skillet. You *do not* have to cook the other side. Place the finished skin, uncooked side down, on the plate and cover with the damp kitchen towel, which will soften the edges. Make more skins from the remaining dough, adjusting the heat as needed and stacking one on top of the other. As you get toward the end, the skins will get smaller as there's less dough to work with. Try spiraling the dough from the center outward to create decent-size skins. It's hard to use up all the dough so discard the last bit.

4. Remove the finished skins from the plate, wrap them in a double-folded kitchen towel, and slide them into a zip-top plastic bag. Keep at room temperature if you are going to be using them right away. The skins can be refrigerated for up to 5 days; for less bulk, wrap them in parchment paper. Before using, return them to room temperature. Over low heat, steam stacks of 10 skins at a time in a kitchen towel for 10 minutes to soften them. Once refreshed, keep them soft in the warm steamer as you work.

Shanghai Pork, Bamboo, and Mushroom Spring Rolls
Shànghǎi Chūnjuǎn

Makes 18 to 20 rolls, serving 4 to 6 as a light main course, 6 to 8 for a snack

There are numerous fillings for fried spring rolls, and this one is my take on an old-fashioned Shanghai filling. The surf-and-turf combination of pork and shrimp is punctuated by earthy bamboo shoots and shiitake mushrooms. Whereas the Cantonese filling on page 79 is savory-sweet (and can be used here), this filling is more robust and offers wonderful depth, so much so that dunking them in a touch of vinegar is all you need to create a wonderful mouthful.

Most spring roll fillings are cooked first because the frying is fast, and you want to ensure that the meat is cooked and that there's a minimum of moisture, so the skins don't soften up too much as they sit once out of the fryer. When preparing this and other similar fillings, cut the main ingredients so that they match in size and roll up well. I typically buy pork tenderloin steaks and freeze them for 10 to 15 minutes to make them easier to cut. Canned bamboo shoots work well so long as they first are boiled briefly to eliminate any tinny flavor. Spring rolls are great as a snack but also terrific for a light lunch along with a green salad.

FILLING

1/2 teaspoon sugar

1 1/2 tablespoons plus 1/2 teaspoon cornstarch

3 large dried shiitake mushrooms, reconstituted and liquid reserved (see page 13), stemmed, and cut into shreds to match the pork (about 1/3 cup)

1 tablespoon light (regular) soy sauce

1/2 pound pork tenderloin, cut into 2-inch-long matchsticks

1/4 pound medium shrimp, peeled, deveined, and coarsely chopped (3 1/2 ounces net weight)

3 tablespoons canola oil

2 quarter-size slices fresh ginger, smashed with the side of a knife

2 cloves garlic, lightly crushed with the side of a knife

1/2 cup shredded bamboo shoots

1/2 pound bean sprouts

3/4 teaspoon salt

18 to 20 Shanghai Spring Roll Skins (page 81)

1 large egg, lightly beaten

Canola or peanut oil, for deep-frying

1/4 cup Chinese black vinegar or balsamic vinegar

1. To make the filling, combine the sugar, the 1/2 teaspoon cornstarch, and the soy sauce in a bowl. Add the pork and shrimp and stir to coat well. Set aside.

2. Put the remaining 1 1/2 tablespoons cornstarch into a small bowl and dissolve it in 3 tablespoons of the reserved mushroom soaking liquid. (Use water or stock if you mistakenly discarded the liquid.) Set aside.

3. Heat 1 1/2 tablespoons of the oil in a large skillet over high heat. Add the ginger and garlic and cook, stirring constantly, for about 30 seconds or until fragrant. Remove the garlic and ginger with a slotted spoon and discard. Add the pork and shrimp mixture, stirring constantly to separate the pork into shreds and shrimp into nuggets, and cook just through, about 1 1/2 minutes. Transfer to a platter.

continued

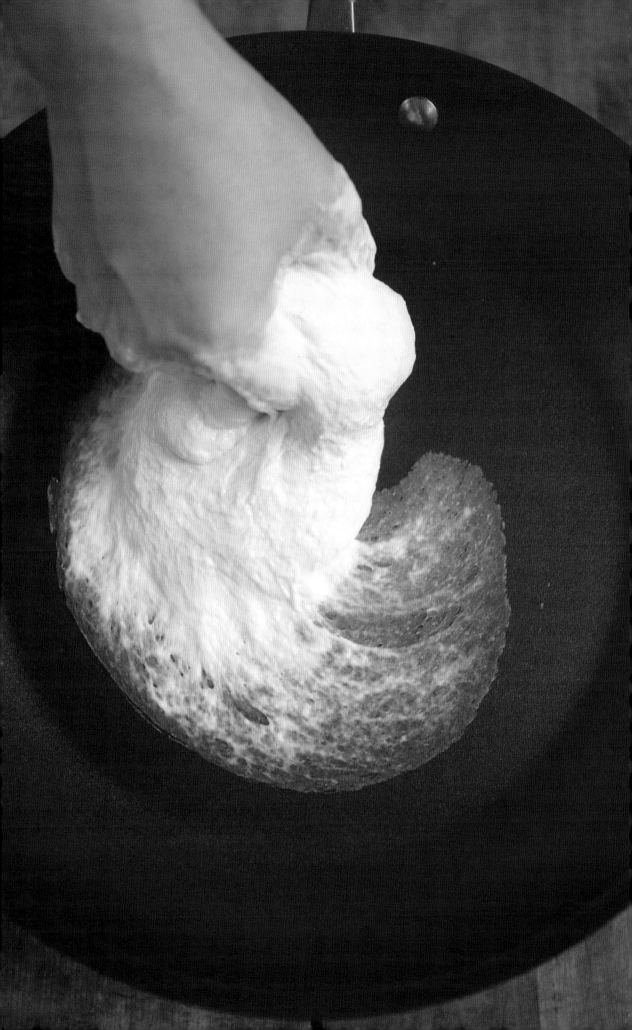

Add the remaining 1 1/2 tablespoons oil to the skillet. When the oil is hot, add the mushrooms, bamboo shoots, bean sprouts, and salt. Cook, stirring constantly, for about 5 minutes, or until the bean sprouts are soft and just cooked through. The mixture will be about half of the original volume. Return the pork and shrimp to the skillet and stir to combine. When heated through, about 45 seconds, lower the heat slightly. Give the cornstarch mixture a stir and pour over the filling mixture. Cook for about 30 seconds, to bind the mixture. Transfer to a platter and spread out. Set aside to cool completely before using. You should have about 3 cups. (The filling can be prepared 2 days in advance, covered, and refrigerated after cooling. Return to room temperature before wrapping.)

4. **Before assembling** the spring rolls, line a baking sheet with parchment paper. For each spring roll, place a skin, smooth side down, on your work surface. Place a generous 2 tablespoons of filling slightly below the center of the skin. Follow the directions on page 75 to create a cigar shape. Before folding in the sides, brush some beaten egg on all of the exposed edges to ensure a good seal. Set the finished rolls, seam side down, on the prepared baking sheet. Keep them covered with a kitchen towel to prevent drying. (To freeze, put them on a baking sheet, about 1/2 inch apart, and slide them into the freezer. After they have hardened, about 1 hour, transfer them to a zip-top bag and keep frozen. Fry them unthawed. They will take a little longer than 3 minutes but will be just fine.)

5. **Heat 1 inch** of oil in a wok, saucepan, or deep skillet over medium-high heat to about 350°F on a deep-fry thermometer. (If you don't have a deep-fry thermometer, stick a *dry* bamboo chopstick into the oil; if bubbles rise immediately to the surface and encircle the chopstick, the oil is ready.) Slide in a few spring rolls and fry, turning as needed, for about 3 minutes, or until golden brown and very crisp. Remove from the oil and drain. Return the oil to temperature, then repeat with the remaining rolls. After all the rolls are fried, you may refry them for 30 seconds in 350°F oil to quickly reheat. (Alternatively, keep the rolls in a warm oven during frying.)

6. **Serve the spring rolls** hot, whole or halved diagonally, with the vinegar as a dipping sauce.

Filipino Shrimp, Meat, and Vegetable Spring Rolls
Lumpia

Makes 18 to 20 rolls, serving 4 to 6 as a light main course, 6 to 8 for a snack

Many Asian cooks have incorporated Chinese spring rolls into their repertoires, but those of Filipino descent have embraced the rolls with the most zeal and flair. Derived from *lūnpiá*, a term from the Fujian (Hokkien) Chinese dialect, *lumpia* are one of the quintessential foods of the Philippines. In fact, I've seldom been to a Filipino celebration where there isn't a platter of crisp *lumpia*, whether it be large ones like these or the diminutive finger-size *lumpia* Shanghai, which is obviously named after its Chinese parent. Banana-filled *lumpia* is a deliciously popular sweet snack called *turon* (page 194). Unfried *lumpia sariwa* are made by rolling up a lettuce leaf and filling of vegetables and meat in a spring roll skin.

Fillings for fried *lumpia* vary from cook to cook, but they often have trademark Filipino touches, such as lots of fried garlic and onion. Simply seasoned, the meat (pork, chicken, or beef), shrimp, and vegetable mixture is precooked but not bound by cornstarch. Thinly sliced green beans are particularly pretty in the rolls and a touch of *patis* (fish sauce) adds another Filipino note. Vinegar is a favorite seasoning in the Philippines, so it's apropos to dip the finished rolls in a tangy soy and garlic sauce. But if you'd like extra tropical flair, dunk the rolls in the Sweet and Sour Sauce on page 217 made with pineapple juice, ginger, and chile.

FILLING

3 tablespoons canola oil

1/2 yellow onion, finely chopped

4 cloves garlic, minced

1/2 pound ground chicken or pork, coarsely chopped to loosen

2/3 pound medium shrimp, peeled, deveined, and cut into pea-size pieces (9 ounces net weight)

3 large dried shiitake mushrooms, reconstituted (see page 13), stemmed, and cut into fine shreds (about 1/3 cup)

1 carrot, coarsely grated (scant 1/2 cup)

1/4 pound green beans or yard-long beans, trimmed and diagonally sliced into long thin pieces

3/4 teaspoon salt

Generous 1/2 teaspoon black pepper

1 1/2 teaspoons sugar

2 teaspoons fish sauce

18 to 20 Shanghai Spring Roll Skins (page 81)

1 large egg, beaten

3 tablespoons unseasoned rice or distilled white vinegar

3 tablespoons regular (light) soy sauce

1 large clove garlic, finely minced

Canola or peanut oil, for deep-frying

1. To prepare the filling, heat the oil in a large skillet over medium-high heat. Add the onion and garlic and cook, stirring constantly, for about 3 minutes, or until the onion is translucent and sweet smelling and the garlic is beginning to turn blond. Add the chicken and cook for 1 minute, or until halfway cooked. Mash, stir, and poke the meat with a spatula to break it into small pieces. Add the shrimp and cook for 30 seconds, or until it begins to turn color. Add the mushrooms, carrot, and green beans. Give the mixture a big stir and sprinkle in the salt, pepper, sugar, and fish sauce.

continued

Continue cooking, stirring constantly, for about 4 minutes, or until the meat is cooked through and the vegetables are tender. Transfer to a platter, spread it out, and set aside to cool completely before using. You should have about 3 cups. (The filling can be prepared up to 2 days in advance, covered, and refrigerated after cooling. Return to room temperature before wrapping.)

2. Before assembling the spring rolls, line a baking sheet with parchment paper. For each spring roll, place a skin, smooth side down, on your work surface. Place a generous 2 tablespoons of filling slightly below the center of the skin. Brush some beaten egg on all of the exposed edges to ensure a good seal and roll to create a cigar shape, following the directions on page 75. Set the finished rolls, seam side down, on the prepared baking sheet. Cover with a kitchen towel to prevent drying. (To freeze, put them on the prepared baking sheet, about 1/2 inch apart, and slide them into the freezer. After they have hardened, about 1 hour, transfer them to a zip-top freezer bag and keep frozen. Fry them unthawed. They will take a little longer than 3 minutes but will be just fine.)

3. To make the dipping sauce, combine the vinegar, soy sauce, and garlic in a communal dipping sauce bowl and set at the table.

4. To fry, heat 1 inch of oil in a wok, saucepan, or deep skillet over medium-high heat to about 350°F on a deep-fry thermometer. (If you don't have a deep-fry thermometer, stick a *dry* bamboo chopstick into the oil; if bubbles rise immediately to the surface and encircle the chopstick, the oil is ready.) Slide in a few spring rolls and fry, turning as needed, for about 3 minutes, or until golden brown. Remove from the oil and drain. Repeat with the remaining rolls. After all the rolls are fried, you can fry them again for 30 seconds at 350°F to reheat, as necessary.

5. Serve hot, whole or cut in half diagonally, with the sauce.

3 Stuffed Buns

In the early 1990s in Dali, a town in southwestern China, I experienced the perfect bun dough. In raw form, the huge mound of dough sat on the bun maker's counter, alive with yeasty goodness. Formed into small filled buns the size of golf balls, then steamed, the tasty dough was spongy, slightly chewy, and just a tad sweet. The cooking setup was simple: a propane-powered burner and a tower of bamboo steamers. My friends and I came back for more every day during our weeklong stay.

Ever since then, I had been looking for that same dough in commercial Chinese steamed *bāo*, which means bundle and parcel in Mandarin and is the generic Chinese term for buns. I did not find the ideal dough in the United States until I started some serious experiments of my own. It turns out that to make a great yeasted bun dough that holds up well under steam heat and tastes good, you need just a handful of ingredients, and you can use a food processor, too. Dough for baked *bāo* is straightforward as well. These two master dough recipes lead off this chapter, followed by a handful of tasty fillings that can be used in both types of dough. The final recipe in the chapter makes unusually delicious pan-fried buns.

Stuffed buns originated in China, perhaps as far back as the third century C.E., and have since spread throughout East and Southeast Asia. There are innumerable variations, and these doughs, fillings, and cooking techniques offer a solid foundation for exploring the broad spectrum of *bāo*.

Basic Yeast Dough

Fāmiàn

Makes 1¹/₄ pounds; enough for 32 small, 16 medium, or 12 large buns

There are several methods for making Chinese yeast dough, some of which employ starters and leavening, such as lye water and ammonium carbonate. This dough uses ingredients available at regular American supermarkets, and the results match the best I've experienced in China.

Many Asian cooks employ—to great success—a cakey, snowy-white Cantonese-style dough made from low-gluten cake flour or from a quickie flour and baking powder blend. This dough is different; it has more depth, and its loft and resilience comes from combining yeast and baking powder; fast-rising yeast works like a champ. All-purpose flour with a moderate amount of gluten, such as Gold Medal brand widely available at supermarkets, is what I prefer for this dough. Use bleached flour for a slightly lighter and brighter finish.

1¹/₂ teaspoons rapid-rise (instant) dry yeast

³/₄ cup lukewarm water

2 tablespoons canola oil

2 tablespoons sugar

2 teaspoons baking powder

12¹/₂ ounces (2¹/₂ cups) bleached or unbleached all-purpose flour

1. **Put the yeast** in a small bowl, add the water, and set aside for 1 minute to soften. Whisk in the oil to blend and dissolve the yeast. Set aside.

2. **To make the dough** in a food processor, combine the sugar, baking powder, and flour in the work bowl. Pulse two or three times to combine. With the motor on, pour the yeast mixture through the feed tube in a steady stream and allow the machine to continue running, for about 20 seconds, or until the dough starts coming together into a ball. (If this doesn't happen, add lukewarm water by the teaspoon.) Let the machine continue for 45 to 60 seconds to knead most of the dough into a large ball that cleans the sides of the bowl; expect some dangling bits. Press on the finished dough; it

should feel medium-soft and tacky but should not stick to your finger.

To make the dough by hand, combine the sugar, baking powder, and flour in a large bowl. Make a well in the center and pour in the yeast mixture. Slowly stir with a wooden spoon, moving from the center toward the rim, to work in all the flour. (Add lukewarm water by the teaspoon if this doesn't happen with relative ease.) Keep stirring as a ragged, soft mass forms. Then use your fingers to gather and pat the dough together into a ball. Transfer to a work surface and knead for about 5 minutes, or until smooth, fingertip soft, and slightly elastic. (You shouldn't need any additional flour on the work surface if the dough was properly made. Keep kneading and after the first minute or two, the dough shouldn't stick to your fingers. If it does, work in a sprinkling of flour.) Press your finger into the dough; the dough should spring back, with a faint indentation remaining.

3. **Regardless of the** mixing method, lightly oil a clean bowl and add the dough. Cover with plastic wrap and put in a warm, draft-

free place (for example, in an oven with the light on) to rise for about 45 minutes, or until nearly doubled. The dough is now ready to use.

4. **Though the dough** can be left to sit for an hour or so after it has doubled, it's best to have the filling already prepared, especially if it requires cooking and cooling.

Alternatively, punch down the dough, cover with plastic wrap, and refrigerate overnight. Return the dough to room temperature before using.

FITTING DUMPLINGS INTO YOUR LIFE

During the course of developing recipes for this book, I prepared and ate a lot of dumplings, and so did my friends, family, and recipe testers. On their own, dumplings make great snacks any time of the day, and I can attest to that as I taste-tested freshly cooked ones throughout the day. Feel free to serve any of the savory dumplings in this book as an appetizer or first course. Each of the sweet dumplings can be presented for dessert or as part of afternoon tea.

But one of the great things about dumplings is that you can easily make an entire meal based around them. Just remember that in one savory filled dumpling, you have both protein and starch. Add a simple vegetable dish, and you're done.

For example, in advance of poaching or steaming dumplings, I often blanch green vegetables such as broccoli, Chinese broccoli (*gai lan*), or green beans in the pot of boiling water. I either serve the veggie as-is, dipped in the same dipping sauce as the dumplings, or I quickly stir-fry it with garlic and oyster sauce or sesame oil and salt.

Instead of featuring a dumpling as a meal's main dish, present it as a side dish. For example, Sticky Rice and Chicken in Lotus Leaf (page 170) is relatively starchy, making it a perfect accompaniment to a pork roast.

Sometimes, dumplings can be a meal unto themselves. My husband and I are quite satisfied making a meal of warming bowls of savory dumplings in soup. We often enjoy steamed and baked buns on road trips and as airplane fare.

Steamed Filled Buns

Zhēng Bāo

Makes 32 small or 16 medium buns

Because ovens were rare, Chinese cooks have been steaming their bread dough for thousands of years, most likely since wheat-milling technology arrived in northern China by way of the Silk Road. There are many ways to present the steamed bread, and the Chinese knack for stuffing it with a savory or sweet filling is perhaps the most well known and well loved. The filled buns, or *bāo*, are a delicious, convenient fast food in many parts of Asia, where you can buy them from street vendors and snack shops.

Here in the States where stopping at a neighborhood *bāo* stand isn't the norm, I make the buns myself in small batches and enjoy them for lunch or as road food, whether I'm driving or flying. They can be reheated until soft, allowed to cool, and then kept in a plastic bag until you're ready to eat.

Medium-size buns are the easiest to make, so you may want to start with those. After you've made buns with the various fillings presented here, create your own fillings. To make steamed rolls that can be used for mini sandwiches, see the Note below.

1¹/₄ pounds Basic Yeast Dough (page 92)

FILLING

1¹/₃ cups Char Siu Pork Bun Filling (page 100), Vegetable and Tofu Bun Filling (page 101), or Curried Chicken Bun Filling (page 102) for savory buns *or* 1¹/₃ cups Sweetened Red Bean Paste (page 203) or Sweetened Mung Bean Paste (page 204) for sweet buns

1. **Transfer the dough** to a very lightly floured work surface, gather it into a ball if needed, and then pat it to flatten it into a thick disk. Cut the disk in half and cover half with plastic wrap or an inverted bowl to prevent drying while you work on the other half.

2. **Roll the dough** into a 12-inch log, then cut it into 8 or 16 pieces for medium or small buns, respectively. (Halve the log first to make it easier to cut into even-size pieces. The tapered end pieces should be cut a little longer than the rest.) Lightly roll each piece between your hands into a ball and then use the palm of one hand to flatten it into a ¹/₄-inch-thick disk.

Use a wooden dowel–style rolling pin to roll the pieces into circles, about 2¹/₂ inches in diameter for small or 3¹/₄ inches in diameter for medium buns. The rim should be thinner than the center; keeping a 1-inch-wide belly in the center to ensure consistent thickness between the bottom and top of the bun. The finished circle will be thick, and it will rise as it sits. (For guidance on rolling, see "Forming Wrappers from Basic Dumpling Dough," step 5, page 24.) Lay the finished circles out on your work surface, lightly dusting their bottoms with flour if you fear they will stick.

3. **Cut parchment paper** into 2¹/₂ or 3-inch squares (for small or medium buns, respectively) before beginning to assemble the buns.

4. **To assemble the buns,** hold a dough circle in a slightly cupped hand. Use a spoon or fork to center about 2 teaspoons of filling for small buns, or about 4 teaspoons of filling for medium

continued

buns, on the dough circle, pressing down very gently and keeping about 1/2 to 3/4 inch of the dough clear on all sides; your hand will automatically close slightly. Use the thumb of the hand cradling the bun to push down the filling while the other hand pulls up the dough edge and pleats and pinches the rim together to form a closed satchel (see page 52). Completely enclose the filling by pinching and twisting the dough closed.

Place the finished bun on a parchment paper square, pleated side up or down; in general, Chinese steamed savory buns are placed pleated side up, while sweet ones are cooked pleated side down to distinguish one from the other. You can put the buns with the parchment paper squares directly into a steamer tray, spacing them 1 inch apart and 1 inch away from the edge to accommodate the rising dough, or on a baking sheet. Repeat with the remaining dough circles and then cover with the steamer tray lid or loosely cover with plastic wrap or a kitchen towel. Set in a warm, draft-free place (for example, the oven with the light on) for 30 minutes to rise until nearly doubled in size. Meanwhile, work on the other dough half to form the remaining buns.

5. About 10 minutes before the rising time is over, get the equipment ready for steaming (see page 17 for guidance on steaming). When the buns have sufficiently risen, steam up to 2 trays of them at a time, 12 minutes for small buns or 15 minutes for medium buns. Cooked buns will have puffed up and will look dry.

Remove each tray and use a metal spatula to transfer the buns, still on their parchment paper squares, to a wire rack to cool for 5 minutes. Put more buns on the trays and repeat the steaming, replenishing the water as needed, until all the buns are cooked.

6. Arrange the buns, still on the parchment, on a platter and serve hot or warm. Remove the parchment before eating the buns out of hand.

Note: The best way to reheat leftover buns is to steam them for 5 to 8 minutes. Leftover buns can be refrigerated for up to a week or frozen for up to a month.

VARIATION: UNFILLED STEAMED BUNS

To make rolls that can be used to hold slices of Char Siu Pork (page 224), roasted duck, or braised pork belly, cut the dough into 16, 24, or 32 pieces for large, medium, or small rolls, respectively. Then roll out the dough pieces to form circles that are a scant 1/4 inch thick. There's no need to make a belly here. Brush a little canola oil on one-half of the dough circle to prevent it from sticking and make it easier to pry open later. Fold the circle over into a semicircle and then place on a parchment paper square. Place in a bamboo steamer or on a baking sheet, let it rise for 20 to 30 minutes, and then steam for 6 to 8 minutes, until puffy and dry looking. The buns will resemble pairs of thick lips when done. Serve the rolls with the sliced meat or preassemble the little sandwiches for your guests. Moisten the roll with some of the cooking juices, if available.

Baked Filled Buns

Jú Bāo

Makes 32 small or 16 medium buns

Baked buns, called *guk bau* in Cantonese, are a wonderful southern Chinese creation. They can be filled with a whole host of things, including sweet bean pastes and savory preserved pork shreds. Some have a crumbly crust that's akin to coffee cake topping.

My favorite renditions are slightly shiny and sticky from having been brushed with a lightly sweet honey glaze. Whatever the filling inside, whether it is spicy chicken curry, roast pork, vegetables, or bean pastes, you can't lose. Commercially produced Chinese baked buns are nearly cloying and super soft, whereas these have a delicate flavor and texture resembling that of challah.

DOUGH

10 tablespoons whole milk

4 tablespoons butter or canola oil

2 teaspoons rapid-rise (instant) dry yeast

2^1/2 tablespoons lukewarm water

1 large egg

2^1/2 tablespoons sugar

12^1/2 ounces (2^1/2 cups) bleached or unbleached all-purpose flour, plus more as needed

FILLING

1^1/3 cups Char Siu Pork Bun Filling (page 100), Vegetable and Tofu Bun Filling (page 101), or Curried Chicken Bun Filling (page 102) for savory buns *or* 1^1/3 cups Sweetened Red Bean Paste (page 203) or Sweetened Mung Bean Paste (page 204) for sweet buns

1 large egg, lightly beaten

2 tablespoons honey mixed with 1 tablespoon warm water

1. For the dough, melt the butter with the milk in a saucepan over medium heat. Set aside to cool for about 5 minutes, or until warm (about 110°F). If using oil, combine it with the milk and heat until warm.

2. Put the yeast in small bowl, add the water, and set aside for 1 minute to soften. Whisk in the milk mixture and the egg to blend.

3. Combine the sugar and flour in a food processor. Pulse two or three times to blend. With the machine running, pour the yeast mixture through the feed tube in a steady stream. After a sticky mass of very soft dough forms, about 5 seconds, continue processing for 45 to 60 seconds to form a smooth, slightly sticky dough that mostly cleans the bowl. The finished dough should stick a bit to your finger when pressed.

Alternatively, to make the dough by hand, combine the sugar and flour in a large bowl. Make a well in the center and pour in the yeast mixture. Slowly stir with a wooden spoon to work in all the flour. (Add water by the teaspoon if this doesn't happen with relative ease.) Keep stirring as a ragged, soft mass forms. Then use your fingers to gather and pat the dough into a ball. Transfer to a work surface and knead for about 5 minutes, or until smooth, fingertip soft, and slightly elastic. (You should not need any additional flour on the work surface if the dough was properly made. Keep kneading and after the first minute or two, the dough should not stick to your fingers. If it does, work in a sprinkling of flour.) Press your finger into the dough; it should spring back, with a faint indentation remaining.

continued

4. **Regardless of the mixing** method, lightly oil a clean bowl and add the dough. Cover with plastic wrap and put in a warm, draft-free place (for example, the oven with the light on) to rise for about 45 minutes, or until nearly doubled. (Or, punch the dough down after rising, cover with plastic wrap, and refrigerate overnight. Return the dough to room temperature before using.)

5. **Line 2 baking sheets** with parchment paper before beginning to assemble the buns.

6. **Remove the dough** from the bowl and put on a lightly floured surface. Knead it a few times, then cut it in half. Cover one-half with plastic wrap or an inverted bowl to prevent drying.

Roll out the dough into a 12-inch log, and then cut it into 8 or 16 pieces for medium or small buns, respectively. (Halve or quarter the log first to make it easier to cut even-size pieces. The tapered end pieces should be cut a little longer than the rest.) Lightly roll each piece between your hands into a ball and then flatten each one into a $1/4$-inch-thick disk.

Use a wooden dowel–style rolling pin to roll the pieces into circles, about $2^{1}/2$ inches in diameter for small or $3^{1}/4$ inches in diameter for medium buns. The rim should be thinner than the center; keep a 1-inch-wide belly. The finished circle will rise as it sits. (For guidance on rolling, see "Forming Wrappers from Basic Dumpling Dough," step 5, page 24.) Lay the finished circles out on your work surface, lightly dusting their bottoms with flour if you fear they will stick.

7. **To form a bun**, hold a dough circle in a slightly cupped hand. Use a spoon or fork to center about 2 teaspoons of filling for small buns, or about 4 teaspoons of filling for medium ones, on the dough circle, pressing down very gently and keeping about $1/2$ to $3/4$ inch of the dough clear on all sides; your hand will automatically close slightly. Use the thumb of the hand cradling the bun to push down the filling while the other hand pulls up the dough edge and pleats and pinches the rim together to form a closed satchel (see page 52). Pinch and twist the dough closed at the end.

Place the bun pleat side down on the prepared baking sheet. Repeat with the remaining dough circles, spacing them $1^{1}/2$ inches apart on the baking sheet. Loosely cover with plastic wrap or a kitchen towel. Set in a warm, draft-free place (for example, the oven with the light on) for 30 minutes to rise. Meanwhile, work on the other dough half to form more buns.

8. **To bake the buns**, about 10 minutes before the rising time is over, position a rack in the middle of the oven and preheat to 350°F. (Let the buns finish rising at room temperature if you've had them in the oven.)

9. **Bake one baking sheet** at a time, brushing the top and side of each bun with the egg right before baking. Bake small buns for about 14 minutes and medium buns for about 18 minutes, or until a rich golden brown; the cooked buns sound hollow when tapped on the bottom. Remove them from the oven, set on a rack, and let cool for 5 minutes.

10. **Brush the honey** mixture on the buns for a sweet-glaze finish that will also soften the crust. Enjoy warm and out of hand. Refrigerate leftover buns for up to a week and reheat at 350°F for 8 to 10 minutes, until hot. When making the buns in advance, wait to brush on the glaze until after you've reheated the buns. These buns may also be frozen for up to a month. Thaw them completely before reheating.

Char Siu Pork Bun Filling
Chāshāo Bāo

Makes 1¹/₃ cups

Whether steamed or baked, buns stuffed with Cantonese char siu pork are among my favorite dim sum. I rarely pass up the opportunity to savor how the spongy, slightly sweet dough complements the savory-sweet, rich meat. For spectacular buns, make this filling with homemade roast pork (page 224); in fact you can prepare a triple batch of filling from a single recipe of roast pork. If you elect to use store-bought pork, wait to salt the filling until after it is done and you can taste it to see what it needs; the meat is often well seasoned already.

FLAVORING SAUCE

1 tablespoon sugar

1 pinch of salt

1 pinch of white pepper

1 tablespoon light (regular) soy sauce

2 teaspoons oyster sauce

1 tablespoon water

2 teaspoons canola oil

2 scallions (white and green parts), chopped

1/2 pound Char Siu Pork, homemade (page 224) or store-bought, diced

1 tablespoon Shaoxing rice wine or dry sherry

1¹/₂ tablespoons cornstarch dissolved in 2 tablespoons water

1. **To make the** flavoring sauce, combine the sugar, salt, white pepper, soy sauce, oyster sauce, and water in a small bowl. Stir to dissolve the sugar and set aside.

2. **Heat the oil** in a medium skillet over medium heat. Add the scallions, and cook, stirring constantly, for about 30 seconds, or until aromatic and slightly softened. Add the pork and combine well. Add the flavoring sauce and cook, stirring frequently, for about 2 minutes, or until the pork is heated through.

Meanwhile, add the rice wine to the dissolved cornstarch. When the pork is hot enough, add the wine and cornstarch mixture. Cook for another 30 seconds, stirring constantly, until the mixture comes together into a mass that you can mound. Transfer to a bowl and set aside to cool completely before using. (The filling can be prepared up to 2 days in advance, covered with plastic wrap, and refrigerated. Return to room temperature before using.)

Vegetable and Tofu Bun Filling

Cài Bāo

Makes 1¹/3 cups

When you buy stuffed buns in Asia, there is usually a vegetarian option that features vegetables and pressed tofu. The fragrant, tasty filling is delightful and satisfying enough to please meat lovers. While you can feature just one vegetable, such as a leafy green, I like to create a varied filling that's full of surprising textures and flavors. It's important to cut the vegetables and pressed tofu into small, thin pieces so that the cooked filling is easy to measure and wrap up in the dough.

FLAVORING SAUCE

2 teaspoons sugar

¹/2 teaspoon black or white pepper

3 tablespoons water

2 tablespoons plus 1 teaspoon light (regular) soy sauce

1¹/2 teaspoons sesame oil

2 tablespoons canola oil

1 fat scallion (white and green parts), chopped

1 cup lightly packed finely shredded cabbage (omit thick center spines)

3 ounces brown pressed tofu, cut into ¹/4-inch-wide sticks and then sliced crosswise into thin, small pieces

¹/2 cup thinly sliced carrot (cut to match the tofu in size)

¹/2 cup thinly sliced small white mushrooms (halve crosswise before slicing)

2 teaspoons cornstarch dissolved in 1 tablespoon water

1. **To make the** flavoring sauce, combine the sugar, pepper, water, soy sauce, and sesame oil in a small bowl, stirring to dissolve the sugar. Set aside near the stove.

2. **Heat the canola oil** in a medium skillet over medium-high heat. Add the scallion and cook, stirring constantly, for about 30 seconds, or until aromatic and slightly softened. Add the cabbage, tofu, carrot, and mushrooms. Stir to combine and add the flavoring sauce. Bring the mixture to a fast simmer, then allow it to bubble away, stirring frequently, for about 3 minutes, or until the liquid has reduced by about one-third, and the vegetables are cooked through.

Give the cornstarch mixture a final stir and add it to the filling mixture. Cook, stirring, for another 30 seconds, or until the filling coheres. Transfer to a bowl and set aside to cool completely until using. (Just like the other bun fillings, this one can be prepared up to 2 days in advance, covered with plastic wrap, and refrigerated. Return it to room temperature before using.)

Curried Chicken Bun Filling

Gālí Jī Bāo

Makes 1¹/₃ cups

Cantonese cooks have been creating curried *bāo* fillings for years, but for buns with both a Southeast Asian and an Indian edge, stuff them with this curried chicken filling that contains plenty of spice and a touch of coconut-milk richness.

The ingredient list looks daunting only because of the number of spices, a combination that yields aromatic, flavorful results. If you have a good curry powder, such as Sun Brand, feel free to substitute 1 tablespoon for the spices below; decrease the amount of salt if the curry powder contains salt already. Or skip the toasting and grinding and substitute equal amounts of ground spices for the whole ones, using two pinches of black pepper for the peppercorns. The flavors will still be good.

1¹/₂ teaspoons coriander seed

¹/₄ teaspoon cumin seed

¹/₈ teaspoon fennel seed

3 black peppercorns

¹/₄ teaspoon ground cayenne

¹/₄ teaspoon ground turmeric

1 pinch of ground cloves

1 pinch of ground cinnamon

1 shallot, chopped (¹/₄ cup)

1 tablespoon chopped fresh ginger

1 clove garlic, chopped

1¹/₂ teaspoons water

1 tablespoon canola oil

²/₃ pound boneless skinless chicken thighs, chopped into peanut-size pieces

¹/₂ teaspoon salt

³/₄ teaspoon sugar

3 tablespoons coconut milk

2¹/₂ teaspoons cornstarch dissolved in 1 tablespoon water

2 tablespoons coarsely chopped fresh cilantro

1. Toast the coriander seed, cumin seed, fennel seed, and peppercorns in a small dry skillet over medium heat for 1 to 2 minutes, until fragrant. Use a clean, dry coffee grinder or mortar and pestle to pulverize. Transfer to an electric mini-chopper and add the cayenne, turmeric, cloves, cinnamon, shallot, ginger, garlic, and water. Process to a paste, scraping down the sides occasionally. (Or add the ingredients, except the water, to the mortar and pestle. Pound, then add the water to make a paste.) Transfer to a small bowl and set aside.

2. Heat the oil in a medium skillet over medium heat. Add the spice paste and cook, stirring frequently, for about 5 minutes, or until it has darkened and become richly fragrant. Add the chicken, salt, and sugar, stirring to combine well. Cook for 2 to 3 minutes, stirring, until the chicken is cooked halfway through. Add the coconut milk, and cook for another 2 to 3 minutes, until the chicken is done and has released some of its juices. Cook for 1 minute more to intensify the flavors. Stir the cornstarch mixture and add it to the skillet. Stir to distribute and cook for about 30 seconds, or until the filling has thickened into a mass.

Remove from the heat and stir in the cilantro. Transfer to a bowl and set aside to cool completely before using. (The filling can be prepared up to 2 days in advance, covered with plastic wrap, and refrigerated. Return to room temperature before using.)

Filipino Chicken and Egg Buns

Siopao

Makes 12 large buns

Nowhere else in Asia has Chinese *bāo* been embraced and appropriated to the extent that it has been in the Philippines. An extremely popular snack, Filipino *siopao* tend to be large, sometimes the size of a softball. They are filled with all kinds of things, including slightly sweet meat and gravy mixtures (*asado siopao*), dense meatloaf-like concoctions (*bola-bola siopao*), and even *balut*, the beloved partially incubated duck egg. Quite often in Filipino meat-filled buns, there's a wedge of boiled egg inside, which is why I've included it in this chicken rendition for a mother-and-child reunion of sorts.

Siopao dough can be made from rice flour, which results in superwhite buns, but I prefer wheat-flour buns because they have a chewier texture and more flavor.

FILLING

2 teaspoons light (regular) soy sauce

2 teaspoons lightly packed light brown sugar

2 teaspoons oyster sauce

1 pinch of salt

1/4 teaspoon black pepper

1 1/2 tablespoons canola oil

2 scallions (white and green parts), chopped

1 large clove garlic, minced

1/2 pound boneless, skinless chicken thighs, cut into peanut-size pieces

1 tablespoon cornstarch dissolved in 1 1/2 tablespoons water

1 1/4 pounds Basic Yeast Dough (page 92)

2 hard-cooked eggs, peeled and cut lengthwise into 6 wedges each

1. To make the filling, in a small bowl, combine the soy sauce, brown sugar, oyster sauce, salt, and pepper. Set these seasonings aside.

2. Heat the oil in a medium skillet over medium heat. Add the scallions and garlic, and cook, stirring constantly, for about 30 seconds, or until aromatic and slightly softened. Add the chicken, stir, and add the seasoning mixture. Cook, stirring frequently, for about 2 minutes, until the chicken is cooked through. Give the cornstarch mixture a final stir and add to the chicken. Continue cooking for about 30 seconds, until the filling has thickened.

Transfer to a bowl and set aside to cool completely before using. (The filling can be prepared up to 2 days in advance, covered with plastic wrap, and refrigerated. Return to room temperature before using.) There should be a generous cup of filling.

3. Transfer the dough to a very lightly floured work surface, gather it into a ball if needed, and then pat it to flatten it to a thick disk. Cut the disk in half and cover one-half with plastic wrap or an inverted bowl to prevent drying while you work on the other half.

4. Roll the dough into a 12 to 14-inch log, and then cut it into 6 pieces. (Halve the log first to make it easier to cut even-size pieces. The tapered end pieces should be cut a little longer than the rest.) Lightly roll each piece into a ball and then use the palm of one hand to flatten each one into a 1/4-inch-thick disk.

Use a wooden dowel–style rolling pin to roll the pieces into circles about 3 3/4 inches in diameter. The rim of each circle should be

continued

thinner than the center; keeping a 1^1/$_2$-inch-wide belly in the center ensures consistent thickness all over the finished bun. The finished circle will be thick and it will rise as it sits. (For guidance on rolling, see "Forming Wrappers from Basic Dumpling Dough," step 5, page 24.) Lay the finished circles out on your work surface, lightly dusting their bottoms with flour if you fear them sticking.

5. Cut twelve 3^1/$_2$-inch squares of parchment paper and set aside. To assemble the buns, hold a dough circle in a slightly cupped hand. Use a spoon to center 1^1/$_2$ teaspoons of filling on the dough circle, pressing down very gently and keeping about ^{1}/$_2$ to ^{3}/$_4$ inch of the dough clear on all sides; your hand will automatically close slightly. Add a wedge of egg, with the curved side down so that when you gather up the dough, the egg will naturally bend and match the round bun shape. Put 1 tablespoon of filling atop the egg.

Use the thumb of the hand cradling the bun to push down the filling while the fingers of the other hand pull up the dough edge and pleat and pinch the rim together to form a closed satchel (see page 52). Completely enclose the filling by pinching and twisting the dough closed.

Place the finished bun on a piece of parchment, pleated side down. You can put the bun, still on the parchment paper, directly into a steamer tray or on a baking sheet. Repeat with the remaining dough circles, spacing them 1 inch apart and 1 inch away from the edge to allow the dough to comfortably rise. Cover with the lid or loosely cover with plastic wrap or a kitchen towel. Set in a warm, draft-free place (for example, the oven with the light on) for 30 minutes to rise until nearly doubled. Meanwhile, work on the other dough half to form the remaining buns.

6. About 10 minutes before the rising time is over, ready the water for steaming (see page 17 for guidance on steaming). When the buns have risen, steam them, up to 2 trays at a time, for about 18 minutes, or until they have puffed up and look dry.

Remove each tray and use a metal spatula to transfer the buns, on the parchment paper, to a wire rack to cool for 5 minutes. Put more buns on the trays and repeat the steaming, replenishing the water as needed, until all the buns are cooked.

7. Arrange the buns, still on the parchment, on a platter and serve. Remove the parchment before eating the buns out of hand. Refrigerate leftover buns and steam them for 6 to 8 minutes to reheat.

Panfried Pork and Scallion Mini Buns

Shēng Jiān Bāozi

Makes 32 small buns

If you like pot stickers and steamed buns, you'll love these spongy-crisp panfried treats from Shanghai, where typically they are cooked in humongous shallow pans (much like large paella pans) with wooden lids. These buns are made of yeast dough that is filled with an aromatic pork mixture and then fried and steamed in a skillet. Cooking under cover with a bit of water delivers plenty of moisture to puff up the buns. Ground beef chuck or chicken thigh can stand in for the pork in this recipe.

A *bāozi* is a mini *bāo* (bun) and for that reason, I like to keep these true to their name and shape small ones. However, you can elect to form sixteen medium-size (2³/₄-inch) buns. Roll the dough circles out to 3¹/₄ inches in diameter and use about 4 teaspoons of filling for each bun; increase the water and cooking time a tad.

FILLING

10 ounces fatty ground pork, coarsely chopped to loosen

2 teaspoons minced fresh ginger

1/4 cup finely chopped Chinese chives or scallions (white and green parts)

1/4 teaspoon plus 1/8 teaspoon salt

1/8 teaspoon white pepper

1/2 teaspoon sugar

1 tablespoon light (regular) soy sauce

2 teaspoons Shaoxing rice wine or dry sherry

2 teaspoons sesame oil

1 tablespoon water

1¹/4 pounds Basic Yeast Dough (page 92), preferably made with unbleached flour

1 tablespoon finely shredded fresh ginger

1/4 cup Chinkiang vinegar or balsamic vinegar

Light (regular) soy sauce (optional)

Chile Oil (page 216) (optional)

3 to 4 tablespoons canola oil

1. To make the filling, combine the pork, ginger, and Chinese chives in a bowl. Use a fork or spatula to stir and mash the ingredients together.

2. Combine the salt, white pepper, sugar, soy sauce, rice wine, sesame oil, and water in a small bowl and stir to combine well. Pour over the meat mixture, then vigorously stir to create a compact mixture. Cover the filling with plastic wrap and set aside for 30 minutes, or refrigerate overnight, returning it to room temperature before assembling the buns. There should be 1¹/3 cups of filling.

3. Transfer the dough to a very lightly floured work surface, gather it into a ball if needed, and then pat it to flatten it to a thick disk. Cut the disk in half and cover one-half with plastic wrap or an inverted bowl to prevent drying while you work on the other half.

4. Roll the dough into a 12 to 14-inch log, and then cut it into 16 pieces. (Halve the log first to make it easier to cut even-size pieces. The tapered end pieces should be cut a little longer than the rest.) Lightly roll each piece between your hands into a ball, then flatten each one into a 1/4-inch-thick disk.

continued

Use a wooden dowel–style rolling pin to roll the pieces into circles, each about 2½ inches in diameter. The rim of each circle should be thinner than the center; keeping a 1-inch-wide belly ensures consistent thickness all over the bun. The finished circle will thicken as it sits. (For guidance on rolling, see "Forming Wrappers from Basic Dumpling Dough," step 5, page 24.) Lay the finished circles out on your work surface, lightly dusting their bottoms with flour if you fear them sticking.

5. **Line a baking sheet** with parchment paper and lightly dust with flour. To assemble a bun, hold a dough circle in a slightly cupped hand. Use a bamboo spatula, dinner knife, or spoon to center about 2 teaspoons of filling on the dough circle, pressing down very gently and keeping about ½ to ¾ inch of the dough clear on all sides. Use the thumb of the hand cradling the bun to push down the filling while the other hand pulls up the dough edge and pleats and pinches the rim together to form a closed satchel (see page 52). Pinch and twist to completely close. Place the bun, pleated side down, on the baking sheet. Repeat with the remaining dough circles and filling. Loosely cover the buns with plastic wrap and let rise in a warm, draft-free spot for 30 minutes, or until about 50 percent larger than their original size. Meanwhile, make buns from the remaining dough and filling.

6. **While the buns rise,** divide the ginger and vinegar between 2 bowls. Taste and if the vinegar is too tart, add water by the teaspoon. Set these at the table along with the soy sauce and chile oil for guests to mix their own sauce.

7. **To panfry the buns,** use a medium or large nonstick skillet; if both sizes are handy, cook 2 batches at the same time. Heat the skillet(s) over medium heat and add 1 tablespoon of canola oil for a medium skillet and 1½ tablespoons for a large one. Add the buns one at a time, arranging them, pleated side up, ½ inch apart; they will expand during cooking. (In general, medium skillets will fit 8 or 9 buns; large skillets will fit 12 or 13 buns.) Fry the buns for 1 to 2 minutes, until they are golden or light brown on the bottom. Gently lift to check the color.

8. **Holding the lid** close to the skillet to lessen the spattering effect of water hitting hot oil, add enough water to come up the side of the buns by ¼ inch, about ¼ cup. The water and oil will sputter a bit. Cover with a lid or aluminum foil, placing it very slightly ajar to allow steam to escape, so condensation doesn't fall on the buns and perhaps cause their collapse. Let the water bubble away until it is mostly gone, about 6 minutes.

9. **When you hear** sizzling noises (a sign that most of the water is gone), remove the lid. Let the dumplings fry for about 1 minute, until the bottoms are brown and crisp. At this point, you can serve the buns, crisp bottoms up like pot stickers. Or, you can use chopsticks to flip each bun over (separate any that are sticking together first) and then fry the other side for about 45 seconds, or until golden.

10. **Turn off the heat,** wait for the cooking action to cease, and transfer the buns to a serving plate. Display them with a golden side up. Serve with the gingered vinegar, chile oil, and soy sauce. Eat these buns with chopsticks—they're a little greasy on the fingers.

Reheat leftovers with some oil and water in a nonstick skillet, as you would a pot sticker.

4 Rich Pastries

Whereas the dumplings showcased in the first three chapters can be described as homey, comforting, and satisfying, these rich pastries are just plain sinful. You cannot go wrong with dough that has been enriched by fat, whether it's butter, shortening, or lard, then filled with well-seasoned fillings that range from curried potatoes and daikon radish and smoky ham to chile-inflected canned sardines.

Health-conscious cooks may want to stick with lighter choices, and I've provided options and a "Lazy Day Tip" to assist you. But for those who want to indulge and learn some nifty Asian cooking methods, progress to the two flaky dough recipes and abandon any fear of fat or frying. The scrumptious results will be well worth it.

Beef, Sweet Potato, and Raisin Turnovers

Empanadas

Makes 12 pastries

Like fried *lumpia* (see page 87), these savory-sweet turnovers are beloved Filipino snacks. Empanadas in the Philippines are usually deep-fried, as they are in other places, such as Argentina, where the Spanish pastry has also been adopted. Filipino-American cooks, however, mostly wrap theirs in a short pastry crust and bake them, with delicious results.

If you've never had Asian pastries like those in this section, this is a good one to start with because it is easy to prepare and love. For richer, deep-fried empanadas, swap the filling below for the one used in the Shrimp, Pork, and Jicama Turnovers (page 118) or Curry Puffs (page 125) recipe. Feel free to substitute other ground meat for the beef.

DOUGH

8³/₄ ounces (1³/₄ cups) bleached all-purpose flour

1¹/₂ teaspoons to 1 tablespoon sugar (use 1 tablespoon for a stronger savory-sweet contrast)

¹/₂ teaspoon salt

3 tablespoon shortening, chilled

¹/₄ cup unsalted butter, chilled and cut into ¹/₄-inch pieces

1 large egg yolk combined with 5 tablespoons ice water

FILLING

1 tablespoon canola oil

2 tablespoons finely chopped yellow onion

1 clove garlic, minced

3 ounces ground beef (preferably chuck)

¹/₃ cup diced sweet potato (orange-flesh variety preferred)

¹/₄ cup water

2 teaspoons light (regular) soy sauce

1 pinch of salt

¹/₈ teaspoon black pepper

2 tablespoons raisins

1 large egg, separated

All-purpose flour, for dusting

1. To make the dough in a food processor, combine the flour, sugar, and salt in the work bowl and pulse 2 or 3 times to combine. Add the shortening and process for 10 seconds to combine. Sprinkle in the butter pieces and pulse 10 to 15 times, until the mixture is pale yellow and resembles coarse crumbs. Break apart pieces larger than a pea. Transfer to a bowl. (Alternatively, put the ingredients in a bowl and use a pastry blender or your fingers in a quick rubbing motion to combine the ingredients.)

Work in the egg mixture, one-third at a time, using a rubber spatula to fold, mash, and press the ingredients together after each addition. When all the liquid has been incorporated, you should be able to press the dough into a ragged mass with the spatula. If not, work in additional ice water by the teaspoon. Transfer the dough to a work surface (no flouring is needed) and very gently knead the dough into a ball. Pat the dough ball into a 5-inch disk. Wrap in plastic and refrigerate for at least 1 hour, or up to 2 days.

2. Meanwhile, to make the filling, heat the oil in a medium skillet over medium heat. Add the onion and garlic and cook, stirring constantly, for 2 to 3 minutes, until the onion is translucent and sweet smelling and the garlic begins to turn blond. Add the beef, and use a wooden

continued

spoon or spatula to stir and mash the meat into small pieces. Cook for 30 to 60 seconds, until most of the meat has begun to brown. Add the sweet potato, water, soy sauce, salt, and pepper. Stir, lower the heat slightly, and cover. Cook for about 4 minutes, or until the potato is nearly tender; there should still be some liquid remaining.

Uncover, add the raisins, and continue cooking, stirring constantly, for about 1 minute, or until the potato is tender and there is very little liquid left. Remove from the heat and use the spoon or spatula to mash half of the potato and make the mixture cohere a bit. Transfer to a small bowl and set aside to cool completely before using. You should have about 3/4 cup. (The filling can be prepared up to 2 days in advance and refrigerated. Return it to room temperature before using.)

3. **If the dough** was refrigerated for longer than 1 hour, let it sit at room temperature until malleable. Position a rack in the middle of the oven and preheat to 375°F. Line 2 baking sheets with parchment paper. Lightly beat the egg white and keep it nearby.

4. **Unwrap the dough** and put it on a lightly floured work surface. Gently squeeze on the dough to elongate it. Roll it into a 12-inch log. Use a knife to cut the log into 12 pieces. (Halve the log first to easily cut even-size pieces. The tapered end pieces should be cut a little longer than the rest.) Loosely cover the dough pieces with plastic wrap or a kitchen towel to prevent drying.

5. **Work with half** of the dough pieces at time, keeping the others loosely covered. Use an Asian-style wooden rolling pin to roll each piece of dough into a circle 3 1/2 inches in diameter and just a bit thicker in the center than at the rim. Use a minimum amount of flour to dust your work surface and rotate the circle. Roll from the center outward as you would a basic dumpling wrapper (see page 24).

Holding a wrapper in one hand, use a spoon to position about 1 tablespoon of filling slightly off-center on the wrapper, pressing down very gently and keeping about 1/2 to 3/4 inch of wrapper clear on all sides. Brush egg white on half of the rim and then bring up the other half to meet it and close. Press with your fingers to create a half-moon (see page 26), sealing the rim well and creating a 1/2-inch brim. For extra security, use your thumb and index fingers to form a rope edge (see page 51) or press with the tines of a fork. Place the turnover, pretty rope edge facing up, on the prepared baking sheet. Repeat with the remaining wrappers, spacing them about 2 inches apart, before working on the second half of dough. Assembled empanadas can be frozen on the baking sheet until hard (about 2 hours), transferred to a zip-top freezer bag, and kept frozen for up to 1 month; partially thaw before brushing with egg and baking.

6. **Lightly beat the egg** yolk and brush it on the turnovers, taking care to cover the spine. Bake 1 baking sheet at a time for 20 to 22 minutes, until golden brown. Put the baking sheet on a rack and cool for about 10 minutes before eating. Empanadas are great at room temperature, too.

LAZY DAY TIP

Use a high-quality prepared pie crust when you have no time to make dough from scratch.

Simple Flaky Pastry

Makes 1/2 pound

Many rich, filled Asian pastries, such as Indian *samosas* (page 115) and Vietnamese *bánh quai vạc chiên* (page 118), employ straightforward dough made of wheat flour, fat, and water. Some cooks use oil for richness, but vegetable shortening creates a wonderful crispness. Pastries made with this dough are not blistery, but rather smooth and undulating with delicate puffy bubbles.

Though you can make the dough by machine, the quantity of ingredients involved doesn't justify the cleanup. I actually prefer the simplicity of preparing dough by hand because it is quick and fun. Rather than cutting the shortening into the flour, you rub the ingredients together to evenly coat the flour—a method referred to as *moyan dena* by Indian cooks. Despite this being a flaky pastry, the dough is kneaded to develop gluten so that it can hold up well during frying. A bit of leaven ensures a light texture. The resulting dough is strong, yet flaky and crisp.

5 ounces (1 cup) bleached or unbleached all-purpose flour

1/4 teaspoon salt

1/8 teaspoon baking powder

3 tablespoons solid vegetable shortening, at room temperature

1/4 cup water

1. Combine the flour, salt, and baking powder in a large bowl. Stir with one hand to blend. Add the shortening, breaking it into 2 or 3 manageable chunks. To combine the ingredients, pick up some flour and shortening and quickly rub it between your hands in a gentle sliding motion from the heel of your hand to your fingertips. Work over the bowl so that the mixture falls back into the bowl. Continue picking up and rubbing more of the mixture until you no longer see lumps of shortening. This process takes less than 1 minute.

2. Work in the water, one-third at a time, using your fingers or a spatula to moisten the flour mixture after each addition. When all the water has been incorporated, you should be able to press the ragged mass of dough and all the bits into a ball.

3. Transfer the dough to an unfloured work surface; it should not stick. Knead the dough for 5 minutes, until it is relatively smooth and somewhat elastic. Push your finger into the dough; it should slowly bounce back with a noticeable dent left behind. Wrap in plastic wrap and set aside at room temperature for at least 30 minutes and up to 2 hours before using. (The dough can be refrigerated overnight. Return to room temperature before using.)

Spicy Potato Samosas

Aloo Samosa

Makes 12 pastries

Bite into a freshly fried samosa, and you'll realize that the quintessential Indian snack is no simple food. When made well, the crisp shell is delicately rich and flaky. The filling inside varies, but a tangy potato mixture is the most common. Many believe that samosas arrived in India via the ancient trade routes that linked West Asia with Central Asia and South Asia. In fact, related pastries are called *sanbusak* in the Middle East and *samsa* in Central Asia.

Samosas are fabulous alone or with a dab of mint and/or tamarind chutney. Add some chai tea, and you have a perfect snack. Or serve them with a salad for a great lunch. Many cooks use russet (baking) potatoes, but I prefer Yukon Golds for their flavor and cheery yellow color. Choose potatoes of the same size to ensure that they're done at the same time.

FILLING

10 ounces Yukon Gold potatoes (2 medium)

1 1/2 tablespoons canola oil

1 1/4 teaspoons coriander seed

1/2 teaspoon cumin seed

1/4 cup finely chopped yellow onion

1 teaspoon minced fresh ginger

1/4 cup frozen green peas, thawed

1 tablespoon finely chopped fresh cilantro

Generous 1/2 teaspoon salt

1/4 teaspoon cayenne

Heaping 1/2 teaspoon garam masala (page 219)

1 1/2 teaspoons fresh lemon or lime juice

1/2 pound Simple Flaky Pastry (page 113)

Canola or peanut oil, for deep-frying

2/3 cup Fresh Mint Chutney (page 219) (optional)

1 1/3 cups Tamarind and Date Chutney (page 220) (optional)

1. To make the filling, put the potatoes in a pot and add water to cover by 1 1/4 inches. Bring to a boil over high heat and boil for about 20 minutes, or until the potatoes are tender. Test by piercing each with a knife. Drain and briefly set aside to cool, then slip off their skins. Cut out any unsightly eyes. Allow the potatoes to cool completely and firm up (refrigerate them overnight, if you want) before cutting them into 1/4 to 1/2-inch cubes. You should have a generous 1 1/2 cups. Set aside.

2. Heat the oil in a medium skillet over medium-high heat. Add the coriander and cumin seeds and fry for about 30 seconds, until very fragrant and slightly darkened. Add the onion and ginger, and cook, stirring constantly, for about 2 minutes, or until soft, compacted, and frothy. Add the potatoes and cook, stirring frequently, for about 4 minutes, or until a number of the pieces are tinged golden brown.

Remove from the heat and stir in the peas and cilantro. Sprinkle on the salt, cayenne, and garam masala. Stir and finish with the lemon juice. Cool for a few minutes, taste, and make any flavor adjustments. Aim for a slightly intense flavor because it will mellow a tad Transfer to a bowl and set aside to cool completely before using. You should have about 1 2/3 cups. (The filling can be prepared up to

continued

2 days in advance, covered in plastic wrap, and refrigerated. Return it to room temperature before using.)

3. **If the dough** was refrigerated, return it to room temperature before using. Line a baking sheet with parchment paper.

On an unfloured or very lightly floured surface, roll the dough into a 6-inch log. Use a knife to cut the log into 6 pieces. (Halve the log first to easily cut even-size pieces. The tapered end pieces should be cut a little longer than the rest.) Cover with plastic wrap or a kitchen towel to prevent drying.

Working with half of the dough pieces at a time, flatten each piece of dough with the palm of your hand. Use a rolling pin to roll the dough into a 6-inch-diameter circle; roll from the center to the edge to create a nice circle. There is no need to make it thicker in the middle. Use a knife to cut it in half. Set aside. A little overlapping is fine; the wrappers should not stick together. Repeat with the other 2 dough pieces to create 6 half-circle wrappers. Keep covered to prevent drying.

Because the wrappers tend to shrink after rolling, I like to reroll each one to ensure it is fully 3 inches wide; the length is not as important. For each samosa, drape a wrapper over your fingers with the curved edge toward your thumb and the midpoint of the straight edge over your index finger. Use your finger to moisten half of the straight edge facing you with water.

To create the cone, bring the dry half of the straight edge to the front and overlap the moistened edge by about 1/4 inch. Use your fingers to press the tip closed and apply pressure along the seam both inside and outside the cone to yield a solid seal.

Support the cone as you fill it by holding it in one hand about halfway up from the tip.

Use a spoon to put 2 generous tablespoons of the potato mixture inside the cone, tapping it down lightly. Moisten half of the rim of the cone with water and then press the edge together to seal well. (The pastries will still be tasty if the seal breaks during frying; they'll just be a little greasy.) Put the finished pastry, seam side down, on the prepared baking sheet. Fill the remaining 5 wrappers before rolling and filling the other 6 dough pieces.

You do not need to cover the assembled pastries as they wait to be fried. In fact, the crust fries up nice and flaky if left out to dry for about 20 minutes (about the amount of time it takes to shape all the samosas); turn them once so all sides dry out a bit. Cover them with a kitchen towel if they have to wait longer, lest they overdry and lose their seal.

4. **Put a paper** towel–lined platter next to the stove. Pour oil to a depth of 2 inches into a wok, deep saucepan, or Dutch oven and heat over medium-high heat to about 310°F on a deep-fry thermometer. Frying for a long time at a moderately low temperature between 300° and 330°F ensures delicate, flaky results. (If you don't have a deep-fry thermometer, stick a *dry* bamboo chopstick into the oil; if it takes 2 to 4 seconds for bubbles to rise to the surface and encircle the chopstick, the oil is ready.)

Working in batches of 4 to 6 to avoid crowding, gently drop the pastries into the hot oil and immediately lower the heat slightly. The samosas will float to the top after about 15 seconds. Spoon hot oil over the puffy tops 2 or 3 times; this facilitates even cooking. The temperature will drop initially and then slowly rise. Expect to gradually lower the heat to keep the oil around 330°F. (If you don't have a thermometer, do the chopstick test a couple of times as the dumplings cook; if bubbles rise immediately to the surface and encircle the chopstick, the oil is too hot.)

Fry, turning them often and pressing them down below the oil level, for about 10 minutes total, or until golden brown. Use a skimmer to scoop up and transfer them to the platter to drain and cool. Adjust the heat before frying more.

5. Allow the pastries to cool for about 5 minutes before serving with the chutneys.

Refrigerate leftover pastries. They are best reheated by frying for about 2 minutes in 2 inches of 350°F oil. For less hassle—and less crisp results—reheat the samosas in a 350°F oven or toaster oven, turning midway, for about 12 minutes, or until gently sizzling and hot.

Shaping Samosas

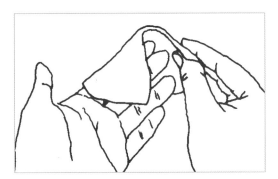

1. Drape a wrapper over your fingers, moisten half of the straight edge facing you, and overlap the dry and moistened halves of the edge by about 1/4 inch.

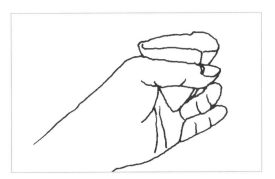

2. Press the tip closed and seal by pressing the seam both inside and out. Support the cone as you fill it by holding it in your hand.

Shrimp, Pork, and Jicama Turnovers
Bánh Quai Vạc Chiên

Makes 12 pastries

Certain childhood treats stick with you, and for me these crisp turnovers are a tasty reminder of our life in Saigon. Sister Thien, our cook, and a family friend whom we called Uncle Thu, would make the dough and fill it with this delectable mixture of shrimp, pork, and jicama. Although they were hot right out of the oil, I could barely wait to dive in. My piggishness often led to a burned tongue.

These are not easy to find abroad in expatriate Vietnamese enclaves, and I wasn't able to rediscover the flavor and texture from my youth until I made them myself. For a baked version, substitute this filling for the one in the empanada recipe (page 111). Note that in the central region of Vietnam, *bánh quai vạc* is the name of unrelated rice- or tapioca-based dumplings.

FILLING

1 tablespoon canola oil

2 tablespoons finely chopped shallot

1 clove garlic, minced

2 ounces ground pork, coarsely chopped to loosen

3 ounces medium shrimp, peeled, deveined, and chopped into pea-sized pieces (2¹/2 ounces net weight)

Scant ¹/4 cup finely diced jicama

Generous ¹/4 teaspoon salt

¹/8 teaspoon black pepper

¹/4 teaspoon plus ¹/8 teaspoon sugar

1 heaping tablespoon chopped scallion (green part only)

¹/2 pound Simple Flaky Pastry (page 113)

Canola or peanut oil, for deep-frying

1. To make the filling, heat the oil in a medium skillet over medium heat. Add the shallot and garlic and cook, stirring constantly, for 2 to 3 minutes, until the shallot is soft and sweet smelling, and the garlic is beginning to turn blond. Add the pork, and use a wooden spoon or spatula to stir and mash the meat into small pieces. Cook for 30 to 60 seconds, until most of the meat no longer looks raw. Add the shrimp, jicama, salt, pepper, and sugar. Cook,

stirring frequently for 4 minutes, or until the jicama is tender. Turn off the heat and stir in the scallion to wilt it slightly. Transfer to a small bowl, partially cover to prevent drying, and set aside to cool completely before using. You should have about ³/4 cup. (The filling can be prepared up to 2 days in advance, covered in plastic wrap, and refrigerated. Return it to room temperature before using.)

2. If the dough was refrigerated for longer than 1 hour, return it to room temperature before using. Line a baking sheet with parchment paper.

Working on an unfloured or very lightly floured surface, gently squeeze and then roll the dough into a 12-inch-long log. Use a knife to cut the log into 12 pieces. (Halve the log first to easily cut even-size pieces. The tapered end pieces should be cut a little longer than the rest.) Cover with plastic wrap or a kitchen towel to prevent drying.

Working with half of the dough pieces at a time, flatten each piece of dough with the palm of your hand. Use a skinny Asian rolling pin to roll the dough into a 3¹/4 to 3¹/2-inch-diameter circle, making it just slightly thicker in the middle and rotating the wrapper as you work. (For guidance, see "Forming Wrappers from Basic Dumpling Dough," steps 4 and 5, page 24.) Set each wrapper aside. A little overlapping is fine; the wrappers should not stick together. Cover to prevent drying.

3. **To assemble a turnover,** hold a wrapper in a slightly cupped hand. Use a spoon to scoop up 1 tablespoon of filling and position it slightly off-center toward the upper half of the wrapper, pressing down gently and keeping about 1/2 to 3/4 inch of wrapper clear on all sides. As you work, your hand should naturally close a bit more to keep the turnover in shape.

Moisten the top rim of the wrapper with water and then bring up the side of the wrapper that is closest to you and firmly press to create a half-moon (see page 26), sealing the rim well and creating a 1/2-inch brim. For extra security, use your thumb and index fingers to form a rope edge (see page 51) or press with the tines of a fork. Place the finished turnover on the prepared baking sheet. Repeat with the other 5 wrappers before making and filling the 6 wrappers from the remaining dough.

Once shaped, keep the finished turnovers uncovered for about 20 minutes (the amount of time it takes to assemble all the turnovers), turning them once so they dry a bit on all sides; this helps the crust fry up nice and flaky. Cover the turnovers with a kitchen towel if they have to wait longer, lest they overdry and lose their seal.

4. **Put a paper** towel–lined platter next to the stove. Pour oil to a depth of 1 1/4 inches into a wok, deep saucepan, or Dutch oven and heat over medium-high heat to about 310°F on a deep-fry thermometer. Frying for a long time at a moderately low temperature between 300° and 330°F ensures delicate, flaky results. (If you don't have a deep-fry thermometer, stick a *dry* bamboo chopstick into the oil; if it takes 2 to 4 seconds for bubbles to rise to the surface and encircle the chopstick, the oil is ready.)

Working in batches of 4 to 6 to prevent crowding, gently drop the turnovers into the hot oil and immediately reduce the heat slightly. They will float to the top after about 15 seconds. Spoon hot oil over the puffy tops 2 or 3 times; this facilitates even cooking. The temperature will drop initially and then slowly rise. You will probably need to gradually lower the temperature to keep it around 330°F. (If you don't have a thermometer, do the chopstick test a couple of times as the dumplings cook; if bubbles rise immediately to the surface and encircle the chopstick, the oil is too hot.)

Fry, turning the turnovers often and pressing them down below the oil level, for about 10 minutes total, or until golden brown. Use a skimmer to scoop them up and transfer them to the platter to drain and cool. Adjust the heat before adding another batch.

5. **Allow the turnovers to** cool for about 5 minutes before serving. Refrigerate leftover turnovers and reheat by frying for about 2 minutes in 1 1/4-inches of oil at 350°F or baking in a 350°F oven, turning midway, for about 12 minutes, or until gently sizzling and hot. The first method refreshes best, but the second one is less hassle.

Chinese Flaky Pastry
Sū Bǐng Pí

Makes 1 pound

Literally translated as "crisp skin for cakes," this northern Chinese flaky pastry employs techniques similar to those for French puff pastry to create tender, layered pastry. What's unusually clever about the Chinese approach is that aside from the usual letter-type folds and turns, the dough is rolled into a cylinder as part of forming the wrappers. The cylinder can then be cut in ways that allow you to form pastries with layers that fall in a spiral or linear pattern.

When deep-fried, this pastry becomes super-rich, but surprisingly not greasy. It may also be baked, though the result is not as spectacular. Some cooks don't add sugar and salt, but I find seasoning the dough sparks the flavor. For the best results, use lard rather than vegetable shortening.

If you have ever found making puff pastry difficult because of the firmness of the butter, this dough is a godsend. It comes together quickly and is amazingly easy to work by comparison.

OUTER DOUGH

5 ounces (1 cup) bleached all-purpose flour

1 1/2 teaspoons sugar

1/4 teaspoon salt

1 tablespoon chilled lard or solid vegetable shortening, cut into 1/2-inch pieces

5 tablespoons warm water

INNER DOUGH

3 3/4 ounces (3/4 cup) bleached all-purpose flour

6 tablespoons chilled lard or solid vegetable shortening, cut into 1/2-inch pieces

1. To make the outer dough, combine the flour, sugar, and salt in a food processor and pulse 2 or 3 times to combine. Sprinkle in the pieces of lard and process for 10 seconds to blend well, or until the mixture looks like coarse meal. (Alternatively, put the ingredients in a bowl and use a pastry blender or your fingers in a quick rubbing motion to combine the flour and shortening.)

Transfer the mixture to a bowl, make a well in the center, and work in the water 1 tablespoon at a time. Use a spatula or wooden spoon to stir, fold, and push the ingredients into a ragged mass. Transfer to a lightly floured work surface and gently knead for about 2 minutes to create a very soft, smooth, and slightly elastic dough. Press your finger into the dough; it should slowly bounce back, leaving a faint indentation. Cover with plastic wrap or an inverted bowl and set aside at room temperature to rest for 20 to 30 minutes.

2. Meanwhile, to make the inner dough, put the flour in the food processor and sprinkle in the lard pieces. Process for 10 seconds to blend and generate a mealy, lumpy, very soft mixture. Transfer to a bowl (the same one as before is fine) and use the spatula to mix and combine well. (Alternatively, put the ingredients in the bowl and use the spatula or back of the wooden spoon to mash the ingredients together until no flour is visible.) It will resemble soft cookie dough.

Gather and pat the dough into a rough ball. Push it from the bowl onto a lightly floured work surface. Gently pat and roll the dough into a smooth ball and set aside. Wrap in plastic wrap if the outer dough needs to rest longer.

3. To encase the inner dough in the outer dough, roll the outer dough into a 6- to 7-inch-diameter circle. (Try your best to work on a minimally floured surface at all times, to prevent the dough from absorbing too much flour and toughening.) Center the ball of inner dough on top and then gently pull up and press the outer dough, pinching the ends together to completely encase the inner dough. Hold the dough in both hands to make this easier.

Use a rolling pin to gently roll the dough into an oblong, about 8 inches wide and 12 inches long. Start each pass from the center and move toward one of the edges before rolling back again. Try to square off the sides and lift up the dough occasionally to prevent sticking. If a bit of the inner dough leaks out, pat some flour on it to seal. Fold the dough into thirds, like a letter, with one end toward the middle and the other end on top to cover, resulting in a rectangle about 8 inches wide and 4 inches long. Turn the dough 90 degrees so that one of the unfolded sides points at you. Roll the dough out again to an 8 by 12-inch rectangle, and fold again into a letter. Wrap in plastic wrap and allow to rest in the refrigerator for 1 hour, or overnight, before using. See the following recipes for details on how to manipulate the dough into patterned layers.

Daikon Radish and Smoky Ham Cakes

Luóbo Sī Sū Bǐng

Makes 12 pastries

When I first tasted this Shanghai specialty in Vancouver a few years ago, I wondered how it could have escaped me so long. The stupendous filling is remarkably simple, with a mild bite from the raw daikon radish, smokiness from the ham, and richness from the sesame oil. The pastries can be shaped as rounds with an arty spiral pattern of layers or as oblongs with a handsome linear pattern of layers. They are a classic Chinese banquet morsel, but there's no need to wait for a special occasion. Enjoy them as a snack, accompanied by other dumplings or a clear soup.

FILLING

10 ounces daikon radish, peeled and grated on largest holes of a shredder (a brimming 1¹/₄ cups)

¹/₂ teaspoon salt

2 tablespoons minced Virginia (Smithfield) ham or other salty, smoky ham (use the lean part)

3 tablespoons finely chopped scallion (white and green parts)

1 generous teaspoon sugar

1 pinch of white pepper

1 teaspoon sesame oil

1 pound Chinese Flaky Pastry (page 120)

¹/₄ cup untoasted white (hulled) or black sesame seeds

1 large egg, well beaten

Canola or peanut oil, for deep-frying (optional)

1. **To make the filling**, combine the daikon and salt in a bowl and toss to combine. Set aside for 15 minutes. Pour off the excess water. Transfer the daikon to a cotton (not terry) kitchen towel, hold over the sink, and squeeze to expel excess liquid. Put the daikon into a clean bowl and fluff with your fingers to separate.

2. **Use a fork** or spatula to mix in the ham, scallion, sugar, white pepper, and sesame oil. Taste and, if necessary, adjust the flavors with extra salt for savory depth, sugar to reduce harshness, or sesame oil for richness. The filling

can be prepared up to 2 days in advance and refrigerated. Return it to room temperature before using. You should have about ³/₄ cup.

3. **If the dough** was refrigerated for longer than 1 hour, let it sit out until malleable.

Working on an unfloured or very lightly floured surface, use a rolling pin to gently roll the dough into an 11-inch square. This is easier to do if you work the rolling pin from the midline toward the top or bottom edge, and then roll back to the midline.

Use both hands to lift up the edge closest to you and roll it all the way up to the top to form a cylinder. Roll the cylinder to even it out and lengthen it to about 12 inches long and 1³/₄ inches in diameter.

To form pastries with the layers arranged in a spiral pattern, cut the dough cylinder crosswise into 12 pieces. Then use the palm and/or heel of your hand to flatten each dough piece into a ¹/₄-inch-thick disk.

For pastries with the layers arranged in a vertical pattern, cut the dough cylinder crosswise into 6 pieces. Then halve each piece lengthwise to expose the layers as straight lines. With the cut side down, use the palm of your hand to flatten each piece into an oblong

continued

about 3 inches long and 1³/₄ inches wide. Gather the 4 corners and pinch and press them to mold the dough into a thick disk. Some of the layering will now face you. Flatten the dough pieces into ¹/₄-inch-thick disks.

4. **Work with half** of the dough pieces at a time, keeping the other ones covered with plastic wrap or a kitchen towel. Use a skinny Asian rolling pin (dowel) to roll each one into a circle, about 3¹/₂ inches in diameter. While there's no need to have a pronounced belly here, the edge should be slightly thinner than the center. (See "Forming Wrappers from Basic Dumpling Dough," step 5, page 24, for guidance.)

5. **Line a baking sheet** with parchment paper. Put the sesame seeds in a shallow bowl. To assemble a pastry, hold a wrapper in a slightly cupped hand. Use a spoon to center about 1 tablespoon of filling onto the dough circle, pressing down very gently and keeping about ¹/₂ to ³/₄ inch of wrapper clear on all sides; your hand will automatically close slightly. Use the thumb of the hand cradling the pastry to push down the filling while the fingers of the other hand pull up the dough edge and pleat and pinch the rim together to form a closed satchel (see page 52). Pinch and twist completely closed at the end.

If you have formed spiraling layers, gently flatten the pastry to prevent it from peaking too much during frying. Linear layers will expand horizontally to create oblong pastries during frying. Brush the bottom with the egg, then press it into the sesame seeds to cover the bottom. Set the finished pastry on the prepared baking sheet. Repeat, spacing the pastries about 1¹/₂ inches apart on the baking sheet.

6. **If you are deep-frying** the cakes, put a paper towel–lined platter next to the stove. Pour oil to a depth of 1¹/₂ inches into a wok, deep saucepan, or Dutch oven and heat over medium-high heat to about 300°F on a deep-fry thermometer. Frying at an initial low temperature ensures delicate, flaky results; subsequently increasing the heat prevents the pastries from becoming greasy. (If you don't have a deep-fry thermometer, stick a *dry* bamboo chopstick into the oil; if it takes about 4 seconds for bubbles to rise to the surface and encircle the chopstick, the oil is ready.)

Working in batches of 4 to 6 to prevent crowding, gently add the cakes to the hot oil and immediately *decrease* the heat to low to steady the temperature, which will quickly rise. The cakes will slowly bubble at first. Let them fry, occasionally turning gently, moderating the heat as needed to keep it at 300°F, for about 3 minutes, or until they are light golden. Then raise the heat to medium-high and fry for 5 to 6 minutes, until golden brown and flaky. Let the temperature eventually hover around 340°F. (Without a thermometer, do the chopstick test a couple of times as the dumplings cook; bubbles that rise after about 1 second signal 340°F.) Transfer the cakes to the platter. Adjust the heat between batches.

Alternatively, to bake the cakes, position a rack in the upper third of the oven and preheat to 400°F. Brush the tops with egg and then bake for 15 minutes. Lower the heat to 350°F and bake for 15 minutes, or until golden.

7. **Whether frying or baking,** allow the cakes to cool for 5 minutes before serving. They are good warm or at room temperature, too. Leftovers can be refrigerated for several days and reheated in the oven at 350°F for 15 minutes, or until gently sizzling and heated through.

Curry Puffs
Karipap
Makes 12 pastries

Stuffed with intriguing spice-laden fillings, curry puffs are a very popular snack in Malaysia, Singapore, and Thailand. In food-crazy Singapore, there are even plastic curry puff molds available for cooks to make perfect-looking puffs.

The filling varies, but the most popular ones feature potato or sardines, both of which are lifted from their humble origins with a heavy dose of fragrant spices and/or chile heat. The dough depends on the cook, who may prepare French-style puff pastry with margarine and bake the results, stick with simple flaky pastry (page 113) to produce old-fashioned crisp fried puffs, or employ Chinese flaky pastry to yield puffs whose shape resembles magnificent clam shells. For a spectacular treat, I prepare curry puffs with Chinese flaky pastry. These deep-fried wonders are out of this world.

For old-fashioned puffs, substitute either of the curry puff fillings for the one in the Vietnamese Shrimp, Pork and Jicama Turnover recipe (page 118). See the Lazy Day Tip below for making puffs with commercial puff pastry. Anyone who has made empanadas (page 111) will be a whiz at filling these.

1 pound Chinese Flaky Pastry (page 120)
3/4 cup Potato and Lamb Curry Puff Filling (page 127) or Spicy Sardine Puff Filling (page 129)
Canola or peanut oil, for deep-frying

1. If the dough was refrigerated for longer than 1 hour, let it sit at room temperature until it is malleable. Working on an unfloured or very lightly floured surface, use a rolling pin to gently roll the dough into an 11-inch square. This is easier to do if you work the rolling pin from the midline toward the top or bottom edge, and then roll back to the midline.

Use both hands to lift up the edge closest to you and roll it all the way up to the top to form a cylinder. Roll the cylinder to even it out and lengthen it to about 12 inches long and 1 3/4 inches in diameter. Cut the dough cylinder crosswise into 12 pieces, then use the palm and heel of your hand to flatten each dough piece into a 1/4-inch-thick disk.

2. Work with half of the dough pieces at a time and keep the others covered with plastic wrap or a kitchen towel. Use a skinny Asian rolling pin (dowel) to roll each dough piece into a circle, a good 3 1/2 inches in diameter. Aim for a wrapper with a 1-inch-wide belly; the edge should be thinner than the middle. (For guidance, see "Forming Wrappers from Basic Dumpling Dough," step 5, page 24.)

3. Line a baking sheet with parchment paper. To assemble a puff, hold a wrapper in a slightly cupped hand. Use a spoon to put about 1 tablespoon of filling in the middle, spreading out the filling a bit to make shaping the puff easier and keeping about 1/2 to 3/4 inch of wrapper clear on all sides. As you work, your hand should naturally close a bit more to keep the puff in shape.

Moisten the top rim of the wrapper with water and bring up the wrapper side closest

continued

to you and firmly press to create a half-moon (see page 26 for guidance); the center coil of dough (the belly) should naturally push out a bit like the hinge of a clam shell. Remember to seal each puff well. For extra security, use your thumb and index fingers to form a rope edge (see page 51) or press with the tines of a fork. Place the finished puff on the prepared baking sheet. Repeat with the other wrappers before making and filling the wrappers from the remaining dough.

4. **Before frying the puffs,** put a paper towel–lined platter next to the stove. Pour oil to a depth of 1¹/₂ inches into a wok, deep sauce-pan, or Dutch oven and heat over medium-high heat to about 300°F on a deep-fry thermometer. Frying at an initial low tem-perature ensures delicate, flaky results; subse-quently increasing the heat prevents the puffs from becoming greasy. (If you don't have a deep-fry thermometer, stick a *dry* bamboo chopstick into the oil; if it takes about 4 sec-onds for bubbles to rise to the surface and encircle the chopstick, the oil is ready.)

Working in batches of 4 to 6 to prevent crowding, gently slide the puffs into the hot oil and immediately decrease the heat to low to steady the temperature, which will quickly rise. The puffs will bubble slowly at first. Let them fry, occasionally turning gently, moder-ating the heat as needed to keep the oil tem-perature around 300°F, for about 3 minutes, or until the puffs are light golden. Raise the heat to medium-high and fry for 5 to 6 minutes, until the puffs are golden brown and flaky. Let the temperature hover around 340°F. (If you don't have a thermometer, do the chopstick test a couple of times as the dumplings cook; bubbles that rise after about 1 second signal

340°F.) Use a skimmer to scoop up and trans-fer the puffs to the platter to drain and cool. Adjust the heat before frying more.

5. **Allow the puffs** to cool for about 5 minutes if you are serving them hot. Or present them to your guests warm or at room temperature. Refrigerate leftover puffs for several days and reheat them in the oven at 350°F for about 15 minutes, or until gently sizzling and heated through.

LAZY DAY TIP

Have no shame. Many busy modern Asian cooks turn to ready-made puff pastry for rich treats like curry puffs (page 125) and samo-sas (page 115). Purchase a package (usually about 1 pound) of puff pastry, the all-butter variety, if you can; puff pastry is usually sold as frozen square sheets, rolled to a thick-ness of ¹/₄ inch. Thaw it in the refrigerator.

Line a baking sheet with parchment paper. Preheat the oven according to the package directions (usually 375° to 400°F).

Work with 1 sheet of pastry at a time. Roll a pastry sheet out to about 10 inches square, if it's smaller than that, and then cut it into four 5-inch squares. Put about 1¹/₂ tablespoons of curry puff or samosa filling atop each square, moisten 2 adjoin-ing edges with water, fold the other side over to form a triangle, and press closed. Use the tines of a fork to press on the edges to seal well, then place on a prepared baking sheet. Repeat with the remaining pastry and filling. Brush with beaten egg, then bake for about 15 minutes, until golden brown.

Potato and Lamb Curry Puff Filling
Karipap Daging
Makes 3/4 cup

One of the most common curry puff fillings features well-seasoned potatoes and a little meat. I like to use ground lamb because it pairs terrifically with the bold spice blend that Malay cooks often identify as meat curry powder. I've broken it down for you here, but feel free to substitute 2^1/$_4$ teaspoons of your favorite curry powder (if salt is already in the powder, add salt to taste only after the filling is done). For a vegetarian rendition, omit the meat and increase the potato to ^{3}/$_4$ cup, adding extra water as needed during cooking.

1^1/$_2$ teaspoons coriander seed

^{1}/$_2$ teaspoon cumin seed

^{1}/$_4$ teaspoon fennel seed

4 black peppercorns

^{1}/$_8$ teaspoon ground cayenne

^{1}/$_8$ teaspoon ground turmeric

1 pinch of ground cloves

1 pinch of ground cinnamon

2 tablespoons chopped shallot

2 teaspoons chopped fresh ginger

1 clove garlic, chopped

^{1}/$_4$ cup plus 1 teaspoon water

1 tablespoon canola oil

2 ounces ground lamb or other ground meat, coarsely chopped to loosen

^{1}/$_2$ cup diced Yukon Gold potato

Generous ^{1}/$_4$ teaspoon salt

Brown sugar (optional)

1. Toast the coriander seed, cumin seed, fennel seed, and peppercorns in a dry skillet over medium heat for 1 to 2 minutes, until fragrant. Use a clean, dry coffee grinder or mortar and pestle to pulverize. Transfer to an electric mini-chopper and add cayenne, turmeric, cloves, cinnamon, shallot, ginger, garlic, and 1 teaspoon water. Process to a paste, scraping down the sides occasionally. (If you've used a mortar and pestle, add all the ingredients, except the water, and pound into a paste. Add the water when done.) Transfer to a small bowl and set aside near the stove.

2. Heat the oil in a skillet over medium heat. Add the spice paste and gently cook, stirring frequently, for 4 to 5 minutes, until it has darkened and become richly fragrant. Add the lamb and use a wooden spoon or spatula to stir and mash the meat into small pieces. Cook for 30 to 60 seconds, until most of the meat no longer looks raw. Add the potato, stir, and then add the ^{1}/$_4$ cup water and salt. Cover, lower the heat slightly, and cook for 5 minutes, or until the potato is tender and there is little liquid remaining.

Remove from the heat and use the spoon or spatula to mash half of the potato and make the mixture cohere a bit. Taste and add extra salt, if needed. Mix in a pinch or two of brown sugar if the filling is too spicy. Transfer to a small bowl and set aside to cool completely before using. The filling can be prepared up to 2 days in advance, covered in plastic wrap, and refrigerated. Return it to room temperature before using.

Spicy Sardine Puff Filling

Karipap Sardin

Makes 3/4 cup

The notion of canned sardines in pastry may seem distasteful, but millions of Southeast Asians consider *karipap sardin* to be delightful soul food. Any fishy intensity is mitigated by a simple combination of supporting ingredients, including ketchup, lime, and fresh chile. Chopped hard-cooked egg adds richness to this quintessential curry puff filling.

For small cans of sardines (5 1/2 ounces, which is about the size of a regular can of tomato paste), head to a Chinese, Southeast Asian, or Latino market. Many Asian cooks prefer Ligo brand. Canned sardines sold at supermarkets come in larger portions, so just use part of the can. This filling is also good on toast.

1 (5 1/2 ounce) can sardines in tomato sauce

1/4 teaspoon sugar

1 pinch of salt

1 tablespoon ketchup

1 teaspoon fresh lime juice

1 tablespoon canola oil

1 shallot, chopped (1/4 cup)

1 medium-hot chile, such as cayenne, Fresno, Holland, or jalapeño, halved lengthwise and thinly sliced

1 hard-cooked egg, coarsely chopped

1. Remove the sardines from the can and reserve the liquid. Use a fork to split open each sardine and lift off the spine bones. Set the flesh aside (there should be about 1/3 cup) and discard the bones.

2. In a small bowl, mix 1 tablespoon of the canning liquid (stir it up before measuring) with the sugar, salt, ketchup, and lime juice. Set this seasoning sauce aside.

3. Heat the oil in a medium skillet over medium heat. Add the shallot and chile and cook, stirring occasionally, for about 3 minutes, or until soft and fragrant. Add the seasoning sauce, and cook, stirring frequently, for about 2 minutes, or until the mixture has reduced and thickened. Add the sardines, stirring gently to break up the flesh into large flakes. Transfer to a bowl and stir in the egg. Cool completely before using. The filling can be prepared up to 2 days in advance, covered, and refrigerated. Return it to room temperature before using.

5 Translucent Wheat and Tapioca Starches

Western cooks mainly think of starches as sauce thickeners, but they are major stars in Asian kitchens, where in addition to their thickening prowess, they are often employed as flour for doughy foods. Many kinds of starches are used, but this chapter focuses on wheat and tapioca starches because they are most often used in dumpling making.

You may be unfamiliar with wheat and tapioca starch dough, but you have probably enjoyed them in Cantonese dim sum favorites, such as *har gow* shrimp dumplings and Chinese chive dumplings. Both rely on a combination of wheat and tapioca starch for their signature translucent skins. In tropical Southeast Asia, tapioca starch is employed for many classic dumplings because it is made from starchy cassava, a tuberous root that proliferates in the region. Thai *saku sai mu* and Vietnamese *bánh bột lọc*, quintessential dumplings in their respective cuisines, use tapioca starch in their chewy wrappers.

Why starches? Because they allow dumpling makers to create dumplings that are attractive, texturally pleasing, and light tasting, with translucent skins that seem to make colorful fillings glow from the inside. Depending on how the starch is manipulated, the resulting dumplings can be soft and yet a touch elastic, making for a delightful eating experience. Lacking gluten, starches yield dumpling skins that are not as hearty as their wheat-flour brethren. They also do not have much flavor so there's greater contrast between skin and filling, which allows the filling to "pop" more in the overall dumpling.

Wheat Starch Dough

Makes a scant 1 pound

This malleable, snowy white dough is the foundation for many Cantonese dim sum favorites, such as Chiu Chow Dumplings (page 137) and Har Gow Shrimp Dumplings (page 135). Wheat starch dough is easy to manipulate; texturally, it is like Play-Doh. In fact, I've seen rabbit-shaped dumplings made from this type of dough. You can definitely sculpt it, though I mostly focus on making sure the filling is sealed up well.

When cooked, this dough has a translucency that allows the filling colors to be visible in a beautiful, impressionistic way. Wheat starch on its own would make a dough that is too firm, so dim sum cooks commonly add elasticity by way of tapioca starch, though cornstarch and potato starch are options, too. The oil lends suppleness and richness.

This dough can be prepared up to 6 hours in advance and kept at room temperature in the plastic bag. When forming wrappers from this dough, do your best to keep the cut dough and formed wrappers covered with plastic wrap to prevent drying.

At Chinese markets, look for plastic bags of wheat starch near other starches and flours; Middle Eastern markets sometimes carry it, too. Tapioca starch is reasonably priced at Chinese and Southeast Asian markets but is also available at health food stores, specialty grocers, and some supermarkets.

4 1/2 ounces (1 cup) wheat starch
2 1/4 ounces (1/2 cup) tapioca starch
1/8 teaspoon salt
About 1 cup just-boiled water (see Note, page 23)
4 teaspoons canola oil

1. In a bowl, combine the wheat starch, tapioca starch, and salt. Make a well in the center and pour in about 14 tablespoons of the water. Use a wooden spoon or rubber spatula to stir the ingredients together. Work at a moderate speed to prevent the fine, lightweight starches from flying. The dough will look translucent first and then become mottled, whitish, and lumpy. You will smell the wheat starch.

Once the water has been incorporated (there may be steam rising from the dough, which is fine), add the oil. Stir to work in the oil. If the dough looks dry, add a little more water. Aim for a medium-firm texture, not a soft and mushy one; work in additional wheat starch by the tablespoon if you add too much water. Press the ingredients together into a rough ball that feels a bit bouncy.

2. Transfer the warm dough to an unfloured work surface and knead for 1 to 2 minutes, until snowy white, smooth, and resembling Play-Doh in texture. When you squeeze on it, it should not crack. If it cracks, very lightly oil one hand and knead it into the dough to increase the dough's suppleness. Depending on the recipe instructions, cut the dough into 3 or 4 pieces. Put them into a zip-top plastic bag and seal well. Set aside for 5 minutes to rest before using.

Dim sum master cooks press pieces of wheat starch dough with an oiled cleaver to make perfect circles, but you can achieve perfection with minimal effort and experience.

Have ready two 6 to 7-inch plastic squares cut from a zip-top bag; smear a little oil on one side of each plastic square to avoid sticking.

1. As specified in the recipe, take a piece of wheat starch dough, roll it on an unfloured work surface into a log, and then cut it into small pieces.

2. To prevent drying and sticking, dab your finger in some canola oil and rub a tiny bit on each of the ends of the dough pieces, pressing each one into a 1/4-inch-thick disk as you work.

3. Place a disk between the squares. Apply moderate pressure with a tortilla press, the flat side of a cleaver, or the bottom of a large measuring cup, a skillet, or a plate. You may have to press more than once to arrive at the desired size. If using the tortilla press, you may turn the dough and press again to arrive at the desired size. With the other implements, press and twist while the pressure is still on to create nice thin circles.

4. Unpeel the plastic and set the slightly shiny wrapper aside. Repeat with the remaining dough pieces. There should be no need to re-oil the plastic between pressings. It is fine to let the wrappers overlap a tad. To prevent the dough from drying out, assemble a batch of dumplings before forming more wrappers from another portion of dough.

Har Gow Shrimp Dumplings

Xiā Jiǎo

Makes 32 dumplings, serving 6 to 8 as a snack

Well known by their Cantonese name *har gow*, these delightful pinkish-white morsels are among the most popular offerings at dim sum houses. They go fast, and I've chased down my fair share of dim sum ladies to get a fresh order. When I started making my own and realized that they can be kept refrigerated and frozen, my fear of *har gow* scarcity diminished.

These are difficult to prepare only if you aim to produce exemplary diminutive ones, which most dim sum places don't. Start out with ones that are a little bigger and scale down as you gain dexterity. You can even make these dumplings as half-moons, and they'll taste swell. Use the best shrimp possible, and immerse the canned bamboo shoots in boiling water to rid it of its tinny flavor before chopping. To make the pork fat easier to mince, blanch it in boiling water for 1 minute, or until firm. Obtain the fat from fatback (I go to a Latino butcher counter) or cut it off a pork chop. Fatty bacon works well, too.

FILLING

2/3 pound medium shrimp, peeled and deveined (9 ounces net weight)

3/4 teaspoon salt

1 1/2 tablespoons minced pork fat or fatty bacon

3 tablespoons finely chopped bamboo shoots

2 teaspoons minced scallion (white part only)

1 1/2 teaspoons cornstarch

3/4 teaspoon sugar

1/8 teaspoon white pepper

1 1/2 teaspoons Shaoxing rice wine or dry sherry

1 teaspoon sesame oil

1 pound Wheat Starch Dough (page 132), cut into fourths

Light (regular) soy sauce, for dipping

Chile Garlic Sauce, homemade (page 216) or store-bought (optional)

1. To make the filling, toss the shrimp with 1/4 teaspoon of the salt, put them in a strainer, and rinse under cold water. Transfer the shrimp to a paper towel and blot dry. Chop the shrimp into peanut-size pieces; halve each shrimp lengthwise first to make it easier. Put the shrimp into a bowl and add the pork fat, bamboo shoots, and scallion. Stir with chopsticks or a fork to evenly distribute the ingredients.

2. In a small bowl, combine the remaining 1/2 teaspoon salt, the cornstarch, sugar, white pepper, rice wine, and sesame oil, stirring to dissolve the cornstarch. Pour the seasonings over the shrimp mixture. Stir with chopsticks or a fork to ensure that all the shrimp are well coated. Cover with plastic wrap and set aside for 30 minutes or refrigerate for up to 4 hours to marinate. Makes about 1 1/3 cups.

3. Working with 1 piece of dough at a time to form the wrappers, roll it on an unfloured work surface into an 8-inch log. Cut the log into 8 equal pieces. Follow the instructions on "Forming Wrappers from Wheat Starch Dough" (page 133) to shape circles that are each 3 to 3 1/4 inches in diameter.

continued

4. **Before assembling** the dumplings, line steamer trays and baking sheets with parchment paper, then oil the paper.

5. **To assemble** a dumpling, hold a wrapper in a slightly cupped hand. Use a bamboo dumpling spatula, dinner knife, or fork to scoop up about 2 teaspoons of filling and place it slightly off-center toward the upper half of the wrapper, gently pressing to flatten slightly and keeping about $1/2$ to $3/4$ inch of wrapper clear on all sides. Then fold, pleat, and press to enclose the filling and create a pleated crescent (see page 29), finishing it by pinching the rim together between your fingers into a thin layer of dough that resembles a crown; this prevents the edge from being unpleasantly thick once cooked. If the skin breaks, dab a tiny bit of oil on the area and try smoothing out and patching up the wrapper. For the pouchy *har gow* shape, lightly press the unpleated side of the dumpling against the knuckle of a bent finger; this will softly arch the dumpling forward. If this shape proves too challenging, simply form a half-moon (see page 26).

Set the finished dumpling in a prepared steamer tray. Assemble more dumplings from the remaining wrappers before working on the next batch of dough. Space them about $1/2$ inch apart; if using a metal steamer tray, keep the dumplings 1 inch away from the edge where condensation will collect. Place overflow dumplings on the baking sheet with a good $1/2$ inch between each and cover with plastic wrap. Once assembled, the dumplings should be cooked as soon as possible, because they cannot be refrigerated uncooked.

6. **Steam the dumplings** over boiling water (see page 17 for guidance) for about 6 minutes, or until they have puffed slightly and are glossy and translucent. Remove each tray and place it atop a serving plate.

7. **Serve hot** with soy sauce and chile garlic sauce. Cooked dumplings can be refrigerated, then steamed for about 3 minutes before serving. Cooked dumplings can also be frozen for up to 1 month, completely thawed in the refrigerator, and steamed for 3 to 5 minutes.

Chiu Chow Dumplings

Cháo Zhōu Fěn Guǒ

Makes 24 dumplings, serving 6 to 8 as a snack

The Cantonese dim sum repertoire would be incomplete without this wonderful contribution from the Chiu Chow, a seafaring people from a region located on the Taiwan Strait. Robustly flavored by briny dried shrimp, this dumpling also tastes light because it's packed with vegetables, including jicama and shiitake mushrooms, and peanuts. The varied texture of the filling gets rounded out by a touch of pork, though you can use any meat. Because there is lots of chopping involved with the filling, make it a couple days in advance to minimize last-minute pressures.

I first enjoyed these nearly twenty years ago in Hong Kong and they instantaneously became one of my favorites. Good renditions were hard to find in the United States, so I began making them myself. Enjoy them alone or with soy sauce and an Asian chile garlic sauce of your choice. If jicama is not available, substitute canned water chestnuts.

FILLING

1/2 teaspoon sugar

1/4 teaspoon white pepper

2 teaspoons oyster sauce

1 teaspoon light (regular) soy sauce

1 tablespoon Shaoxing rice wine or dry sherry

1 tablespoon water

1 tablespoon canola oil

1 clove garlic, minced

1 1/2 tablespoons chopped dried shrimp

1/4 pound ground pork or minced pork shoulder

2 large dried shiitake mushrooms, reconstituted (see page 13), stemmed, and chopped (1/4 cup)

1/2 cup finely diced jicama

2 tablespoons unsalted, roasted peanuts, chopped

1 1/2 teaspoons cornstarch dissolved in 1 tablespoon water

2 tablespoons chopped fresh cilantro or scallion (green part only)

Salt

1 pound Wheat Starch Dough (page 132)

Light (regular) soy sauce, for dipping

Chile Garlic Sauce, homemade (page 216) or store-bought (optional)

1. **To make the filling,** in a small bowl, combine the sugar, white pepper, oyster sauce, soy sauce, rice wine, and water. Stir to dissolve the sugar and set aside.

2. **Heat the oil** in a medium skillet over medium-high heat. Add the garlic and dried shrimp and cook, stirring constantly, for about 30 seconds, or until fragrant. Add the pork and stir and mash to break it up into small pieces. When most of the pork has browned, about 1 minute, add the mushrooms, jicama, and peanuts. Stir to combine and add the seasoning mixture. Reduce the heat slightly and cook, stirring constantly, for about 4 minutes, or until the jicama is tender-crisp and there is little liquid left. Give the cornstarch mixture a final stir and add to the pan. Cook for about 15 seconds to lightly bind. Turn off the heat and stir in the cilantro. Taste and add a pinch or two of salt, to taste. Transfer to a bowl and set aside to cool completely before using. (The filling can be prepared up to 2 days in advance. Return to room temperature before using.) You should have about 1 1/4 cups.

continued

3. **Cut the dough** in thirds. Working with 1 piece of dough at a time to form the wrappers, roll it on an unfloured work surface into an 8-inch log. Cut the log into 8 pieces. Follow the instructions on "Forming Wrappers from Wheat Starch Dough" (page 133) to shape circles that are roughly 3¹/₂ inches in diameter.

4. **Before assembling** the dumplings, line steamer trays and/or baking sheets with parchment paper. Oil the paper lining in the steamer trays.

5. **To assemble** a dumpling, hold a wrapper in a slightly cupped hand. Use a spoon to place 1 scant tablespoon slightly off-center toward the upper half of the wrapper, pressing down gently to compact and keeping about ¹/₂ to ³/₄ inch of wrapper clear on all sides. Bring up the edge and seal to make a half-moon (see page 26). Press the rim to meld the edges into one. You can stop here and place the dumpling on its side in a prepared steamer tray. Or set the dumpling on your work surface and gently scrunch up the rim to create a ruffled edge. Bring up the ends so it sits proudly upright. Set the finished dumpling in a steamer tray. Make more dumplings from the remaining wrappers before working on the next piece of dough. Place them about ¹/₂ inch apart in the steamer; if using a metal steamer tray, keep the dumplings 1 inch away from the edge where condensation will collect. Place any overflow dumplings on the prepared baking sheet, spacing them slightly apart, and cover with plastic wrap.

Continue making dumplings until all the dough and filling are used. Assembled dumplings can sit for about 1 hour before cooking, but do not refrigerate.

6. **Steam the dumplings** over boiling water (see page 17 for guidance) for about 7 minutes, or until they have puffed slightly and are glossy and translucent. Remove each tray and place it atop a serving plate.

7. **Serve hot** with soy sauce and the chile garlic sauce. Cooked dumplings can be refrigerated; steam for about 3 minutes before serving. They can also be frozen for up to 1 month, completely thawed in the refrigerator, and steamed to reheat for 3 to 5 minutes.

GROUND PORK OPTIONS

For many Asian cooks, meat means pork, and there are many different cuts sold at Asian butcher counters. With regard to the ground pork selection, there is usually a fatty one and a lean one. You won't see fat percentages posted, but the costlier ground meat is leaner. There may even be coarsely ground pork that resembles hand-chopped pork. You can also purchase a shoulder roast and have it ground on the spot. It will have a fat content of 15 to 20 percent, making it excellent for juicy dumplings, and it freezes well. I generally prefer fattier ground pork for dumplings, and in certain cases, such as the Shanghai Soup Dumplings (page 59), it's required. For guidance on mincing and chopping meat by hand, see page 158.

Vegetarian Crystal Dumplings
Chai Kuih

Makes 24 dumplings, serving 6 to 8 as a snack

Many Chiu Chow people migrated from mainland China to Southeast Asia, particularly to the Malay Peninsula. That is why you will find Chiu Chow dumplings among the hawker street food offerings in places like Penang. Along with the regular version in the preceding recipe, there is usually a vegetarian option.

Chai kuih (literally "vegetable cake") can be flavored with dried shrimp and oyster sauce, or it can be totally vegetarian. I have presented the latter, though you can certainly add the other seasonings if you wish. The mushroom soaking liquid adds savory depth to this jewel-like filling, so remember to save it after rehydrating the shiitakes.

FILLING

Scant 1/4 teaspoon white pepper

1/2 teaspoon sugar

2 teaspoons light (regular) soy sauce

3 large dried shiitake mushrooms, reconstituted and liquid reserved (see page 13), stemmed, and chopped (generous 1/3 cup)

1 teaspoon sesame oil

1 tablespoon canola oil

2 tablespoons finely chopped shallot

2 cloves garlic, minced

2 dried wood ear mushrooms, reconstituted (see page 13), trimmed, and chopped (3 tablespoons)

2/3 cup finely diced jicama

1/4 cup finely diced carrot

1/4 cup chopped Chinese chives or scallions (green part only)

1 1/2 teaspoons cornstarch dissolved in 1 tablespoon shiitake mushroom soaking liquid or water

Salt (optional)

1 pound Wheat Starch Dough (page 132)

Light (regular) soy sauce, for dipping

Chile Garlic Sauce, homemade (page 216) or store-bought (optional)

1. To make the filling, in a small bowl, combine the white pepper, sugar, soy sauce, 2 tablespoons of the reserved mushroom soaking liquid, and sesame oil. Stir to dissolve the sugar and set aside.

2. Heat the canola oil in a medium skillet over medium-high heat. Add the shallot and garlic and cook, stirring constantly, for 1 to 2 minutes, until fragrant, and a few garlic pieces have turned blond. Add the shiitake mushrooms, wood ear mushrooms, jicama, and carrot. Stir to combine, then pour in the seasoning mixture. Lower the heat slightly and cook, stirring frequently, for about 4 minutes, until the jicama and carrot are tender-crisp. Add the Chinese chives and cook for 15 to 30 seconds, until softened. Give the cornstarch mixture a final stir and add to the pan. Cook for about 15 seconds to lightly bind. Turn off the heat and taste for salt, adding if needed. Transfer to a bowl and set aside to cool completely before using. (The filling can be prepared up to 2 days in advance. Return to room temperature before using.) You should have about 1 1/4 cups.

3. Cut the dough in thirds. Working with 1 piece of dough at a time to form the wrappers, roll it on an unfloured work surface into an 8-inch log. Cut the log into 8 pieces. Follow the instructions on "Forming Wrappers from Wheat Starch Dough" (page 133) to shape circles that are roughly 3 1/2 inches in diameter.

continued

4. **Before assembling** the dumplings, line steamer trays and/or baking sheets with parchment paper, then oil the paper.

5. **To assemble** a dumpling, hold a wrapper in a slightly cupped hand. Use a spoon to place 1 scant tablespoon slightly off-center toward the upper half of the wrapper, pressing down gently to compact and keeping about 1/2 to 3/4 inch of wrapper clear on all sides. Bring up the edge and seal to make a half-moon (see page 26). Press the rim to meld the edges into one. You can stop here and place the dumpling on its side in a prepared steamer tray. Or, set the dumpling down and gently scrunch up the rim to create a ruffled edge. Bring up the ends so it sits proudly upright.

Set the finished dumpling in a steamer tray. Make more dumplings from the remaining wrappers before working on the next piece of dough. Place them about 1/2 inch apart in the steamer; if using a metal steamer tray, keep the dumplings 1 inch away from the edge, where condensation will collect. Place any overflow dumplings on the prepared baking sheet, spacing them slightly apart and cover with plastic wrap.

Continue making dumplings until all the dough and filling are used. Assembled dumplings can sit for about 1 hour before cooking, but do not refrigerate.

6. **Steam the dumplings** over boiling water (see page 17 for guidance) for about 7 minutes, or until they have puffed slightly and are glossy and translucent. Remove each tray and place it atop a serving plate.

7. **Serve hot** with soy sauce and chile garlic sauce. Cooked dumplings can be refrigerated; steam for about 3 minutes before serving. They can also be frozen for up to 1 month, completely thawed in the refrigerator, and steamed to reheat for 3 to 5 minutes.

Scallop Dumplings

Dàizi Jiǎo

Makes 24 dumplings, serve 6 to 8 as a snack

Delectable scallop dumplings often combine scallop and shrimp, but I prefer a filling that features just scallop. The silky plump flesh gets a boost from rehydrated shreds of dried scallop, the stealth ingredient that gives this dumpling its distinctive savory-briny-sweet edge. Shredded carrot imparts a pinky-orange glow.

Dried scallops are sold at Chinese markets in 8-ounce plastic packages in the refrigerated foods section near the dried shrimp, as well as by the ounce. The packaged ones are small, the size of bay scallops. Larger ones, resembling thick checkers pieces, are individually sold by weight because they are pricey; buying two of them, however, is not prohibitively expensive. I mostly purchase little ones, refrigerate them in a zip-top plastic bag, and use a little more than I would otherwise.

The instructions here are for shaping big ruffly dumplings like the Chiu Chow dumplings on page 137. If you prefer cute pleated morsels, substitute this filling for the one in the *har gow* shrimp dumpling recipe (page 135).

FILLING

10 small or 2 regular-size dried scallops, broken into peanut-size pieces with your fingers

2 tablespoons water

2 teaspoons canola oil

1 teaspoon minced fresh ginger

1/3 cup lightly packed grated carrot (use largest hole on grater)

1/4 cup chopped Chinese chives or scallions (green part only)

1 pinch of salt

1 pinch of white pepper

1/2 teaspoon sugar

2 teaspoons cornstarch

1 teaspoon light (regular) soy sauce

11/2 teaspoons oyster sauce

1 teaspoon Shaoxing rice wine or dry sherry

1 teaspoon sesame oil

1/2 pound raw scallops, rinsed, blotted dry with paper towels, and cut into 1/2-inch dice

1 pound Wheat Starch Dough (page 132), cut into thirds

Light (regular) soy sauce, for dipping

Chile Garlic Sauce, homemade (page 216) or store-bought (optional)

1. To make the filling, put the dried scallops in a small dish and add the water; place the dish on a steamer tray. Steam over boiling water for 10 minutes to soften. Uncover and let the scallops cool for 10 minutes in the steamer. Then drain through a mesh strainer over a bowl, reserving the liquid. Crush the scallop chunks between your fingers and do your best to separate them into extra-fine shreds. Set aside.

2. Heat the canola oil in a medium skillet over medium-high heat. Add the ginger and cook, stirring constantly, for about 15 seconds, or until fragrant. Add the reconstituted dried scallops and carrot and stir to combine. Pour in the reserved dried scallop liquid and cook for 1 to 2 minutes, until the carrot is tender-crisp. Add the Chinese chives and cook for 1 more minute, until they have softened and are fragrant. Transfer the mixture to a plate, spreading it out into a thin layer, and let cool completely, about 10 minutes.

3. **In a bowl,** combine the salt, white pepper, sugar, cornstarch, soy sauce, oyster sauce, rice wine, and sesame oil, stirring to dissolve the cornstarch. Add the raw scallops, coat well, and add the cooked carrot mixture. Cover and set aside to marinate for 30 minutes, or refrigerate overnight. You should have about 1¼ cups.

4. **Working with** 1 piece of dough at a time to form the wrappers, roll it on an unfloured work surface into an 8-inch log. Cut the log into 8 pieces. Follow the instructions on "Forming Wrappers from Wheat Starch Dough" (page 133) to shape circles that are roughly 3½ inches in diameter.

5. **Before assembling** the dumplings, line steamer trays and/or baking sheets with parchment paper, then oil the paper.

6. **To assemble** a dumpling, hold a wrapper in a slightly cupped hand. Use a spoon to place 1 scant tablespoon slightly off-center toward the upper half of the wrapper, gently pressing to flatten it into a mound and keeping about ½ to ¾ inch of wrapper clear on all sides. Bring up the edge and seal to make a half-moon (see page 26). Press the rim to meld the edges into one. You can stop here and place the dumpling on its side in a prepared steamer tray. Or set the dumpling on your work sur-face and gently scrunch up the rim to create a ruffled edge. Bring up the ends so it sits proudly upright.

Set the finished dumpling in a steamer tray. Make more dumplings from the remaining wrappers before working on the next piece of dough. Place them about ½ inch apart in the steamer; if using a metal steamer tray, keep the dumplings 1 inch away from the edge, where condensation will collect. Place any overflow dumplings on the prepared baking sheet, spacing them slightly apart, and cover with plastic wrap.

Continue making dumplings until all the dough and filling are used. Assembled dumplings can sit for about 1 hour before cooking, but do not refrigerate.

7. **Steam the dumplings** over boiling water (see page 17 for guidance) for about 7 minutes, or until they have puffed slightly and become somewhat translucent. Remove each tray and place it atop a serving plate.

8. **Serve hot** with soy sauce and chile garlic sauce. Cooked dumplings can be refrigerated; steam for about 3 minutes before serving. They can also be frozen for up to 1 month, completely thawed in the refrigerator, and steamed to reheat for 3 to 5 minutes.

Chinese Chive Dumplings

Jiǔcài Jiǎo

Makes 18 dumplings

You can often spot these crystalline, dome-shaped dumplings from afar because of their contents: emerald green Chinese chives. The garlicky, flat-leaf green is a workhorse ingredient in Chinese dumpling making that commonly plays a supporting role. Here the chives are the star, flavored by a bit of shrimp in regular and dried form to punch things up a bit.

Chinese chive dumplings (called *gow choy gow* in Cantonese) can be served steamed or panfried to a delicate crispness, my preferred option. They do not freeze well, but I've never had a problem gobbling them up quickly.

FILLING

1/2 teaspoon light (regular) soy sauce

1 teaspoon Shaoxing rice wine or dry sherry

3 teaspoons cornstarch

1/3 pound medium shrimp, peeled, deveined, and cut into pea-size pieces (4 1/2 ounces net weight)

1/2 teaspoon sugar

2 pinches of white pepper

2 teaspoons oyster sauce

1/2 teaspoon sesame oil

2 tablespoons water

1 tablespoon canola oil

1 tablespoon finely chopped dried shrimp (optional)

6 ounces Chinese chives, trimmed of thicker bottom portion and cut into 1/2-inch lengths (about 1 3/4 cups)

Salt (optional)

1 pound Wheat Starch Dough (page 132), cut into thirds

About 3 tablespoons canola oil, for panfrying

Light (regular) soy sauce, for dipping

Chile Garlic Sauce, homemade (page 216) or store-bought (optional)

1. To make the filling, in a bowl, combine the soy sauce, rice wine, and 1 teaspoon of the cornstarch, stirring to dissolve the cornstarch. Add the raw shrimp and stir to coat well. Set aside. In another bowl, create a seasoning sauce by stirring together the remaining 2 teaspoons cornstarch, sugar, white pepper, oyster sauce, sesame oil, and water. Set aside.

2. Heat the canola oil in a medium skillet over medium-high heat. Add the dried shrimp and cook, stirring constantly, for about 30 seconds, or until fragrant. Add the Chinese chives and keep stirring and cooking for 1 minute, or until the chives have wilted slightly. Add the raw shrimp and cook for about 1 minute, or until they have just turned orange. Make a well in the center, give the seasoning sauce a stir, and add to the skillet. Cook for about 45 seconds, or until the mixture thickens and coheres. Taste and, if needed, add salt for savory depth. Transfer to a bowl and set aside to cool completely. You should have about 1 1/4 cups.

3. Working with 1 piece of dough at a time to form the wrappers, roll it on an unfloured work surface into a chubby 6-inch log. Cut the log into 6 pieces. Follow the instructions on "Forming Wrappers from Wheat Starch Dough" (page 133) to shape circles that are each about 4 inches in diameter.

continued

4. Before assembling the dumplings, line steamer trays and/or baking sheets with parchment paper. Oil the paper lining in the steamer trays.

5. To assemble a dumpling, hold a wrapper in a slightly cupped hand. Use a spoon to center about 1 tablespoon atop the wrapper, flattening the filling a bit and keeping about 1/2 to 3/4 inch of wrapper clear on all sides. Then fold, pleat, and press to enclose the filling and create a closed satchel (see page 52). Try to make large pleats so that the dumpling is not too thick on one side. After pinching the opening closed, twist off any excess dough and discard.

As you work, set each finished dumpling in a prepared steamer tray, closed side down, and 1/2 inch apart; when using a metal steamer tray, keep the dumplings 1 inch away from the edge, where condensation will collect. Set overflow dumpling on the baking sheet and loosely cover. Assemble more dumplings from the remaining wrappers before working on the next batch of dough.

Once assembled, the dumplings should be cooked as soon as possible, because they cannot be refrigerated uncooked.

6. Steam the dumplings over boiling water (see page 17 for guidance) for about 7 minutes, or until they have puffed slightly and become somewhat translucent.

Remove the trays and place atop a plate if serving as steamed dumplings.

To panfry, remove the trays and let the dumplings cool to room temperature. (They can sit for up to 2 hours.) Use a regular (*not* a nonstick) skillet for better browning. Heat the skillet over medium-high heat and add 1 tablespoon oil for a medium skillet or 1 1/2 tablespoons oil for a large skillet.

When the oil is just about to smoke, add the dumplings, smooth side down, in batches if necessary; it is okay if they touch. Fry for about 3 minutes, or until crisp and tinged golden brown. Flip each over to crisp the sealed (pleated) side for about 2 minutes; reduce the heat if the oil smokes. There is no need to brown the bottom as it will not show. Transfer to a platter.

7. Serve hot or warm with the soy sauce and chile garlic sauce for guests to concoct their own dipping sauce. Cooked dumplings can be refrigerated; steam to reheat for about 3 minutes before serving.

Vietnamese Tapioca Water Dumplings
Bánh Bột Lọc Trần

Makes 32 small dumplings, to serve 4 as a light lunch, 6 to 8 as a snack

It is easy to overindulge in these chewy-soft dumplings because they slip right down your throat. Just as you are savoring the rich scallion oil, well-seasoned filling, and tangy-sweet-spicy dipping sauce, the dumpling is gone, and you must eat another.

The skin of this central Vietnamese specialty is traditionally made of tapioca starch; I add a little wheat starch for firmness, lest the dough become unpleasantly rubbery. Some Viet cooks laboriously wrap each *bánh bột lọc* in a banana leaf and steam them. I don't have such patience and boil mine for the "naked" (*trần*) version. When peeling the shrimp, save the shells for a stock to use in the sauce.

SCALLION OIL

3 tablespoons canola oil

3 scallions, thinly sliced (white and green parts) (³/4 cup)

FILLING

2 teaspoons canola oil

2 tablespoons finely chopped shallot

¹/4 pound ground pork or minced pork shoulder

¹/4 pound medium shrimp, peeled, deveined, and cut into peanut-size pieces (3¹/2 ounces net weight) (reserve shells for stock, see Note)

Scant ¹/4 teaspoon salt

¹/2 teaspoon sugar

¹/4 teaspoon black pepper

2 teaspoons fish sauce

SAUCE

2 tablespoons sugar

2 tablespoons fish sauce

1¹/2 tablespoons unseasoned rice vinegar

¹/3 cup shrimp shell stock (see Note) or water

1 to 2 Thai or serrano chiles, thinly sliced

DOUGH

4¹/2 ounces (1 cup) tapioca starch

3 ounces (²/3 cup) wheat starch

¹/4 teaspoon salt

²/3 cup just-boiled water (see Note, page 23)

2 tablespoons canola oil

1. **To make the scallion oil,** heat the oil in a medium skillet over medium-high heat. When the oil is hot enough to sizzle a scallion ring upon contact, add the scallions and stir immediately to evenly cook. When the scallions have collapsed and are soft, about 30 seconds, transfer to a small heatproof bowl, and set aside to cool completely.

2. **To make the filling,** add the oil to the hot skillet. Add the shallot and cook, stirring constantly, for about 45 seconds, or until fragrant and beginning to brown. Add the pork, stirring and mashing it into small pieces, and cook for about 1 minute, or until it is no longer pink. Add the shrimp, salt, sugar, pepper, and fish sauce. Cook, stirring frequently, for about 4 minutes, or until the flavors have concentrated, there is little liquid left, and the mixture is lightly sizzling. Transfer to a bowl and set aside to cool completely. You should have about 1 cup. (The scallion oil and filling can be prepared up to 2 days in advance and brought to room temperature before using.)

3. **To make the sauce,** combine the sugar, fish sauce, vinegar, and shrimp shell stock in a small bowl. Stir to dissolve the sugar, taste,

continued

and make any flavor adjustments. Add the chiles and set aside until serving time.

4. To make the dough, combine the tapioca starch, wheat starch, and salt. Make a well in the center and pour in the water. Stir until the water has been absorbed and the mixture is lumpy. Add the 2 tablespoons oil and work it in before pressing the ingredients together into a rough ball.

Knead for 1 to 2 minutes on an unfloured work surface, until the dough is snowy white, smooth, and very malleable. Cut into 4 pieces and put in a zip-top plastic bag and seal well. Set aside for 5 minutes to rest before using. This dough can be prepared up to 6 hours in advance and kept at room temperature in the bag.

5. Line a baking sheet with parchment paper.

6. Working with 1 piece of dough at a time to form the wrappers, roll it on an unfloured work surface into an 8-inch log. (If the dough cracks when rolled, a sign of dryness, very lightly oil your hands and knead it into the dough.) Cut the log into 8 pieces. Follow the instructions on "Forming Wrappers from Wheat Starch Dough" (page 133) to shape thick circles that are about $2^{3}/_{4}$ inches in diameter.

7. Once a batch of wrappers is finished, assemble some dumplings. For each dumpling, hold a wrapper in a slightly cupped hand. Position about $1^{1}/_{2}$ teaspoons of filling slightly off-center toward the upper half of the wrapper, gently pressing down to compact and keeping about $1/_{2}$ to $3/_{4}$ inch of wrapper clear on all sides. Bring up the edge and seal to make a half-moon (see page 26 for details on this shape). Seal well by pressing the rim to meld the edges into one. Set the finished dumpling on the

prepared baking sheet. Make more dumplings from the remaining wrappers, set them on the baking sheet spaced apart slightly, and cover them with plastic wrap to prevent drying. Continue making wrappers and assembling dumplings. The dumplings can sit for about 1 hour before cooking but cannot be refrigerated.

8. To cook, fill a large pot two-thirds full with water and bring to a boil. Add the dumplings in batches of 8 to 12; they should float right up to the surface. After the water returns to a boil (cover the pot if it is a slow go), adjust the heat to gently boil the dumplings for 6 minutes, flipping them midway. They are done when glossy and the rims look mostly clear.

Meanwhile, partially fill a bowl with warm water and set near the stove. Spread about one-third of the scallion oil garnish on 2 serving plates and set nearby.

Use a slotted spoon to scoop up the cooked dumplings, pausing at the top to allow excess water to fall back into the pot. Deposit them in the water bowl and let them sit in the water for about 30 seconds; this removes excess starch. Transfer them to the serving plates. Cover with an aluminum foil tent or inverted bowl while you cook the remaining dumplings.

9. These dumplings are best warm, but are fine at room temperature. Top them with the remaining scallion oil, then present with the sauce. Enjoy with a spoon and fork or chopsticks.

Note: To make shrimp shell stock, put the reserved shrimp shells in a small saucepan and add 1 cup water. Bring to a boil and cook for 5 minutes. Strain through a paper towel–lined mesh strainer and discard the shells. Cool before using in the sauce. Makes about $1/_{2}$ cup.

Thai Tapioca Pearl Dumplings

Saku Sai Mu

Makes 24 dumplings, serving 6 to 8 as a snack

Thai food is full of bold juxtapositions of flavor and texture. For these crystalline dumplings, the chewy skin is made from tapioca pearls (*saku* in Thai). The filling of pork, peanuts, shallot, palm sugar, and fish sauce is crumbly, sweet, salty, and savory. To eat, the dumplings are wrapped in lettuce leaves with fresh herbs and hot chiles.

Saku sai mu is a popular street food in Thailand; here in the States, I have purchased them at Thai markets and snack shops. Making the dumplings at home ensures freshness and availability, and the ingredients can be found at most supermarkets. Hard-core cooks may handmince pork shoulder or chicken thigh and seek out cilantro root and palm sugar from Southeast Asian markets, but ground meat (avoid superlean pork or chicken), cilantro stems, and brown sugar are terrific stand-ins.

DOUGH

1 cup small (1/8-inch) tapioca pearls

1/2 cup just-boiled water (see Note, page 23)

1/4 teaspoon salt

FILLING

1 tablespoon canola oil

1 1/2 teaspoons minced fresh cilantro roots or thicker stems

1 teaspoon minced garlic

3 ounces ground or minced fatty pork or chicken

2 tablespoons finely chopped shallot

2 teaspoons fish sauce

1 tablespoon light brown sugar or palm sugar

1/4 teaspoon white pepper

1 1/2 tablespoons finely chopped unsalted, roasted peanuts

Salt

2 to 3 tablespoons tapioca starch, for dusting

1/4 cup canola oil

1 tablespoon minced garlic

8 to 12 soft lettuce leaves, such as butter or red leaf

6 to 8 sprigs cilantro and/or mint

3 to 5 hot Thai or serrano chiles, cut into 1/4-inch pieces (optional)

1. **To make the dough,** put the tapioca in a bowl and add hot tap water to cover. Swirl twice, then immediate pour into a mesh strainer to drain. Shake the strainer to get rid of excess water. The tapioca will have bloomed and expanded. Wipe the bowl dry and return the tapioca to it. Stir in the just-boiled water and salt, combining well. Cover with plastic wrap and set aside for 1 hour.

2. **Heat the 1 tablespoon** oil in a medium skillet over medium-high heat. Add the cilantro roots and the 1 teaspoon garlic. Cook, stirring constantly for about 1 minute, or until the mixture is fragrant and the garlic is light golden. Add the pork and shallot, stirring and mashing the meat into crumbly bits. Cook for about 1 minute, or until most of the pork has lost its pinkness, then add the fish sauce, brown sugar, and white pepper. Continue cooking, stirring constantly, for about 3 minutes, or until some of the pork has browned and the mixture is hissing and bubbling. Add the peanuts, stirring to combine well. Remove from the heat; taste and add salt and sugar as needed.

continued

Aim for a slightly intense salty-sweet flavor. Transfer to a small plate, spreading the filling out, then set aside to cool completely before using. (The filling can be prepared up to 2 days in advance and refrigerated. Return it to room temperature before using.) Makes an ample 1/2 cup.

3. Line steamer trays and/or baking sheets with parchment paper, then oil the paper.

4. Transfer the tapioca dough to an unfloured work surface. You will initially work with slightly wet hands to prevent sticking and later dust them with tapioca starch to form the dumplings.

Dampen your hands with water and knead the dough for about 1 minute into a bumpy ball of tapioca pearls. It may be a bit pasty and squishy, and that is fine. Cut the dough in half, and return half to the bowl, covering it with plastic wrap.

Working with the other half, dampen your hands again and roll the dough into a 12-inch log. Cut into 1-inch pieces. With damp hands, roll each piece of dough into a ball. Now, wash your hands and dry them thoroughly.

For each dumpling, lightly dust your hands with tapioca starch. Pick up a dough ball and make an indentation in the center with your thumb. Keep your thumb in place as you rotate the dough and press on its walls to create a 1/2 to 3/4-inch deep cup. Holding the cup in the crook of your hand, fill it with about 1 teaspoon of filling, tapping it down lightly. Then close up the opening by pressing the dough inward with your fingers. Should there be a break in the dough, pinch the surrounding pearls together and dab on some tapioca starch to seal. Roll the ball between your hands for an even shape. Set in the steamer tray or

on a baking sheet spaced 1 inch apart. Repeat with the remaining dough pieces before working on the other half of the dough.

The dumplings can be cooked now or frozen. To freeze, place them in the freezer for about 1 hour, until hard. Then put into a zip-top plastic bag, press out excess air before sealing, and freeze for up to 1 month. Thaw completely in the refrigerator before steaming.

5. Steam the dumplings for 20 minutes over boiling water; see page 17 for steaming guidelines. Turn off the heat and remove the steamer lid. After about 3 minutes, the tapioca pearl dough should go from translucent to mostly clear. If it does not, steam for 5 minutes more.

6. As the dumplings steam, make the garlic oil. Combine the remaining 1/4 cup oil and the remaining 1 tablespoon garlic in a small saucepan and heat over medium heat. Let the garlic sizzle for about 2 minutes, or until it is blond. Immediately transfer to a heatproof dish and set aside to cool. Put 2 tablespoons of the garlic oil on a platter and set aside.

7. When the dumplings are done, detach or remove the steamer tray and let cool for 5 minutes before transferring the dumplings to the platter. Present the dumplings warm or at room temperature, with the remaining garlic oil drizzled atop each dumpling. Serve with the garnishes of lettuce, cilantro, and chiles either tucked onto the platter or arranged on a separate plate.

To eat, tear off a palm-sized piece of lettuce and put a dumpling on top. Add a few cilantro and/or mint leaves (pinch their stems off) and a piece of chile. Bundle up the lettuce and enjoy.

Refrigerate leftover dumplings and steam them for about 8 minutes, or until soft again.

6 Transformations of Rice

Rice dishes grace Asian tables throughout the day: there are myriad options for transforming the many varieties of the grain into lovely, delectable foods. This chapter touches upon some of the ways that *Oryza sativa* is employed in savory dumpling making; the sweets chapter offers a few more.

Many of the recipes in this chapter come from southern China and Southeast Asia, where rice is king. Wheat-based dumplings are characteristic of northern Asia, where that grain grows better.

Like wheat, rice can be ground up into flour, and regular rice flour is made from long-grain rice. When the rice is soaked before it is ground, the result is soft, fine flour. Since rice flour can't be made into elastic dough like wheat flour, it is often used in a batter to make tender, steamed rice sheets, which, once cooked, are cut into noodles or dumpling wrappers. The filling often gets rolled up in rice sheet wrappers but sometimes is sprinkled onto the batter during steaming. This chapter opens with a master recipe for steamed rice sheets, followed by a number of ways to employ them for dim sum treats.

The other common kind of rice flour in the Asian kitchen is made from glutinous (sticky) rice, which has a wonderful natural sweetness and chewiness. Glutinous rice flour has many uses in dumpling making because it can be used to make a wrapper that can hold a shape during steaming, poaching, and deep-frying. Cantonese fried sticky rice dumplings are delightful wonders stuffed with savory-sweet fillings such as roasted pork.

Grains of sticky rice are also used for Asian dumplings, many of which are wrapped in leaves such as lotus and banana. Regardless of the leaf used, the leaf wrapper helps to maintain the dumpling's shape, makes the dumpling a portable food, and imparts unique flavor and perfume to the rice. Explore this type of dumpling through Chinese lotus leaf packets of *Nuò Mǐ Jī* (page 170) and Indonesian banana leaf parcels of *Lemper Ayam* (page 173).

Asian markets are the best source for the flours, rice, and specialty ingredients employed in this chapter. Lay in a small supply because a little goes a long way.

Rice Sheet Batter

Hé Fěn Mǐ Jiāng

Makes 1¹/₄ cups, enough for 3 large square noodle sheets

Versatile rice sheets are an integral part of many Asian cuisines; they can be cut into fresh noodles, dried into rice papers or crackers, and used as delicate wrappers for filled treats. Called *ho fun* in Cantonese, the sheets are nothing but big noodles made from silky batters of mostly rice and water.

Many Asian cooks purchase opaque rice sheets, but for the purposes of dumpling making, it is best to prepare them yourself, as this guarantees freshness and a terrific toothsome texture. You need just a few for an abundance of tasty shrimp- or beef-filled rolls like the ones found at dim sum parlors. The sheets can be cooked and filled hours in advance of serving. A quick steaming is all they need right before serving.

I have tried soaking and grinding raw rice for this batter but have never been as satisfied with the results as when I use rice flour from Thailand. The flour is both consistent and convenient. Look for it at Asian markets in plastic bags, typically with red lettering. Adding cornstarch and tapioca starch to the batter contributes to the sheets' resilience and slight translucence. When starting out, make a double batch of batter so you can get plenty of practice.

2¹/₂ ounces (¹/₂ cup plus 1 tablespoon) rice flour (any Thai brand such as Erawan)

1 tablespoon cornstarch

1 tablespoon tapioca starch

¹/₈ teaspoon salt

1 tablespoon canola oil

1 cup water

1. Combine the rice flour, cornstarch, tapioca starch, and salt in a bowl. Make a well in the center and add the oil. Steadily whisk in the water to make a thin, silky batter. If the oil hasn't been broken up into minute droplets by the time you are done, whisk for about 15 seconds more.

2. Set aside at room temperature for 30 minutes to allow the starches to bloom. The batter can be prepared up to 4 hours in advance, covered, and left at room temperature.

How to Make Rice Sheets

Professional cooks steam rice sheets atop a piece of cloth set on a special perforated pan, but most home cooks use square baking pans. A nonstick metal pan works best because it is light and easy to move with tongs. A glass pan is okay, especially with nonstick cooking spray applied to the bottom to ensure a clean release.

Square pans work well for all the recipes here, though you can use a round one for the unfilled Dried Shrimp and Scallion Rice Rolls (page 162). My inexpensive nonstick square pan has sloping walls measuring 8 inches at the top and 7 inches at the bottom.

If the baking pan fits your steamer tray, use the steaming method. Review the guidelines on page 17 before you start if you need to brush up on steaming techniques. Otherwise, use the poaching method.

1. To steam, bring the water to a rolling boil with the steamer tray in place. Put the pan inside the tray, cover, and preheat for 2 minutes.

Alternatively, to poach the noodle sheet, select a wide deep pot, covered roasting pan, or electric skillet inside which your baking pan will fit. Fill the pot or pan with enough water so that the baking pan floats nicely but there is plenty of room for steam to circulate when the lid is on. Bring the water to a boil, put the pan in the water, and lower the heat to gently simmer. Cover to preheat the pan for 2 minutes.

2. Regardless of cooking method, lower the heat before removing the lid for safety. If water dripped into the pan, use tongs or potholders to grab the pan and pour the water out.

Because the batter separates and settles as it sits, stir it with a ladle until there is no drag, then ladle enough batter into the pan to cover the bottom by about $1/8$ inch. For my square baking pan, I use about 6 tablespoons (a generous $1/3$ cup) of batter. If the pan is not completely flat, the batter will not cover the bottom at first. Let the batter begin to set for 5 to 10 seconds, then use tongs to tilt the pan to evenly spread the batter and film the bottom.

3. Adjust the heat to a boil for steaming or gently simmer for poaching, then cover and cook for about 5 minutes, or until the noodle sheet has set and bubbled up. If you touch it, it shouldn't stick to your finger. Lower the heat or turn it off, then use tongs to remove the pan. Set aside for 2 to 3 minutes, until the rice sheet is cool enough to handle. A completely cool rice sheet will lift off more easily from the pan but a warm rice sheet will roll up and seal better. To hasten cooling, set the pan in a bowl of cold water for a few minutes.

4. Run a thin-rimmed rubber spatula or metal icing spatula around the edge of the noodle sheet to detach it from the pan. Pry up two of the corners (select thicker ones) and use your fingers to peel off the noodle sheet. Place it bottom side down on a work surface and let it cool for a few minutes (use the waiting time to wash and dry the pan and start steaming another sheet) before proceeding as directed in the recipe. Repeat for the other sheets. If you are stacking the sheets, put parchment paper between each one to make separating them easier.

The recipes in this book call for filling the sheets soon after they are cooked, but you can keep cooked sheets at room temperature for up to 12 hours. Wrap the stack in parchment paper and seal them in a zip-top plastic bag, or place in an airtight plastic container. They can be individually steamed, placed on an oiled plate or piece of parchment paper set in a steamer tray, over low heat for 1 to 2 minutes to regain their softness. Refrigerated sheets harden and are best cut up and treated like fresh noodles for panfried noodles or soup.

Shrimp Rice Noodle Rolls

Xiā Cháng

Makes 12 rolls, serving 4 to 6 as a light snack

Asian dumplings are often prepared with chopped shrimp, but these rolls are filled with whole shrimp and always seem extra decadent. Called *har cheung* in Cantonese, they are a perennial favorite dim sum—delighting diners with the orange-pink glow of the shrimp beneath the sheath of rice sheet. On their own, the rolls will seem very mild flavored. But finishing them with the sweet soy sauce makes all the elements sing.

36 medium shrimp (about 1 pound), peeled and deveined

1/4 teaspoon salt

1 teaspoon oyster sauce

1 teaspoon sesame oil

2 teaspoons canola oil

11/4 cups Rice Sheet Batter (page 154)

1/2 cup Sweet Soy Sauce (page 217)

1 to 2 tablespoons thinly sliced scallion (green part only)

Chile Garlic Sauce, homemade (page 216) or store-bought (optional)

1. **Toss the shrimp** with the salt. Put in a strainer, rinse under cold water, then transfer to a paper towel and blot dry. Put the shrimp in a bowl and coat well with the oyster sauce and sesame oil. Set aside for 30 minutes to marinate.

2. **Heat the canola oil** in a medium skillet over medium-high heat. Add the shrimp and cook, stirring a few times, for about 1 minute, or until just cooked through. Transfer to a bowl and set aside to cool.

3. **Prepare the rice sheets** using the instructions in "How to Make Rice Sheets" on page 155. You can make the rolls in between making each sheet, while the sheets are still warm, or after they are all done and completely cool. However, the rolls seal best when the sheet is warm.

4. **Before assembling the rolls,** lightly oil a plate. Cut a rice sheet into 4 (31/2 inch) squares. Line 3 shrimp up in a horizontal row along the lower edge of one of the squares. Bring up the lower lip of the sheet and roll it over, along with the shrimp, to close. There should be a 1/2 inch overlap of rice sheet when you are done. Place the finished roll on the plate, seam side down, and repeat with the other squares before moving on to the next rice sheet. Use a new oiled plate after filling one up. It is fine for the rolls to touch.

When making the rolls in advance, lightly coat them with oil to prevent drying. Cover and set aside for up to 3 hours. They can be refrigerated for up to 8 hours and returned to room temperature before steaming.

5. **Put the plates** of rolls in steamer trays and steam over boiling water (see page 17 for guidance) for 3 to 4 minutes, until the rolls are soft and heated through. Remove the plates from the steamer trays or keep them in the trays and bring to the table. Keep the rolls whole or cut them into thirds, so that there is one shrimp in each section of each roll. Pour the sweet soy sauce over the rolls (it will pool on the plate) and garnish with the scallion. Serve immediately with the chile garlic sauce. Use both chopsticks and spoons to eat these rolls, lest the shrimp slip out of the wrapper.

Beef and Orange Rice Rolls
Niú Ròu Cháng

Makes 12 rolls, serving 4 to 6 as a light snack

Rice roll fillings are often precooked and reheated through steaming, but this popular one involves a filling of raw beef and orange zest that requires steaming to complete the cooking. For efficiency, professional Chinese cooks typically add the raw beef to the rice sheet about 30 seconds into cooking, but that is a difficult technique. Filling cooked sheets and then steaming them to cook the beef is easier and the results are the same.

You do not have to use the baking soda in the filling, but some Chinese cooks use it as a meat tenderizer and to lend a silky texture. The beef should be hand- or machine-chopped so it isn't too finely textured and clumpy (see page 158 for guidance).

FILLING

Generous 1/4 teaspoon finely grated fresh orange or tangerine zest

Scant 1/2 teaspoon sugar

1/8 teaspoon salt

1/8 teaspoon white pepper

1/4 teaspoon baking soda (optional)

1 teaspoon cornstarch

1/2 teaspoon soy sauce

2 teaspoons water

1 1/2 teaspoons canola oil

1 scallion (white and green parts), finely chopped

1/3 pound minced or coarsely chopped beef steak, such as sirloin or bottom sirloin

1 1/4 cups Rice Sheet Batter (page 154)

1/2 cup Sweet Soy Sauce (page 217)

1 to 2 tablespoons thinly sliced scallion (green part only)

Chile Garlic Sauce, homemade (page 216) or store-bought (optional)

1. To make the filling, in a bowl, combine the orange zest, sugar, salt, white pepper, baking soda, cornstarch, soy sauce, water, and oil. Stir to dissolve the cornstarch. Add the scallion and beef and mix well with a fork or spatula. Set aside to marinate for 30 minutes, or cover with plastic wrap, refrigerate overnight, and return to room temperature before using. You should have about 3/4 cup.

2. Prepare the rice sheets using the instructions in "How to Make Rice Sheets" on page 215. You can make the rolls in between making each sheet, while the sheets are slightly warm, or after they are all done and completely cool. However, the rolls seal best when the sheet is warm.

3. Lightly oil a plate. To assemble the rolls, cut a rice sheet into 4 (3 1/2 inch) squares. Arrange 1 tablespoon of the beef along the midline of one of the squares. Avoid pressing the meat into a compact log because it is not really a sausage. Bring up the lower edge of the rice sheet to partially cover the filling and roll to close. The finished roll will look flat, and there should be about a 1/2-inch overlap of rice sheet when you are done. Place the finished roll on the prepared plate, seam side down, and repeat with the other squares before moving on to the next rice sheet. Oil a new plate and use after you have filled one up. It is fine for the rolls to touch.

continued

When you are making the rolls in advance, lightly coat them with oil to prevent drying, cover with plastic wrap, and refrigerate for up to 8 hours. Return to room temperature before steaming.

4. **To finish cooking** the rolls, steam the plates of rolls over boiling water (see page 17 for guidance) for about 5 minutes, or until the beef is cooked through and the rolls are soft. Remove the plates of rolls from the steamer trays or keep them in the trays. Keep the rolls whole or cut them into thirds with a knife or scissors. Pour the sweet soy sauce over the rolls, letting it pool in the plates, and garnish with the scallion. Serve with the chile garlic sauce.

MINCING AND CHOPPING MEAT BY HAND

Meat that is minced and chopped by hand lends a wonderfully varied texture to dumplings. There is usually little meat involved in dumpling making, so the task is not as time-consuming as you might think. Use boneless skinless chicken thigh, pork shoulder (blade) steak, or beef steak. Trim away any gristly bits but keep the fat, and cut the meat into pea-size pieces. Mound them up in a pile and use a rocking motion to move the knife blade from one side of the pile to the other. Occasionally pause and lift the meat with the blade and fold it over on itself to maintain a moderately compact mass. For a minced texture, chop until you have a coarse paste-like consistency that is not as fine as regular ground meat. For a hand-chopped texture, aim for a coarser finish.

When chopping a large quantity of meat, use two knives of the same weight and size, working as if you are drumming. Or, put the cut pieces of meat in a food processor or electric mini-chopper and pulse. The resulting texture is not uniform, but the process is more convenient.

Chicken and Vegetable Rice Rolls
Jī Sī Cháng

Makes 12 rolls, serving 4 to 6 as a light snack

Chinese cooks use rice sheets as wrappers for not only shrimp and beef, but also tasty stir-fries like this one. The chicken and vegetable mixture here could be used as a filling for deep-fried spring rolls, but it is also wonderful in this delicate treatment: encased in rice sheets and steamed.

The chicken and vegetables are cut into matchsticks to complement the shape of the roll. To cut the chicken, freeze it first for 5 to 10 minutes, slice it, and then stack the slices and slice again into thick matchsticks. Pork tenderloin or beef flank can be substituted for the chicken. For a vegetarian version, replace the chicken with 2/3 cup packed shredded bamboo shoots (boil for 1 minute first to eliminate the tinny flavor) and decrease the cornstarch to 2 teaspoons.

FILLING

2 pinches of salt

1 tablespoon plus 1 teaspoon cornstarch

2 tablespoons plus 2 teaspoons water

5 1/2 teaspoons canola oil

1/4 pound boneless, skinless chicken breast, cut into matchsticks

1 teaspoon light (regular) soy sauce

1 tablespoon oyster sauce

1/2 teaspoon sugar

1 pinch of white pepper

2 large dried shiitake mushrooms, reconstituted (see page 13), stemmed, and cut into thin strips (1/4 cup)

2 1/2 inches carrot, cut into fine matchsticks

1 rib celery, strings removed with vegetable peeler, cut into matchsticks

1 scallion (white and green parts), cut into thin strips to match the celery

1 1/4 cups Rice Sheet Batter (page 154)

1/2 cup Sweet Soy Sauce (page 217)

1 to 2 tablespoons chopped fresh cilantro or thinly sliced scallion (green part only)

Chile Garlic Sauce, homemade (page 216) or store-bought (optional)

1. **To make the filling,** in a bowl, combine the salt, the 1 teaspoon cornstarch, the 2 teaspoons water, and 1 1/2 teaspoons of the oil. Stir to dissolve the cornstarch. Add the chicken and stir to coat well. Set aside to marinate for 15 minutes, or cover and refrigerate for several hours, returning it to room temperature before cooking.

2. **Combine the remaining** 1 tablespoon cornstarch, remaining 2 tablespoons water, the soy sauce, oyster sauce, sugar, and white pepper. Stir to dissolve the sugar. Set the seasonings aside.

3. **Heat 2 teaspoons** of the oil in a medium skillet over high heat and add the chicken. Cook, stirring constantly, for about 45 seconds, or until the chicken has mostly lost its raw color. Transfer to a plate. Lower the heat to medium-high, add the remaining 2 teaspoons of oil, and then the mushrooms, carrot, and celery. Cook, stirring frequently, for about 2 minutes, until the vegetables are tender-crisp. Add the scallion, stir, and then return the chicken to the skillet. Combine well, then add the seasonings.

continued

Cook for about 30 seconds, stirring, or until the mixture has thickened. Transfer to a plate, spreading it out, and set aside to cool completely before using. Or, cover and refrigerate overnight, returning the filling to room temperature before using it. You should have 1 heaping cup.

4. **Prepare the rice sheets** using the instructions in "How to Make Rice Sheets" on page 155. You can make the rolls in between making each sheet, while the sheets are still warm, or after they are all done and completely cool. The rolls seal best when the sheet is warm.

5. **Lightly oil a plate.** To assemble the rolls, cut a rice sheet into 4 (3^1/$_2$-inch) squares. Center 1^1/$_2$ tablespoons of filling along the midline of one of the squares. Bring up the lower edge of the rice sheet to partially cover the filling and roll to close. There should be about a ^{1}/$_2$-inch overlap of rice sheet when you

are done. Place the finished roll on the oiled plate, seam side up, and repeat with the other squares before moving on to the next rice sheet. Oil a new plate and use after you have filled one up. It is fine for the rolls to touch.

When making the rolls in advance, lightly coat them with oil to prevent drying, cover with plastic wrap, and set aside for up to 3 hours. They can be refrigerated for up to 8 hours and returned to room temperature before steaming.

6. **Before serving,** put the plates of rolls in steamer trays and steam over boiling water (see page 17 for guidance) for 3 to 4 minutes, until the rolls are soft and heated through. Remove the plate of rolls from the steamer tray or keep them in the trays and bring to the table. Keep the rolls whole or cut them into thirds with a knife or scissors. Liberally pour the sweet soy sauce over the rolls, letting it pool in the plates, then garnish with the scallion. Serve immediately with the chile garlic sauce.

Dried Shrimp and Scallion Rice Rolls

Xiā Mǐ Cháng

Makes 3 rolls, serving 4 to 6 as a snack or with 2 or 3 other dishes

Commonly sold on Styrofoam trays at Chinese and Southeast Asian markets, these opaque white rice rolls flecked with orange dried shrimp and green scallion are a terrific southern Chinese snack. Purchased ones are seldom as tasty as homemade because producers tend to be skimpy with the dried shrimp, which give the rolls their oomph.

These steamed rolls can be eaten as is, dipped in sweet soy sauce. Or they can be panfried to a delicate crisp. When served with other dishes, a few rolls are all you will need. For a light main course with a salad, double or triple the recipe.

2 tablespoons minced dried shrimp

2 scallions (white and green parts), finely chopped

1¹/4 cups Rice Sheet Batter (page 154)

1/4 cup Sweet Soy Sauce (page 217)

1 teaspoon toasted, hulled (white) sesame seeds (optional)

Chile Garlic Sauce, homemade (page 216) or store-bought (optional)

1. In a small bowl, combine the dried shrimp and scallions. Set aside near the stove.

2. Follow the instructions in "How to Make Rice Sheets" on page 155 to prepare each rice sheet. After pouring the batter into the baking pan and spreading it out to cover the entire surface of the pan, let the batter set for 5 to 10 seconds. Then sprinkle one-third of the shrimp and scallion mixture on the surface. Cover and cook the rice sheet for 5 minutes, or until translucent and set.

3. Remove the pan from the steamer tray or pot, if poaching, and cool for 2 to 3 minutes on a rack, until cool enough to handle the rice sheet. Meanwhile, lightly oil a plate. Remove the rice sheet from the pan as directed on page 155 and place it on a work surface with the smoother bottom-side down.

Gently roll up the rice sheet as you would a scroll of paper. If you roll it up too tightly, it will be too heavy, so leave it loose in the center. Aim for 1-inch-diameter rolls. Place the finished roll on the prepared plate, seam side down, before making another one, washing and drying the pan first.

If you are not serving the rolls right away, lightly coat them with oil to prevent drying, cover with plastic wrap, and set aside at room temperature for up to 4 hours. They can be refrigerated but will harden, and the best way to revitalize them is by panfrying (see the Note below).

4. Serve the rolls at room temperature. Or, warm them by steaming them for about 2 minutes, if needed. Use a knife to cut them into 1-inch pieces and return them to their plate. Drizzle on the sweet soy sauce and finish with a sprinkling of the sesame seeds. Present with the chile garlic sauce.

Note: To panfry the rolls, first cut each in half. Heat 2 to 3 teaspoons of oil in a nonstick skillet over medium heat and panfry the rolls for 2 to 3 minutes per side, until lightly crisp and a bit golden. Cut the rolls into 1-inch pieces and serve on a plate with a drizzle of the sweet soy sauce, a shower of sesame seeds, and a side of chile garlic sauce.

Fried Sticky Rice Dumplings

Xián Shuǐ Jiǎo

Makes 20 dumplings, serving 6 to 8 as a snack

Traditionally a Cantonese Lunar New Year treat, but now a standard dim sum offering, these remarkable football-shaped dumplings have a tender, crisp skin that yields to a wonderful sweet chewiness when you bite into them. Light brown sugar helps to color the dough during frying and adds a bit of sweetness—a contrast with the savory pork or vegetable filling.

I usually avoid these dumplings (called *haam sui gok* in Cantonese) at dim sum restaurants because they tend to be leaden and overly greasy. However, made at home, they are irresistible. Make sure to prepare the filling before making the dough.

DOUGH

5 3/4 ounces (generous 1 1/4 cups) glutinous (sweet) rice flour (any Thai brand such as Erawan)

2 1/4 ounces (1/2 cup) wheat starch

1/4 cup lightly packed light brown sugar

1/4 teaspoon salt

2 tablespoons lard or solid vegetable shortening, cut into 4 chunks

2/3 cup just-boiled water (see Note, page 23)

1 cup Char Siu Pork and Mushroom Filling (page 166) or Vegetable and Shrimp Filling (page 167)

Canola oil, for deep-frying

Light (regular) soy sauce (optional)

Chile Garlic Sauce, homemade (page 216) or store-bought (optional)

1. To prepare the dough, combine the rice flour, wheat starch, brown sugar, and salt in a bowl. Make a well in the center and add the lard. Pour the water into the well; the lard will begin to melt. Stir to dampen and combine all the ingredients. After a crumbly mixture forms, switch to stirring and pressing to gather all the bits into a rough dough. Knead the mixture into a ball while it is still in the bowl, then transfer to a work surface. Knead for about 1 minute to form a smooth dough. Cover with plastic wrap and set aside for 5 minutes to cool.

2. Work with half of the dough and keep the other half covered. Roll the dough into a 10-inch log. Cut it into 10 equal-size pieces and then roll each piece into a ball.

3. Line a plate or baking sheet with parchment paper. To assemble a dumpling, take a ball of dough, make an indentation in the center with your thumb, and then work the dough with your fingers to form a shallow, 2 3/4-inch-wide bowl. Fill the cavity with 2 rounded teaspoons of filling, pressing down gently. It will seem very full. Press and pinch the edges closed to form a football (see page 164 for guidance). Set the finished dumpling on the prepared plate. Repeat with the remaining dough balls before working on the other half of the dough. Loosely cover the finished dumplings with plastic wrap to prevent drying.

4. Put a paper towel–lined platter next to the stove. Pour oil to a depth of 1 1/4 inches into a wok, deep saucepan, or Dutch oven and heat over medium-high heat to about 350°F on a deep-fry thermometer. (If you don't have a thermometer, stick a *dry* bamboo chopstick into the oil; if bubbles rise immediately and encircle the chopstick, the oil is ready.)

continued

Divide the dumplings into 3 or 4 batches. Gently drop one batch of dumplings into the oil. They will bubble in the oil for a few minutes before rising to the top. If any stick together, nudge them apart. Fry, turning them frequently to ensure even cooking, for 5 to 6 minutes, until puffy, golden brown, and crisp. Using a skimmer, scoop up the dumplings from the oil and set them on the paper towels to drain. Adjust the heat before frying more.

5. Let the dumplings cool for a few minutes before serving. Serve them whole or use scissors or a knife to cut each in half. Enjoy with a dip in soy sauce and chile garlic sauce.

Note: Reheat leftover dumplings by refrying in 375°F oil for about 2 minutes or baking in a preheated 375°F oven or toaster oven for 10 to 15 minutes.

Master Shape: Football

To make a football-shaped dumpling, take a ball of dough and make an indentation in the center with your thumb. Keeping that thumb in place, rotate the dough, pressing on its walls with the other fingers to form a wide bowl. Eventually, the dough will resemble a shallow mushroom cap. If you end up with a flat circle, that is fine; the difference is that the dumpling will be a little longer, like a large grain of rice and less football like. Put the filling in the cavity, then press and pinch the edges closed, taking care to seal the edges so they meld together and form a chubby football. There will be a little ridge along the top where the dumpling seals. Set it on your work surface and neaten it up so it sits upright.

Shaping Footballs

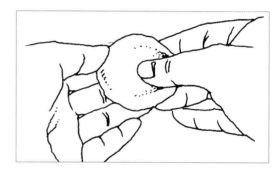

1. Rotate the dough as you press on its walls to create a shallow bowl.

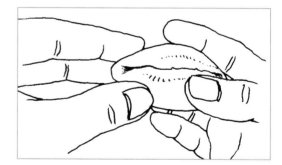

2. Press and pinch the dough closed, forming a chubby football.

Char Siu Pork and Mushroom Filling

Chăshāo Xián Shuĭ Jiăo

Makes about 1 cup

Earthy and well-seasoned, this filling features char siu pork and shiitake mushrooms. The five-spice power adds sweet perfume, while the dried shrimp injects a note of the sea. Feel free to vary this filling by substituting a combination of chopped raw pork and shrimp for the roasted pork below.

SEASONING SAUCE

1/2 teaspoon sugar

2 pinches of Chinese five-spice powder (optional)

1 pinch of white pepper

1 1/2 teaspoons cornstarch

2 teaspoons oyster sauce

1/2 teaspoon light (regular) soy sauce

1/2 teaspoon sesame oil

1 teaspoon Shaoxing rice wine or dry sherry

1 tablespoon water

2 teaspoons canola oil

2 teaspoons finely chopped dried shrimp

1 scallion (white and green parts), finely chopped

1/4 pound Char Siu Pork, homemade (page 224) or store-bought, diced

2 large dried shiitake mushrooms, reconstituted (see page 13), stemmed, and chopped (1/4 cup)

1. **To make the seasoning sauce,** in a small bowl, combine the sugar, five-spice powder, white pepper, cornstarch, oyster sauce, soy sauce, sesame oil, rice wine, and water, stirring to dissolve the cornstarch. Set the sauce aside.

2. **Heat the canola oil** in a medium skillet over medium-high heat and add the dried shrimp and scallion. Cook for about 20 seconds, or until the scallion has just softened. Add the pork and mushrooms, and cook for about 1 minute, stirring frequently, to heat through. Give the seasoning sauce a stir and add to the skillet. Cook for another 30 seconds, or until the mixture has cohered. Transfer to a plate or small bowl and set aside to cool completely before using. (The filling can be prepared up to 2 days in advance, covered with plastic wrap, and refrigerated. Return to room temperature before using.)

Vegetable and Shrimp Filling
Shū Cài Xián Shuǐ Jiǎo

Makes about 1 cup

Cantonese deep-fried sticky rice dumplings can be filled many ways, but there is usually chopped rehydrated shiitake mushroom and a little chopped dried shrimp for savory oomph. With those two ingredients in this vegetable-laden alternative, you won't miss the meat.

SEASONING SAUCE

Scant 1/2 teaspoon salt

1 teaspoon sugar

2 pinches of white pepper

1 1/2 teaspoons cornstarch

1/2 teaspoon sesame oil

1 teaspoon light (regular) soy sauce

2 tablespoons water

1 tablespoon canola oil

1 clove garlic, minced

1 tablespoon finely chopped dried shrimp

2 scallions (white and green parts), chopped

1/4 cup finely diced carrot

2/3 cup diced jicama

2 large dried shiitake mushrooms, reconstituted (see page 13), stemmed, and chopped (1/4 cup)

1. **To make the seasoning sauce,** in a small bowl, combine the salt, sugar, white pepper, cornstarch, sesame oil, soy sauce, and water, stirring to dissolve the cornstarch. Set the sauce near the stove.

2. **Heat the canola oil** in a medium skillet over medium-high heat. Add the garlic, dried shrimp, and scallions. Cook, stirring constantly, for about 30 seconds, or until the scallions have just softened.

3. **Add the carrot,** jicama, and mushrooms. Cook, stirring frequently, for about 4 minutes, or until the jicama and carrot are tender-crisp. Give the seasoning sauce a stir and then add to the skillet. Cook for another minute, or until the mixture coheres. Transfer to a bowl and set aside to cool completely before using. (The filling can be prepared up to 2 days in advance, covered with plastic wrap, and refrigerated. Return to room temperature before using.)

Steamed Sticky Rice Dumplings
with Shrimp and Pork
Bánh Ít

Makes 12, serving 4 as a light main course, 6 as a snack

Whereas fried sticky rice dumplings have their alluring crispy-chewy skins, steamed sticky rice dumplings are as soft and comforting as a well-worn pair of jeans. They retain the charming soft texture and natural sweetness of sticky rice. I grew up breakfasting on Vietnamese *bánh ít* ("small dumplings"), though they can certainly be a satisfying brunch, lunch, or snack food. Filled with a surf-and-turf mixture of shrimp, pork, and wood ear and shiitake mushrooms, these dumplings are enjoyed warm, dipped in a pool of soy sauce and pepper. The banana leaf imparts a wonderfully tealike quality to the dumplings during the cooking process.

These are easy to make, especially when the filling is prepared a day in advance. Viet cooks often use boiling water to create glutinous rice dough, but the dough is easier to handle and control when cold water is used. I combine two kinds of glutinous rice flour (see page 15) to arrive at a texture that is pleasantly chewy, not overly sticky. The rice flours are available at Asian markets, as is fresh or frozen banana leaf.

FILLING

1 tablespoon canola oil

1/4 cup finely chopped yellow onion

3 ounces ground pork, fattier kind preferred, coarsely chopped to loosen

1 dried wood ear mushroom, reconstituted (see page 13), trimmed, and finely chopped (about 1 1/2 tablespoons)

2 dried shiitake mushrooms, reconstituted (see page 13), stemmed, and chopped (about 3 tablespoons)

1/4 pound medium shrimp, peeled, deveined, and cut into pea-size pieces (3 1/2 ounces net weight)

1 teaspoon fish sauce

Scant 1/4 teaspoon salt

1/2 teaspoon black pepper

DOUGH

8 5/8 ounces (1 1/2 cups) Mochiko Blue Star brand glutinous (sweet) rice flour

3 3/8 ounces (3/4 cup) glutinous (sweet) rice flour (select a Thai brand such as Erawan)

1/2 teaspoon salt

1 cup plus 2 tablespoons water

12 circles, each 3 1/2 inches in diameter, cut from fresh or thawed, frozen banana leaf, rinsed and wiped dry

Canola oil, for oiling the leaves

Light (regular) soy sauce or Maggi Seasoning Sauce (optional)

Black pepper (optional)

1. To make the filling, heat the oil in a medium skillet over medium heat. Add the onion and cook, stirring occasionally, for 1 to 2 minutes, until soft and fragrant. Add the pork, pressing and poking it to break it up into small pieces. When the pork is halfway cooked, about 1 minute, add the wood ear mushroom, shiitake mushrooms, and shrimp. Stir to combine well, then sprinkle in the fish sauce, salt, and pepper. Continue cooking for 2 to 3 minutes, until the shrimp turns pink. Transfer to a bowl and set aside to cool completely before using. (The filling can be prepared up to 2 days in advance, covered in plastic wrap, refrigerated,

and returned to room temperature before use.) You should have about 1 1/2 cups.

2. **To make the dough,** stir together the two rice flours and salt. Make a well in the center, pour in the water, and stir with a spatula until a clumpy dough forms. Use your hands to knead the dough into a rough mass. Turn out the dough and all the unincorporated bits onto a work surface and knead with both hands for about 2 minutes, until you have a soft, smooth ball that feels like modeling clay. If needed, add water by the teaspoon or a bit of rice flour (either kind is fine) to achieve the correct consistency. Pinch the finished dough; it should barely stick to your fingers.

Shape the finished dough into a log, and then cut it into 12 pieces. Roll each piece into a rough ball and set aside for a moment.

3. **Arrange the banana** leaf circles in a single layer on the counter and very lightly brush the top of each with oil to prevent the dumplings from sticking. Have a small bowl of water handy for moistening your fingers.

4. **To form a dumpling,** lightly wet your fingertips and then gently press a piece of dough from the center toward the rim to create a 3-inch circle that is slightly thinner at the middle than at the rim; as you press, rotate the dough to make a nice circle. (It is like shaping a tiny pizza.)

Gently cup one hand and put the dough circle in that hand, placing it toward the fingertips, which will cradle the dumpling as you shape it. Place a scant 2 tablespoons of filling in the center. Lightly press on the filling

with the back of the spoon to create a shallow well; your hand will naturally cup a little tighter. Use your free hand to push and pinch the dough together to completely enclose the filling. You will end up with a 2-inch ball. Pass the ball between your hands a few times to smooth out the surface, and then center it on a banana leaf circle. A bit of lumpiness is fine.

Repeat with the remaining dough and filling. Place the dumplings in steamer trays, spacing them 1 inch apart; when using a metal steamer tray, keep the dumplings 1 inch away from the edge, where condensation will collect.

5. **Steam the dumplings** over boiling water (see page 17 for guidance) for 15 minutes, or until they have expanded and no longer look chalky. Detach the steamer trays and then use a metal spatula, sliding it under the banana leaf circles, to transfer the dumplings to a cooling rack or serving plate. Let them firm and cool for 5 to 10 minutes, during which time they will shrink slightly, become less sticky to the touch, and form a shiny skin.

6. **Serve these dumplings** atop the banana leaf circles and invite guests to use chopsticks or forks to lift them from the leaf (they come off easily); they should set the leaf aside as it is not eaten. The dumplings are good as they are, but they are even tastier dipped in a pool of soy sauce and pepper.

Leftover dumplings can be stacked and refrigerated in an airtight container for about 5 days. Return them to room temperature before reheating in the steamer for about 3 minutes.

Sticky Rice and Chicken in Lotus Leaf
Nuò Mǐ Jī

Makes 8 packets, serving 8

Opening up a steamed lotus leaf packet and inhaling its alluring musty fragrance is part of many Cantonese dim sum rituals. Inside, the sticky rice is stained a rich brown from the leaf, and once you start digging toward the center with chopsticks, there is a treasure trove of succulent ingredients.

Figuring out what comprises the filling is most fun. Chicken is often included, as *jī* (fowl) is part of these packets' name in Mandarin; they are called *lo mai gai* in Cantonese. Chicken is commonly combined with shiitake mushrooms and Chinese sweet sausage, as is done here. But cooks can add a myriad of other boldly flavored or rich ingredients, such as roasted char siu pork (page 224), roast duck, dried shrimp, salted egg yolk, and chestnuts. Lotus leaf packets can be made large enough for several people to share, but I prefer to present a small one to each guest. I freeze extras as a homemade convenience food to be later revived and packed into a lunch box or enjoyed on the road.

At Chinese and Southeast Asian markets, you will find the sticky rice and dried sweet sausages. Packages of fanlike dried lotus leaves are usually near the dried mushrooms; they are inexpensive and last indefinitely if stored in a dry spot. If you are making lotus packets for the first time, soak a couple of extra leaves in case you tear them.

2 cups sticky rice (long-grain or short-grain variety)

SEASONING SAUCE

1 tablespoon cornstarch

2 teaspoons oyster sauce

1/2 teaspoon sugar

1 1/2 teaspoons rice wine

1/8 teaspoon white pepper

1 1/2 teaspoons light (regular) soy sauce

1/2 teaspoon dark soy sauce

1/4 cup water

FILLING

1/2 teaspoon cornstarch

1 teaspoon oyster sauce

1/2 teaspoon sesame oil

1/4 teaspoon sugar

1 teaspoon Shaoxing rice wine or dry sherry

6 ounces boneless, skinless chicken thigh, cut into 1/2-inch dice

1 tablespoon canola oil, plus more for smearing

1 clove garlic, minced

1/2 teaspoon minced fresh ginger

2 Chinese sweet sausages, diced (see Note)

2 large dried shiitake mushrooms, reconstituted (see page 13), stemmed, and chopped (1/4 cup)

1/4 pound medium shrimp, peeled, deveined, and cut into 1/2-inch pieces (3 1/2 ounces net weight)

Generous 1/2 teaspoon salt

1 cup water

4 dried lotus leaves

1. Put the rice in a bowl and add water to cover by 1 inch. Let stand for at least 2 hours (or even overnight) at room temperature.

2. Make the seasoning sauce by combining the cornstarch, oyster sauce, sugar, rice wine, white pepper, light and dark soy sauces, and water. Stir to dissolve the cornstarch. Set aside near the stove.

3. **To make the filling,** in a bowl, stir together the cornstarch, oyster sauce, sesame oil, sugar, and rice wine. Add the chicken and stir to coat well. Let marinate for 15 minutes.

4. **Heat the canola oil** in a medium skillet over high heat. Add the garlic and ginger and cook for about 15 seconds, or until aromatic. Add the chicken and cook for about 30 seconds, stirring constantly, until it is barely cooked. Add the Chinese sausages and mushrooms, and continue cooking for 30 seconds, or until the sausage is glistening and the fat is clear. Add the shrimp and cook for 1 minute, or until the shrimp turns pink. Make a well in the center, give the seasoning sauce a last stir, then pour it into the well. Stir to combine and cook for about 30 seconds, or until the mixture coheres and the chicken is cooked through. Transfer to a bowl or plate and set aside to cool completely. (The filling can be prepared up to 2 days in advance, covered, and refrigerated. Return to room temperature before using.) You should have about 2 cups.

5. **Drain the rice** in a mesh strainer and rinse under cold running water. Let it sit for 1 to 2 minutes, then give it a good shake to expel water. Select a high-sided round cake pan or metal bowl that fits into your steamer tray and put the rice in it. Toss with the salt and add the water. Put into the steamer tray and steam over boiling water (see page 17 for guidance) for 25 minutes. After about 8 minutes, stir the rice with a spatula to ensure even cooking. The rice is done when it is translucent and soft. Turn the heat off, give the rice a stir, and let it sit, covered, for 10 minutes to finish cooking. If the rice seems dry, sprinkle 1 or 2 tablespoons of water onto the hot rice, cover, and let it rest for a few minutes to soften more.

Detach the steamer tray and set it aside to cool the rice for about 15 minutes. If you are not using the rice right away, keep the rice in the steamer; make sure it is cool enough to handle before using. Use a spatula or knife to divide the rice into 8 portions.

6. **While the rice steams,** cut each lotus leaf down the middle into 2 double-layered fans. You will have 8 pieces of lotus leaf in total. Soak them in hot water for 30 minutes to soften them; I use a large roasting pan or bowl. Submerge the leaves completely by putting a plate on top.

Remove the leaves from the water, rinse them, then shake off excess water. Use scissors to cut off about 1 1/2 inches of the pointy bottom (this is hard to fold). To separate the double layers of each piece of leaf, cut each piece in half where the leaf was folded by the packing company. Then trim any excessively ragged edge. You should now have 16 pieces of leaf, each one representing one-quarter of the original whole leaf. Stack the pieces with the darker side facing up so that when you wrap the packets, the darker side will color the outer layer of rice a rich brown.

7. **For each packet,** use 2 pieces of lotus leaf. Arrange them, darker side facing up, on your work surface with the narrow ends pointing toward you and with an overlap of about 5 inches; the arrangement will look like a large open fan. Smear a little oil over the surface of the leaves to prevent sticking. Wet your fingertips, take half of one portion of rice, put it on the center of the leaf, and press it into a 3 by 4-inch rectangle. Center 1/4 cup of filling atop the rice; a measuring cup is handy for this. Take the remaining half portion of rice and press it into a 1/4-inch-thick layer that is big enough to drape over the filling. Place atop the filling.

Wrapping up the rice is as simple as wrapping a gift. First bring the bottom portion of leaf up and over the rice. Keeping one hand on

continued

the center to steady the packet, use the other hand to fold in one of the side flaps of leaf. Fold in the other side flap and finish by bringing the top down; tuck in the leaf as needed to create a neat rectangular shape. Place it seam side down in a steamer tray or on a baking sheet. Repeat with the remaining leaves, rice, and filling to make more.

If you are not steaming right away, slide the packet into an airtight plastic container or zip-top plastic bag and refrigerate for up to 3 days. Return to room temperature before steaming. To freeze for up to 3 weeks, wrap each packet in plastic wrap and then put into a zip-top freezer bag and freeze; bring to room temperature before steaming.

8. To meld the flavors and heat, steam the packets over boiling water for 15 minutes, or until heated through and soft. Transfer to a serving plate and invite guests to help themselves. They should open the packets up and dig in with chopsticks, fork, or spoon. The leaf is inedible.

Note: Available either shrink-wrapped or free of packaging at Chinese and Southeast Asian markets, Chinese sweet sausages are dried and look shriveled up and hard. Don't be put off by their appearance. *Lop chong* (the Cantonese name) are rich, savory, and absolutely delicious. They are made with pork, chicken, pork liver, or duck liver and are about six inches long. I prefer the standard pork sausages; they taste sweet and have a nice amount of fat without the heaviness of liver. Check the ingredients listing for rice wine, which makes for extra tasty sausages. Refrigerate the sausages for weeks or freeze them for months.

Sticky Rice and Spiced Chicken in Banana Leaf
Lemper Ayam

Makes 8 packets, serving 4 to 6 as a snack or side dish

Banana leaf packets of coconut sticky rice are prepared in many parts of Southeast Asia. These spectacular ones from Indonesia are filled with intensely flavored chicken. Among my favorites, they are a fine example of Indonesian cooks' ability to create foods that are lusty, earthy, and chock-full of complexity. *Lemper ayam* are a popular snack and can be simply steamed or grilled; during cooking the banana leaf imparts a deep tealike flavor to the rice.

For the best, most robust flavor, grind the spices from seed and use the galangal and kaffir (*makrut*) lime leaf; these latter ingredients are available at Southeast Asian markets and specialty-food stores, as are the candlenuts and banana leaf. Traditional Indonesian cooks use toothpicks to close up the ends of the banana leaf, whereas many modern cooks staple them shut. Serve the packets alone or as an interesting side dish.

1¹/₂ cups sticky rice (long-grain or short-grain variety)

FILLING

Salt

¹/₂ pound boneless, skinless chicken thighs

1 tablespoon whole coriander seed or ground coriander

1 teaspoon whole cumin seed or ground cumin

1 large shallot, coarsely chopped (¹/₃ cup)

3 cloves garlic, coarsely chopped

2 candlenuts or unsalted macadamia nuts, coarsely chopped

1 medium-hot chile, such as cayenne, Fresno, Holland, or jalapeño, coarsely chopped

1-inch piece fresh or thawed, frozen galangal, peeled and coarsely chopped (optional)

2 teaspoons water

2 tablespoons canola oil

4 whole fresh or thawed, frozen kaffir lime leaves (optional)

¹/₄ cup coconut milk

¹/₂ teaspoon salt

¹/₂ cup coconut milk

¹/₄ cup water

8 (6 by 9-inch) pieces fresh or thawed, frozen banana leaf, trimmed of brown edges, rinsed, and wiped dry

1. **Put the rice** in a bowl and add water to cover by 1 inch. Let stand for at least 2 hours (or even overnight) at room temperature.

2. **To make the filling,** fill a small saucepan half full of water and add 1 teaspoon salt. Bring to a rolling boil and add the chicken. Adjust the heat to gently simmer and cook the chicken for 15 to 20 minutes, until you can stick a chopstick into the thickest part and there is very little resistance. Transfer the chicken to a bowl and set aside to cool. Discard or save the broth for another use.

When cool enough to handle, hand-shred the chicken, aiming for thick matchsticks. As you work, discard unsightly blood vessels and sinew, but keep some fat for richness.

3. **Make a flavoring** paste for the filling by grinding the coriander and cumin seeds to a powder. (If you are using ground spices, just put them right into the mini-chopper.) Transfer to an electric mini-chopper and add the shallot, garlic, candlenuts, chile, galangal, and water. Process to a soft texture resembling that

continued

of oatmeal, pausing as needed to scrape down the sides. If needed, add extra water by the teaspoon to move things along. (When using a mortar and pestle, pound the spices, then work in the other paste ingredients, adding the water gradually.)

4. **Heat the oil** in a medium skillet over medium-low heat. The oil is ready when a bit of flavoring paste sizzles gently on contact. Add the paste and fry, stirring frequently, for 5 to 7 minutes, until the mixture no longer smells raw but is wonderfully fragrant. Add the lime leaves and cook for 1 minute, or until you can smell their heady scent. Add the coconut milk, stir to combine, and add the chicken and a generous 1/4 teaspoon salt. Cook, stirring frequently, for about 8 minutes, or until the liquid has evaporated and the mixture is relatively dry. The chicken shreds should be clearly visible, with a few of them standing out from the mixture. Transfer to a plate and discard the kaffir leaves. Taste and add salt, if necessary. (The filling can be prepared up to 2 days in advance, covered, and refrigerated. Return to room temperature before using.) There should be about 1 cup.

5. **Drain the rice** in a mesh strainer and rinse. Let it sit for 1 to 2 minutes, then give it a good shake to expel water. Put the rice in a high-sided round cake pan or metal bowl that fits into your steamer tray. Toss with the salt, then add the 1/2 cup coconut milk and 1/4 cup water. Put into the steamer tray and steam over boiling water (see page 17 for guidance) for 25 minutes. After about 8 minutes, stir the rice with a spatula to ensure even cooking. The rice is done when it is translucent and soft. Turn the heat off, give the rice a stir, and let it sit, covered, for 10 minutes to finish cooking. If the rice seems dry, sprinkle 1 or 2 tablespoons of water onto the hot rice, cover, and rest for a few minutes to soften more.

Detach the steamer tray and set it aside to cool the rice for about 15 minutes. If you are not using it right away, keep the rice in the steamer; make sure it is cool enough to handle before using. Use a spatula or knife to divide the rice into 8 portions.

6. **Use one piece** of banana leaf for each packet. (If the banana leaves feel stiff, soften them by passing each over the flame of a gas stove or a hot electric burner.) Put a leaf on your work surface, smoother side up and one of the longer sides closest to you. Wet your fingertips, take about two-thirds of one portion of rice, put it on the center of the leaf, and press it into a 3 by 5-inch rectangle. Center about 2 tablespoons of filling atop the rice, spreading and pressing it into a log shape. Take the remaining one-third portion of rice and press it into a 1/4-inch-thick layer, big enough to drape over the filling. Place on top of the filling.

Bring the lower flap of banana leaf over the rice and tuck it underneath to create a tubular shape. Then roll it closed. If you like, fold the open ends together so that they form a boat shape. Otherwise, keep the ends open. Secure each end closed with a round wooden toothpick or staple. Repeat to make the remaining 7 packets.

If you are not cooking them right away, slide the packets into an airtight plastic container or zip-top plastic bag and refrigerate for up to 3 days. If the rice hardens and you plan to grill them, steam the packets into softness for 4 to 6 minutes first.

7. **To cook the packets,** you can steam them over boiling water for 4 to 6 minutes. Turn off the heat and wait for the steam to subside before lifting the lid, and then carefully lift it

away from you to avoid condensation dripping onto the dumplings. The packets should be soft and heated through. Steaming preserves the flavors of the delicate coconut rice and robust filling well.

Or, add a little edge by grilling each packet over a medium-hot fire, seam side down, for 4 to 7 minutes, until the leaf has browned or is somewhat charred on the ends; a longer grilling allows the banana leaf to impart a stronger tea-leaf aroma and flavor to the rice, but the delicateness of the rice and filling diminish.

Flip the packet over and grill for 2 to 4 minutes more, until the leaf is browned or lightly charred. (Alternatively, roast the packets on a baking sheet in the upper third of the oven at 500°F for 4 to 6 minutes on each side, until the packets gently hiss and the leaf is tinged brown and crispy.)

Regardless of cooking method, serve the packets warm or at room temperature. Remove the toothpicks or staples, unwrap, and enjoy with a fork. Remember that the leaf is inedible.

7 Legumes and Tubers

Dumplings are by nature starchy foods, but the sources of the starch are not always grains. In fact, Asian cooks often use legumes and tubers to create extraordinary dumplings. Just like wheat and rice, such ingredients are first rendered into a fine texture and then turned into dough or batter.

Legumes—beans and lentils—have a crucial role in Asian cuisines, particularly because they are nutrient-rich protein substitutes. Dumplings exploit their buttery richness in myriad ways, such as steamed Chinese buns filled with sweetened red bean filling (page 203) or mung bean filling (page 204). The recipes in this chapter showcase the Indian knack for using legumes in delightful snacks. Delicate mung beans, arguably one of the workhorses of the Asian kitchen, are soaked and ground to make tender *moong dal vada*. Spiced potato dumplings (*batata vada*) get a thin coating of batter made from garbanzo bean flour.

When selecting tubers for dumplings, dryish varieties are preferred because they will not generate an overly soft dough that is difficult to handle. Steamed and mashed tubers, such as sweet potato and taro root, are mixed with flour to make a malleable dough. The resulting dumplings showcase the essence of the tuber.

For instance, Malay *cucur badak* has a chewy soft shell of sweet potato that marvelously contrasts with the spicy, fluffy filling of lemongrass and coconut. Cantonese taro puffs, a dim sum classic, celebrate the ancient tuber by capturing its nutty sweetness in the dough, which flowers to form a crisp shell during cooking. Taro root has long been a staple for people in China and Southeast Asia, perhaps since prehistoric times before rice was used, and sweet potato, native to the Americas, was introduced to Asia in the sixteenth century. Both have sustained Asia's populations and expanded its cuisines.

All the recipes in this chapter are deep-fried, and there is no alternative cooking method. The delicious results are not greasy, and the cooking smell is inviting. If you are new to deep-frying, see page 18 for helpful tips.

Fried Mung Bean Dumplings

Moong Dal Vada

Makes 16 to 18 dumplings, serving 4 to 6 as a snack

These flavorful little fried dumplings and the spiced potato balls on page 183 are members of the *vada* family of Indian snacks. They vary in size and shape, with some resembling doughnuts, but they often feature a thick batter of ground legumes and are deep-fried to yield chewy-crisp skins. Whereas potato *batata vada* is coated with a batter made from garbanzo bean flour, this preparation is all about the nutty richness of mung beans.

Moong dal vada are easy to prepare and really quite approachable; yellow split hulled mung beans are sold at Asian markets as well as health food stores. Get the beans soaking (I have had them sit for 16 hours) and the rest comes together quickly with the help of a food processor. These dumplings are best hot from the oil, but they are not bad reheated, either.

1/2 cup yellow split hulled mung beans

1/4 cup finely chopped yellow onion

1 hot green chile, such as Thai or serrano, finely chopped

1 tablespoon minced fresh ginger

2 tablespoons lightly packed chopped fresh cilantro (leaves and stems)

3 tablespoons water

1/4 teaspoon plus 1/8 teaspoon salt

1/8 teaspoon baking soda

11/2 tablespoons all-purpose bleached or unbleached flour

Canola or peanut oil, for deep-frying

1/3 cup Tamarind and Date Chutney (page 220) and/or Green Chutney (page 221)

1. Rinse the mung beans, put them in a bowl, and add water to cover by 11/2 inches. Soak for at least 4 hours, or as long as 16 hours.

2. When you are ready to fry, drain the beans in a mesh strainer. Combine the onion, chile, ginger, and cilantro in a bowl and set nearby.

3. Give the mung beans a few last shakes to expel excess water and then put into a food processor. Add the water, salt, and baking soda. Process to a slightly creamy texture, like that of polenta. When pinched between your fingers, the beans should feel soft but slightly coarse. Pause the machine as needed to scrape down the sides of the bowl.

When you are satisfied with the texture of the beans, add the flour and pulse a few times to incorporate. Transfer to the bowl of onions and aromatics. Use a spatula to gently fold and combine the ingredients. Set aside.

4. Pour 1 inch of oil into a medium saucepan, wok, or deep skillet. Heat over medium-high heat until 320° to 340°F on a deep-fry thermometer. (If you don't have a thermometer, stick a *dry* bamboo chopstick into the oil; if it takes 1 to 2 seconds for bubbles to rise to the surface and encircle the chopstick, the oil is ready.) Lower the flame slightly to steady the heat.

5. Line a plate with paper towels and place near the stove. To make each dumpling, you'll need two spoons. Scoop up about 1 tablespoon of batter with one spoon and pass the batter back and forth 1 or 2 times between the two spoons to create a neat mound. Then use one spoon to

continued

gently scoot the batter from the other spoon into the hot oil; do this close to the oil surface to maintain the round shape. The dumplings will not be uniform, but do your best to make them equivalent in size and shape. Repeat, and fry as many dumplings as can fit without crowding, about 6 to 8 per batch.

Fry, stirring and turning the dumplings often, for about 3 minutes, or until slightly puffed up and golden brown. Use a slotted spoon or skimmer to remove the dumplings from the oil and put them on the towel-lined plate to drain and cool. Adjust the heat before frying more.

6. **Serve hot with** both or one of the chutneys. Leftover dumplings can be refrigerated, returned to room temperature, and reheated in a 350°F oven for about 6 minutes, or until hot; prolonged reheating will turn the dumplings chewy and unpleasant.

Tangy Spiced Potato Dumplings

Batata Vada

Makes 18 to 20 dumplings, serving 4 to 6

A favorite Indian snack, *batata vada* are thinly coated by a batter made with garbanzo bean flour, which fries up crisp and then settles into a delicate chewiness. Inside, the cheery yellow potato filling (colored by turmeric) speckled by mustard seed bursts with flavor from chile, ginger, lime juice, and fresh herbs. Each one is a small eating adventure in trying to parse the individual elements while enjoying the synergistic whole. You can make the experience more fun with plops of chutney.

Called *bondas* in Southern India and *batata vada* in Northern India, these dumplings are beloved all over the country. In Bombay, they are shaped as patties and served in a bun as a hamburger-like sandwich called *vada pao*. Garbanzo bean flour (called *bésan* in Hindi) is available at Indian grocery stores and health food markets. It has numerous uses in Indian cuisine, as a thickener as well as in batters for fried snacks.

FILLING

3 medium red (boiling) potatoes (1¼ pounds)

1 teaspoon plus scant ½ teaspoon salt

1 tablespoon canola oil

1 teaspoon brown or black mustard seeds

1 to 3 hot green chiles, such as Thai or serrano, finely chopped

2 to 3 teaspoons minced fresh ginger

¼ teaspoon ground turmeric

10 to 12 curry leaves, chopped (optional) (see Note)

2 or 4 tablespoons finely chopped fresh cilantro, leafy tops only (use larger quantity if not using curry leaves)

1½ tablespoons fresh lime juice

¼ pound (1 cup) garbanzo bean flour

½ teaspoon salt

Scant ¼ teaspoon ground turmeric

¼ teaspoon baking soda

½ cup water

Canola or peanut oil, for deep-frying

⅔ cup Tamarind and Date Chutney (page 220) and/or Green Chutney (page 221)

1. To make the filling, peel and quarter the potatoes. Half-fill a medium pot with water and add the 1 teaspoon salt. Bring the water to a boil and add the potatoes. After the water returns to a boil, adjust the heat to bubble gently for about 20 minutes, or until the potatoes are tender but not falling apart; test by sticking a thin-blade knife into a piece of potato.

Drain and transfer to a bowl. Partially cover with a foil tent or pot lid to keep warm. Set aside.

2. Heat the oil in a medium skillet over medium-high heat until nearly smoking. Add the mustard seeds, lower the heat to medium, and partially cover. When the seeds sputter and pop, giving off a nutty aroma, you can shake the skillet or briefly remove it from the heat to mitigate the drama.

When the noise stops, add the chile and ginger. Cook, stirring, for about 30 seconds, or until fragrant. Remove from the heat and stir in the turmeric, curry leaves, and cilantro.

Add to the potato, then sprinkle in the remaining scant ½ teaspoon salt and lime

continued

juice. Mash the potato to combine the ingredients. Aim for a fairly smooth mixture with small chunks of potato to lend a nice texture. Taste and if needed, add extra salt and/or lime juice for depth and tang; the lime juice also cuts some of the heat.

3. **Use your hands** to shape the potato mixture into sixteen balls, each about 1¹/₂ inches in diameter. As you work, set the finished balls on a baking sheet or platter. Set near the stove.

4. **To make the** batter, whisk together the garbanzo bean flour, salt, turmeric, and baking soda. Whisk in the water to create a mustard-colored batter that resembles thick pancake batter. Add additional water by the teaspoon if it is too thick. Set near the stove.

5. **Line a plate** with paper towels and place near the stove. Pour 2 inches of oil into a medium saucepan, wok, or Dutch oven. Heat over medium-high heat to about 350°F on a deep-fry thermometer. (If you do not have a deep-fry thermometer, stick a *dry* bamboo chopstick into the oil; if bubbles rise immediately to the surface and encircle the chopstick, the oil is ready.)

Fry in batches of 5 to 8, as many as can comfortably fit in the pan. Use your fingers to dip, roll, and coat each potato ball in the batter; the surface will not be evenly coated, and there may be some small peaks of batter, which may fry up as charming horns. Gently slip the dumpling into the hot oil. Fry for 5 to 7 minutes, gently stirring and turning occasionally. After about 3 minutes, the balls should float to the top. When they are golden brown, use a slotted spoon or skimmer to scoop them up and transfer them to the paper towels to drain. Repeat to fry the remaining potato balls; adjust the heat as needed.

6. **Serve the** *batata vada* hot, warm, or at room temperature with both or one of the chutneys. Refrigerate leftovers, bring to room temperature, and reheat in a 350°F oven for about 6 minutes, or until hot.

Note: Resembling tender, svelte bay leaves in looks, but full of lemony zing, slender fresh curry leaves are available at Indian markets and some Southeast Asian markets. Whole branches are sold in plastic bags. Look for fresh, supple leaves and avoid dried ones. They keep well frozen for up to 3 months.

Sweet Potato, Shrimp, and Lemongrass Dumplings
Cucur Badak

Makes 16 dumplings, serving 6 to 8 as a snack

Soft and somewhat elastic on the outside, this Malaysian morsel contains a spritely filling of dried shrimp, shallot, ginger, lemongrass, chile, and grated coconut. After I tasted my first one in Kuala Lumpur, I quickly learned to say "choo-choo ba-dah" like a local so that I could buy them from street vendors whenever possible.

Use the yellow-fleshed sweet potatoes with pale skin because this variety has a lower moisture content and will yield manageable dough that is not too sticky. For the dough, I have provided a range so that you can make dainty or moderate-size dumplings. To determine the amount of flour, use the original weight of the sweet potato. If it weighs 3/4 pound, use 3/4 cup (33/4 ounces) of flour. A 1-pound potato requires 1 cup (5 ounces) of flour.

Whole unpeeled shrimp traditionally crown the dumpling, but modern versions sold by vendors often lack them. If you opt for the charming old-fashioned topping, purchase shell-on white shrimp (not tiger shrimp) which have edible, thin shells; they are sold at Asian markets.

FILLING

3 tablespoons dried shrimp

1 stalk lemongrass

1 shallot, chopped (1/4 cup)

1 tablespoon chopped fresh ginger

1 or 2 red Thai chiles, chopped

2 tablespoons canola oil

1/2 cup fresh or thawed, frozen grated coconut, (see page 225)

1 pinch of ground turmeric

1/2 teaspoon sugar

1/4 teaspoon salt

3/4 to 1 pound yellow-fleshed sweet potato (1 medium or medium-large one)

Generous 1/4 teaspoon salt

33/4 to 5 ounces (3/4 to 1 cup) all-purpose bleached or unbleached flour (see above for amount to use), plus extra as needed

16 medium white shrimp, trimmed of feet and tails (use scissors to snip) (optional)

Canola or peanut oil, for deep-frying

1. **To make the filling,** put the dried shrimp in a small bowl, add warm water to cover, and set aside to soften for 10 to 15 minutes. Rinse, drain well, and roughly chop. Set aside.

2. **Trim the lemongrass** stalk by removing any hard or loose parts that will be difficult to cut. To do that, peel off any dry or loose outer layers. Then, cut off the bottom part between the end and just below the widest point of the bulbous portion. Finish by cutting off the dry, tough portion at the top. The remaining stalk should be smooth and firm.

Cut the trimmed stalk into 3 or 4-inch sections, then halve each lengthwise. Working with two halves at time, put them cut side down, then cut them crosswise into thin half moons; repeat with the other halves. Finish by roughly chopping with a rocking motion of your knife. Measure 3 tablespoons and transfer to an electric mini-chopper; save any remaining lemongrass for another use.

continued

Process the lemongrass to a fine texture, pausing to scrape down the sides as needed. Add the dried shrimp, shallot, ginger, and chiles. Process to a texture to match that of the grated coconut. Occasionally pause and scrape down the bowl to process evenly.

3. **Heat the oil** in a medium skillet over medium-high heat. Add the dried shrimp mixture and cook, stirring often, for about 1 minute, until the mixture is fragrant with the smell of lemongrass and briny shrimp. Add the coconut, turmeric, sugar, and salt, and cook, stirring frequently, for about 3 minutes, until the coconut has absorbed the yellow turmeric color and the overall mixture has dried out a bit and is somewhat fluffy. Remove from the heat, taste, and add extra salt or sugar, as needed. Transfer to a bowl and set aside to cool. Cover and refrigerate overnight if you are making the filling in advance. You should have about 1 cup.

4. **To make the dough,** bring water to a boil for steaming (see page 17 for guidance). Meanwhile, peel the sweet potato, making sure you remove any hard spots that will not mash up later. Cut the potato into 1-inch chunks and then put into a steamer tray. Steam the potato over boiling water for about 8 minutes, or until tender. Test by stabbing a few pieces with a thin-bladed knife. Detach the steamer tray and set aside to cool and dry for 3 to 5 minutes; the potato mashes easily when warm, and a drier potato yields a less sticky dough.

5. **Mash the potato** with the salt to a smooth texture; remove any stringy or hard bits as you mash. Then incorporate the flour, half at a time, to create a medium-firm dough. Use the potato masher or a wooden spoon to combine the ingredients at first and then switch to one hand to knead the dough in the bowl. Gather the dough into a ball and continue kneading it for 4 to 5 minutes on a well-floured surface.

Initially, as the flour becomes hydrated, the dough will soften and become sticky. Work in extra flour as you knead; I typically work in about 2 tablespoons of additional flour. The finished dough should feel medium-soft and supple. Press your finger in and a deep indentation will remain. Cover with plastic wrap or an inverted bowl and set aside to rest for 30 minutes to relax and become earlobe soft. The dough can sit for a few hours at room temperature, but it will soften further and become stickier, requiring you to use extra flour when shaping the dumplings.

6. **Line a baking sheet** with parchment paper and dust the paper with flour. To assemble the dumplings, cut the dough in half, keeping one half covered while you work on the other. Roll the dough into a log and cut it into 8 equal-size pieces. Dust your hands with flour and roll each piece into a ball; if the dough feels sticky, be liberal with the flour.

To make each dumpling, put it on a floured work surface and pat it with your fingers into a circle a scant 1/4 inch thick and 2 1/2 to 2 3/4 inches in diameter. Pick it up and press the rim with your fingertips to widen the circle to 3 to 3 1/4 inches and to make the edge thinner than the center.

Gently cup one hand and put the dough circle in that hand, placing it toward your fingertips, which will cradle the dumpling as you shape it. Place about 1 lightly packed tablespoon of filling in the center. Gently press on the filling with the back of the spoon to create a shallow well; your hand will naturally cup a little tighter. Use your free hand to gather, pleat, and pinch the dough together to completely enclose the filling. Pinch and twist

continued

off any excess dough. If the pleated side feels sticky, press it on some flour. Gently roll the ball between your hands to smooth out the surface. You'll have a 1 1/2 to 1 3/4-inch ball.

Put the ball on your work surface and gently press on it to create a thick disk that is a scant 1 inch thick and 1 3/4 to 2 inches in diameter. If you are using the shrimp garnish, finish the dumpling with a shrimp, bending the shrimp to create a C-shape, and press it into the dough to ensure it sticks. Regardless, put the shaped dumpling on the prepared baking sheet. Repeat to make more dumplings from the cut pieces of dough before working on the remaining half of dough.

7. Line a platter with paper towels and place near the stove. Pour oil to a depth of 1 inch into a medium saucepan, wok, or deep skillet. Heat over medium-high heat to about 325°F

on a deep-fry thermometer. (If you don't have a deep-fry thermometer, stick a *dry* bamboo chopstick into the oil; if it takes about 2 seconds for bubbles to rise to the surface and encircle the chopstick, the oil is ready.)

Fry the dumplings in batches, stirring and turning often, for about 3 minutes, or until browned on both sides. Take care to adjust the heat in between batches; aim to keep the temperature at or below 325°F because a higher temperature browns the dumplings too quickly and creates too many large blisters, which affects their appearance, not their flavor.

8. Drain the dumplings on the paper towels. Let them cool for about 5 minutes before serving. Leftover dumplings can be refrigerated and reheated in a 350°F oven for about 10 minutes, or until hot. They can be frozen for up to a month, too; thaw completely before reheating.

Taro Puffs
Yù Jiǎo

Makes 12 dumplings, serving 4 to 6 as a snack

A perfect taro puff (pictured on page ii) is ethereal; its gossamer shell crisp and not greasy. The underside of the dough is rich and creamy, enveloping a well-seasoned filling.

I eagerly look for *wu gok*, as taro puffs are called in Cantonese, at dim sum restaurants. Unfortunately, most versions are lackluster and leaden by the time I pick them off the cart. Homemade ones are significantly better because they are consistently tasty and hold their crispness for hours. The dough and filling can be prepared in advance and refrigerated for a couple of days. Dumpling assembly is easy, and the deep-frying is fast.

Brown and barrel-shaped with distinctive rings, taro is sold at Asian and Latin markets, often near other tubers like sweet potato. For this recipe, the large variety is used because its flesh is much drier than that of the small taro. Select a firm, full one with no signs of shriveling or molding. When cut open, taro should smell fresh; its flesh should be bright and feel firm like coconut. Store taro in a cool, dry spot and use it within a few days of purchase. Peeled and trimmed taro sold in Cryovac packaging works great.

Feel free to substitute chicken thigh for the pork. Finely chopped bamboo shoots, water chestnut, or rehydrated shiitake mushrooms can replace the shrimp. Weighing the wheat starch and cooked taro and frying at moderately high heat ensures that the puff will hold together.

FILLING

3 ounces well-trimmed pork shoulder, cut into 1/4-inch dice

1 teaspoon dark soy sauce

1/2 teaspoon minced fresh ginger

3 ounces medium shrimp, peeled and deveined (2 1/2 ounces net weight)

1/4 teaspoon plus 1 pinch of salt

1 pinch of white pepper

1/2 teaspoon sugar

1 teaspoon cornstarch

1/4 teaspoon sesame oil

1 1/2 teaspoons oyster sauce

1 teaspoon Shaoxing rice wine or dry sherry

1 tablespoon water

1 tablespoon canola oil

1 tablespoon finely chopped scallion (white and green parts)

DOUGH

1 (3/4 to 1-pound) taro root (use large variety)

1 3/4 ounces (1/3 cup) wheat starch

About 1/3 cup just-boiled water (see Note, page 23)

1/2 teaspoon salt

1 1/4 teaspoons sugar

1/4 cup lard or solid vegetable shortening, at room temperature

Canola or peanut oil, for deep-frying

1. To make the filling, combine the pork, dark soy sauce, and ginger in a bowl. Set aside to marinate.

2. **Toss the shrimp** with the 1/4 teaspoon salt and then rinse. Drain well and pat dry with paper towels. Finely chop and set aside.

continued

3. Make the seasoning sauce by combining the pinch of salt, white pepper, sugar, cornstarch, sesame oil, oyster sauce, rice wine, and water in a bowl. Stir to dissolve the cornstarch. Set aside.

4. Heat the canola oil in a medium skillet over high heat. Add the pork and cook, stirring constantly, for about 1 minute, or until the pork has turned a beautiful glossy brown. Add the shrimp and continue stirring for about 1 minute to cook the shrimp through. Give the seasoning sauce a stir and add to the mixture. Stir for about 15 seconds, or until the mixture has cohered and taken on a sheen. Turn off the heat and stir in the scallion. Taste and add adjust the flavor as necessary. Transfer to a small bowl and let cool completely. Cover and refrigerate for at least 2 hours, and as long as 2 days. You should have about 3/4 cup.

5. To make the dough, trim off the ends of the taro root to reveal the flesh. Stand the taro on its wider end and use a knife in downward motions to remove 1/4 to 1/3 inch of the outer layer, which includes the rough brown skin and a tough ring of flesh where there is a greater concentration of the speckled chocolate brown flecks. As you work all around the taro, your knife blade may sense the density difference between the more tender inner flesh and the harder outer layer. Do not worry about removing it all because you will have another chance later.

Halve the taro lengthwise and then cut into half-circles about 3/4 inch thick. Put into a bowl of water and set aside while you bring water to a boil for steaming (see page 17 for guidance).

6. Drain the taro, put it in a steamer tray (there is no need to line it), and steam over boiling water for 30 to 45 minutes, until the taro is soft. Poke several pieces with a toothpick; there should be no resistance. Depending on your trimming job, some areas at the rim may be hard still. That is fine because you will shortly discard them. Aim for most of the flesh to be soft. The texture of cooked taro will seem dry.

Remove the steamer tray and set aside to cool for about 5 minutes, or until the taro is still warm but cool enough to handle with your fingers. Warm taro mashes easily.

7. While the taro steams, put the wheat starch in a bowl. Gradually add the water, stirring with a wooden spoon or rubber spatula. When the mixture is pasty and has a texture resembling frosting, stop adding water. There may be leftover water. Set aside. Expect the wheat starch to firm up as it sits. Cover if it begins to dry.

8. Pick up each taro piece and crumble and mash it with your fingers into a bowl. It should fall apart easily. Discard all the hard pieces. Tiny firm bits suspended in the mash are fine.

Measure out 1/2 pound (1 packed cup) and transfer to the bowl of wheat starch; discard or save the extra taro for another use. Add the salt and sugar and combine the ingredients with your fingers until well blended. Add the lard and keep mixing and kneading for 1 to 2 minutes, until a soft dough with the texture of mashed potatoes forms. Gather the dough into a ball and put it in a clean, dry bowl. Cover the bowl with plastic wrap and refrigerate for at least 2 hours, and as long as 2 days. Firm dough is easier to work with.

9. When you are ready to form the dumplings, remove the dough and filling from the refrigerator. Line a baking sheet or plate with parchment paper.

On an unfloured work surface, roll the dough into a thick 12-inch log. Cut the log into 12 even-size pieces. Roll each one into a ball and set aside. Chill the dough balls for about 5 minutes to firm them up so that they are easier to manipulate, if you like.

For each dumpling, take a ball of dough and use your thumb to press a well in the center. Then press on the walls with your fingers to form a shallow bowl a good 2 1/2 inches wide and 1/4 inch thick. Put a scant tablespoon of filling in the center and tap it gently to flatten it out. Then bring up the edges of the dough to close up the dumpling. Gently push and press the dough to fully enclose the filling. It should look like a small football (see page 164 for guidance). Put it on the work surface and neaten it up, if you like. Put the finished dumpling on the prepared plate. Repeat with the remaining dough and filling.

10. To fry the dumplings, pour 1 1/2 inches of oil into a medium saucepan. Because the oil will dramatically bubble during frying, make sure that there is at least 2 inches between the top level of the oil and the rim of the pan. Heat over medium-high heat until 360° to 370°F on a deep-fry thermometer. (Without a thermometer, test a dumpling to gauge the oil temperature. The chopstick test here is not as helpful.)

When frying these dumplings, begin at a medium-high oil temperature and then immediately lower the heat after the dumplings have set. This assures that the dumplings do not disintegrate, creates their signature lacy coating, and allows them to adequately cook without browning too fast.

Fry in manageable batches of 3 dumplings. After adding the dumplings to the oil, the oil will rush to a boil, sending the dumplings floating upward. At that point, *lower* the heat to medium-low. Fry for 2 to 3 minutes, until the dumplings are a beautiful brown. If they stick together, nudge them a bit as they fry, and they will eventually separate. Use a slotted spoon or skimmer to lift the dumplings from the oil (you will hear them sizzle still) and drain them on paper towels.

Raise the heat to medium-high to return the oil temperature to a moderately high temperature between batches. Skim and discard any floating bits in the oil, as needed.

11. Serve hot, warm, or at room temperature, as long as the dumplings are crisp. Present on a platter, each one each cut in half with scissors or a knife so it is easy to pick up with chopsticks.

Freshly fried dumplings will hold their crispness for about 3 hours if left at room temperature. To serve them hot, reheat in a 400°F oven for about 5 minutes. Refrigerated ones soften, and the best way to revive them is by refrying in 350°F oil for about 1 minute; the lacy crispness will return.

8 Sweet Treasures

To the uninitiated palate, Asian sweet dumplings may seem very odd. They don't resemble common Western sweet dumplings, such as baked apples wrapped in pastry. They can taste mildly sweet, savory-sweet, tart-sweet, or intensely sweet. The morsels may be cloaked in syrup, deep-fried and hollow, or chewy-soft.

But despite these differences, Asian sweet dumplings please people just as much as their Western counterparts do. Both speak of rich culinary traditions and are treasured reminders of home.

The Asian repertoire of sweet dumplings is vast, not just because Asia itself is huge and varied, but because Asian people love to nibble all day long. It's no wonder that cooks developed a knack for preparing bite-size treats that delight and satisfy. Plus, sweets are considered snack foods and are thus not limited to the dessert course at the end of a meal.

This chapter offers a glimpse into the world of Asian sweet dumplings, with a collection of baked, poached, steamed, and fried morsels. In many respects, they are sweet extensions of the culinary concepts behind savory dumplings.

Filipino *turon* are delectable banana spring rolls. The art of making rich pastries is exemplified in diminutive Singaporean *kuih* tarts, which look like tiny tangerines but are buttery crusts encasing a spiced pineapple jam. Indian *gulab jamun* are deep-fried, rich orbs of reduced milk soaked in fragrant syrup and embody the philosophy of dumpling makers who do more with less.

Sticky rice flour and legumes come together for East and Southeast Asian dumplings that are poached to a silky softness and deep-fried to a glorious crisp. Malay *onde onde* employ sticky rice flour, too, but contain melted palm sugar inside, making for a fun eating experience. The creative and practical use of leaves for dumpling making is highlighted by Thai sticky rice and coconut packets, which rely on banana leaves to shape and aromatize the creamy rice contents.

Round out your dumpling-making skills with a few sweet preparations, a number of which are delicious ancient foods made from a humble handful of ingredients. Once you've made one, it's hard to stop.

Fried Banana Spring Rolls

Turon

Makes 12, serving 4 to 6

Full of flavor and textural contrast, Filipino *turon* embody the Asian knack for taking the commonplace banana and turning it into a spectacular fried treat. A popular street food, these fried rolls benefit from the delicate crispness of Shanghai spring roll skins. The bananas become creamy inside during frying and rather custardlike.

You can eat these rolls alone or gild the lily with a scoop of rich vanilla ice cream or drizzle of caramel *dulce de leche*. Thin strips of jackfruit can be rolled up with the banana, too. The shallow frying can get a little dramatic at the end, but it is well worth the clean-up.

3 ripe, but firm bananas, each about 7 inches long

3 tablespoons dark brown sugar

12 (6 to 7-inch) Shanghai Spring Roll Skins (page 81)

1 large egg, well beaten

Canola or peanut oil, for frying

1. Peel the bananas, removing any strings as you work. Cut each in half crosswise, then halve each lengthwise. You now have 12 pieces. Put the brown sugar on a plate and coat the bananas with the sugar. Most of it will stick to the cut sides. Set aside.

2. Line a baking sheet with parchment paper. For each spring roll, place a skin, smooth side down, on your work surface. Horizontally position a piece of sugared banana slightly below the center of the skin. Bring up the bottom flap to cover the banana, brush some beaten egg on all of the exposed edges to ensure a good seal, fold in the sides, then roll it up cigar style (see page 75 for guidance). Set the finished rolls, seam side down, on the baking sheet. Cover the spring rolls with a kitchen towel to prevent drying.

3. To fry, heat 3/4 inch of oil in a wok, saucepan, or deep skillet over medium-high heat to about 350°F on a deep-fry thermometer. (If you don't have a thermometer, stick a *dry* bamboo chopstick into the oil; if bubbles rise immediately to the surface and encircle the chopstick, the oil is ready.) Fry a few spring rolls at a time to prevent crowding, turning as needed, for about 3 minutes, or until golden brown.

In the last 30 seconds or so, the sugars will have melted and leaked a bit. The frying may get louder and be somewhat dramatic. Slightly reduce the heat to brown the skins sufficiently, if needed. Once the rolls are browned, use a skimmer to scoop them up, *briefly* rest them on paper towel (they will stick to the paper if left too long), then transfer to a communal platter or individual plates. Adjust the oil temperature, as needed, then repeat with the remaining rolls. Let cool for 1 minute before diving in.

Spiced Pineapple-Filled Pastries

Kuih Tart

Makes 32 pastries

Eating is practically a sport in Singapore, and these very popular pastries are part of the city-state's eclectic and irresistible cuisine. Possibly Portuguese in origin, these intensely flavored pineapple tarts come in many shapes, from fancy open-faced tarts to carefully carved tiny pineapples. However, for the Lunar New Year, they're made to resemble tangerines, a symbol of good fortune; in Chinese, tangerine is a homonym for "gold." A decorative clove (not meant for consumption!) sits atop each one to mimic the fruit's stem.

Traditionally, fresh grated pineapple is used, but many modern cooks opt for canned pineapple. A long simmering turns the fragrant pineapple into a lovely amber-colored jam resembling tangerine flesh. Instead of adding food coloring to the egg-yolk glaze to enhance the pastry's appearance, I add a touch of ground annatto seed to brighten up the dough. Without the natural colorant, the pastries still taste great.

FILLING

1 (20-ounce) can crushed pineapple in natural juice, drained and juice reserved

10 tablespoons sugar

1/2 whole star anise (4 robust points)

1 (3-inch) cinnamon stick or piece of cassia bark

2 whole cloves

1 pinch of salt

DOUGH

10 ounces (2 cups) all-purpose bleached flour

3 tablespoons cornstarch

3/4 teaspoon salt

1/8 teaspoon ground annatto (optional) (see Note)

3/4 cup (1 1/2 sticks) plus 1 tablespoon unsalted butter, at room temperature

2/3 cup confectioners' sugar

1 large whole egg plus 1 large egg yolk, lightly beaten

1 1/2 teaspoons vanilla extract

2 large egg yolks, lightly beaten and strained

32 whole cloves

1. To make the filling, put the drained pineapple in a food processor and pulse 10 to 15 times to achieve an even, finely chopped texture.

Transfer to a small saucepan and add the reserved juice, sugar, star anise, cinnamon stick, cloves, and salt. Bring to a boil over medium-high heat, stirring frequently, and taste. If needed, add extra sugar for a tangy-sweet balance. Decrease the heat to medium-low and gently simmer, stirring occasionally, for about 1 3/4 hours total, or until nearly all the liquid has evaporated and the thickened mixture has darkened to an amber-orange color. During the last 30 minutes, stir more often to prevent scorching. Stir the finished jam; it should hold its shape with just a bit of liquid bubbling at the bottom.

2. Remove the cinnamon stick, star anise, and cloves. Transfer to a bowl and set aside for about 2 hours to cool and firm up. Cover and refrigerate up to a week. The jam can be used chilled. Makes about 1 cup.

3. To make the dough, sift together the flour, cornstarch, salt, and annatto. Set aside.

Use an electric mixer to cream together the butter and confectioners' sugar until light

continued

and fluffy. Add the whole egg and egg yolk and vanilla, then beat to blend well. Use a spatula or wooden spoon to mix in the flour mixture, one-third at a time, to create a somewhat sticky dough. The mixture will seem dry at first, but keep stirring and folding to moisten the flour and bring it together into a rough mass that is soft like marzipan. Transfer the dough to a work surface, press it into a ball, and then pat into a 1-inch-thick disk. Wrap in plastic wrap and chill for 1 hour to firm up, or refrigerate for up to 2 days, letting the dough sit out at room temperature for about 1 hour to become malleable.

4. **Line 2 baking sheets** with parchment paper. Unwrap the dough and put it on a lightly floured work surface. Cut it in half; cover one-half and keep it chilled while you work with the other half. Gently squeeze on the dough to elongate it and then roll it into a 1-inch-thick log. Use a knife to cut the log into 16 pieces. (Quarter the log first to easily cut even-size pieces. The tapered end pieces should be cut a little longer than the others.)

Use an Asian dowel-style rolling pin to roll each piece of dough into a 3 to $3^1/4$-inch-diameter circle. As with many dumpling wrappers, these should be thicker in the middle than at the edges. Apply more pressure with your rolling pin on the outer $1/2$-inch border to achieve a thin rim. (For guidance on rolling, see "Forming Wrappers from Basic Dumpling Dough," step 5, page 24.)

5. **To assemble the** pastries, hold a wrapper in one hand and use a bamboo dumpling spatula, dinner knife, or spoon to place a scant $1^1/2$ teaspoons of jam at the center. Smooth and tap the jam into an egg yolk shape,

keeping about $1/2$ to $3/4$ inch of wrapper clear on all sides. To enclose the jam, choose a spot on the wrapper rim, say at 3 o'clock, and fold the wrapper rim toward the center. Keep working around the rim to fold in more of the wrapper, gently pinching and pressing the dough together as you go. You will naturally create small pleats. When all the dough has been folded inward, the jam should be sealed up or nearly sealed up. Use your fingers to lightly pinch or push the dough to cover up any openings. Cup the pastry in your hands and gently roll it around to form a smooth ball. If any holes appear, nudge a bit of dough or pinch off a tiny amount from the bottom to patch. Place the pastry, pleated side down, on the prepared baking sheet. Repeat with the remaining dough, spacing the pastries 2 inches apart on the baking sheet, before working on the other half of dough.

6. **Before baking,** chill the pastries for 15 minutes. Meanwhile, position a rack in the middle of the oven and preheat to 350°F.

7. **Brush the pastries** with egg yolk and stick a clove, ball end down, in the center of each one. Bake for 24 to 26 minutes, until golden. Remove from the oven and cool completely on a rack. During cooling, the pastries darken a tad, cracks shrink, and leaking jam dries. Serve or store in an airtight container.

Note: Purchase ground annatto or whole annatto seeds (also known as achiote) at Asian or Latin markets; also check the Mexican spice section at regular supermarkets. If you have whole seeds, use an electric spice grinder (a coffee grinder dedicated to spices) to pulverize them into a pale orange powder.

Milk Dumplings in Cardamom and Saffron Syrup

Gulab Jamun

Makes 12 dumplings, serving 4 to 6

Cakey, spongy, and deliriously delicious *gulab jamun* is one of India's great contributions to the world of sweets. Shaped as small spheres that are fried and then soaked in a fragrant sugar syrup, the rich brown dumplings are frequently on restaurant menus and are enjoyed during special occasions such as Diwali, the autumn festival of lights, which is also known as the festival of sweets.

The dumplings, traditionally made from *khoya* (milk that has been cooked down), are named for their resemblance to juicy, purple-brown *jamun* fruit. Cardamom is typically part of the sugar syrup, but you can add saffron and/or rose flower water, too; *gulab* means "rose" in Hindi.

Cooking down milk is labor intensive, and many modern Indian cooks instead use nonfat dry milk to great success. The whipping cream lends richness and enhances the milk sugars, which you can smell while making the dough and frying the dumplings. For the rose flower water, I use rose-scented distilled water from France, which is sold in small blue bottles and often found at well-stocked liquor stores. If you are using rose essence, use just a few drops; it is very strong.

DUMPLINGS

$2^1/2$ ounces (1 cup) nonfat dry milk, plus more as needed

$1^1/4$ ounces ($1/4$ cup) all-purpose bleached flour

1 pinch of baking soda

$1/2$ cup whipping cream

Water, as needed

Canola or peanut oil, for deep-frying

SYRUP

$1^1/2$ cups water

$1^1/4$ to $1^1/2$ cups sugar (use maximum if you have a sweet tooth)

3 or 4 whole green cardamom pods, slightly crushed

4 or 5 saffron threads (optional)

About 2 teaspoons rose water (optional)

1 teaspoon finely chopped pistachios, for garnish

1. To make the dumplings, combine the dry milk, flour, and baking soda in a bowl. Stir to blend. Make a well in the center and pour in the whipping cream. Use a wooden spoon or spatula to stir the ingredients together into a rough ball of dough. Switch to using one hand to knead and incorporate all the bits, then transfer the dough to a work surface. Knead the dough until medium-soft and pliable. If it is slightly sticky at first, dust your hands with some dry milk. If the dough is crumbly, work in water by the $1/2$ teaspoon.

2. Roll the dough into a 12-inch log and cut into 12 even-size pieces. Roll the pieces into smooth round balls, each one about 1 inch in diameter. Apply slight pressure as you roll to make each one as crack-free as possible; otherwise, fissures may form during frying. Set the balls on your work surface and loosely cover with plastic wrap or a kitchen towel to prevent drying.

3. Place a paper towel–lined platter near the stove. Pour 1 inch of oil into a shallow sauce-

pan, wok, or deep skillet. Heat over medium-high heat to 290° to 300°F on a deep-fry thermometer. (If you don't have a deep-fry thermometer, stick a *dry* bamboo chopstick into the oil; if it takes about 4 seconds for bubbles to rise to the surface and encircle the chopstick, the oil is ready.) Slow and low-temperature frying guarantees that the dumplings cook all the way through, so they don't collapse later as they soak in the syrup, and the milk sugars caramelize nicely.

When the oil is ready, steady it by decreasing the heat to medium-low. If you like, test-fry one dumpling. After you add it to the oil, it should remain at the bottom for about 20 seconds before rising to the top. If it rises much sooner, the oil is too hot.

Fry the dumplings in 2 batches, stirring often with a slotted spoon or skimmer to ensure even cooking and browning. Adjust the heat as necessary to fry for 4 to 5 minutes, until the dumplings are a lovely reddish brown. Be patient. Lift the fried dumplings from the oil and drain on the paper towels.

4. **To make the syrup,** combine the water, sugar, cardamom, and saffron threads in a shallow, wide saucepan or deep skillet large enough to hold all the dumplings in one layer with a little room for expansion. Bring to a boil, then lower the heat to very gently simmer for 5 minutes.

Add all the fried dumplings and simmer for 15 to 20 minutes, turning them occasionally, until the dumplings are soft and enlarged, and the syrup has thickened a bit.

5. **Remove from the** heat and gently stir in the rose water. Set aside to cool for about 20 minutes before serving; expect the dumplings to shrink during cooling. (The dumplings can be prepared up to 5 days in advance and refrigerated. Return to room temperature and reheat them over medium-low heat, adding a splash of water to move things along, until soft again.)

Serve the dumplings warm or at room temperature. Present 2 or 3 dumplings in individual dessert bowls along with a little syrup; if some cardamom seeds are loose in the syrup, include them; they provide a great burst of flavor. Top each dumpling with a bit of pistachio for color and texture. Enjoy with spoons.

Sesame Seed Balls
Má Tuán

Makes 18 balls

One of the most beloved Asian sweet dumplings is crisp-chewy fried sesame seed balls. A Chinese New Year specialty that may have originated during the Tang Dynasty as palace food, they have been adopted by cooks of countless cultures to be enjoyed year-around. At Cantonese dim sum houses, this treat is called *jin deui* and usually contains sweetened red bean paste. In Vietnam, the filling typically features buttery mung beans. Ground peanuts are a quick and tasty filling option; if you select the peanut filling, use an electric mini-chopper to grind the nuts, sugar, and salt, and aim for a sandy texture. Sesame balls can be made without a filling, though I find those to be a tad lacking.

The sugar used in the rice dough makes for a golden brown skin that slightly shatters with the first bite. Slab brown candy, called *peen tong* in Cantonese and sold at Chinese markets, looks like pieces of parquet flooring. It has a complex flavor not unlike maple sugar and lends a glorious rich brown color to the finished dumplings. When it is unavailable, light brown sugar is a fine substitute. Pressing on the balls during frying is the trick to getting them to expand, resulting in their signature hollow center.

6 tablespoons Sweetened Red Bean Paste (page 203) or Sweetened Mung Bean Paste (page 204), or 1/4 cup coarsely chopped unsalted roasted peanuts ground with 2 1/2 tablespoons sugar and 2 pinches of salt

1/2 pound (generous 1 3/4 cups) glutinous (sweet) rice flour (select a Thai brand such as Erawan)

2/3 cup water

2 slabs Chinese brown candy/sugar, coarsely grated or finely chopped, or 2/3 cup lightly packed light brown sugar

1/3 cup raw hulled (white) sesame seeds

Canola or peanut oil, for deep-frying

1. If you are using one of the bean pastes for a filling, measure 1 level teaspoon of paste for each dumpling and roll each portion into a small ball. Put on a plate, cover, and set aside. If you are using the peanut filling, put it in a small bowl.

2. Put the rice flour in a bowl and make a large well in the center. Have a small bowl of water nearby for wetting your hands later.

Bring the 2/3 cup water to a boil in a small saucepan. Add the candy and stir until completely dissolved. Remove from the heat and pour the sugar syrup into the rice flour. Use a wooden spoon or spatula to combine, stirring and eventually pressing the ingredients into a ball. Transfer to a work surface (the dough will still be warm, so be careful) and knead until smooth.

3. Cut the dough into 3 pieces. Take a piece and give it a gentle squeeze. This dough tends to dry quickly due to the hot water evaporating. If cracks form, wet your hands and squeeze on the dough. Roll it on your work surface into a chubby log about 6 inches long. The extra water should soften and smooth the dough out. Cut the log into 6 even-size pieces. Roll each piece into a ball and cover with plastic wrap to prevent drying. Repeat with the remaining dough pieces to yield 18 balls total.

continued

4. **For each dumpling,** take a ball of dough and make a deep indentation to create a little cup. Aim to make the cup about 1 inch deep. You can build up the wall by pressing it between your thumb and index finger, working all the way around. Put a ball of paste or 1 teaspoon of ground peanut mixture in the well, tapping it down a bit. Close the cup, making sure that the filling is enclosed. Pinch and twist off any extra dough and seal well.

Roll the dumpling between your hands to make it perfectly round and smooth; slightly wet your hands before this final roll if the dough feels dry. Set aside and repeat to make more; cover the filled ones to prevent drying.

5. **Put the sesame** seeds in a small bowl. Dunk each dumpling into the bowl of water, shake off the excess water, and then put it in the bowl of sesame seeds. Dredge the dumpling to coat it well with sesame seeds, then place it back on your work surface. Repeat with the remaining balls. As you gain confidence, you can dunk and coat 2 balls at a time.

Working over the bowl of sesame seeds, now roll each coated ball between your palms to remove excess sesame seeds and ensure that the remaining ones adhere well. Cover the finished coated balls with plastic wrap or a kitchen towel.

6. **To deep-fry** the balls, use a wok or a pot, about 8 inches wide and 5 inches deep (for example, a 4-quart pot). Near the stove, have a platter or baking sheet lined with several thicknesses of paper towel.

Pour in the oil to a depth of 2 1/2 inches. Heat over medium-high heat to just below 350°F on a deep-fry thermometer. (If you don't have a deep-fry thermometer, stick a *dry* bamboo chopstick into the oil; if bubbles rise immediately to the surface and encircle the chopstick, the oil is ready.) Steady the oil temperature by lowering the heat to medium.

Fry the balls, 6 at a time, for 7 to 8 minutes, carefully lowering each one into the oil. The balls will lazily fry at the bottom of the pot for 2 to 4 minutes before floating to the surface. During that period, frequently turn and stir the balls to prevent uneven browning. After they rise, use the back of a metal slotted spoon or spatula to resubmerge each one in the oil and to gently press it against the side of the pan. Press and hold for 1 to 2 seconds and release; you will see the balls expand a bit. They will rotate and swim around the pot so that each can have its turn at being pressed. Keep pressing and releasing until each is about 2 1/2 times its original size; you will develop a rhythm. When the balls are about 2 inches in diameter, stop pressing and let them fry a bit longer until golden brown. Lift them from the oil, letting excess oil drip back into the pot, then place on the paper towels to drain. Fry the remaining sesame seed balls. Adjust the heat during frying so that it remains from 340° to 360°F.

Though you can eat these sesame seed balls at room temperature, when they are warm they are a tad crisper on the outside, which makes a nice contrast with the chewy inside. Do try to eat them the day they are made. If desired, reheat them in a 400°F oven for about 5 minutes until heated through and gently sizzling, or refry in 2 1/2 inches of 350°F oil for about 1 minute; they recrisp as they cool. Cover leftovers with parchment paper and keep at room temperature.

Sweetened Red Bean Paste
Hóng Dòu Shā

Makes 1¹/₃ cups

To those unfamiliar with red bean paste, the concept may seem strange, but millions of people the world over cannot imagine their favorite steamed or baked buns and deep-fried sesame seed balls without this lightly sweet, chocolate-brown filling. The richness comes from the beans themselves and from a touch of oil, though lard would be used by traditionalists. Some cooks use brown or white sugar; I use both for a deep, well-rounded sweetness. Red bean paste is sold canned, but it's overly sweet and incomparable to homemade.

Adzuki beans are available at most natural food stores, specialty grocers, and Asian markets. You can also use the small red beans sold at Chinese markets. Sometimes I add a pinch or two of salt for a savory edge, reflecting a Japanese style of bean paste. The recipe here is more in the sweeter Chinese fashion.

²/₃ cup dried adzuki or small red beans
5 tablespoons white sugar
2 tablespoons firmly packed dark brown sugar
1 to 1¹/₂ tablespoons canola oil

1. **Rinse the beans,** put them in a bowl, and cover them with 1 inch of water. Discard any floaters. Let the beans soak for 6 to 9 hours.

2. **Drain the beans** and put them in a small saucepan. Add water to cover by 2 inches and bring to a boil. Lower the heat to gently simmer for about 1¹/₄ hours, or until the beans are very soft. Some will split open. Press on one, and it should crush easily with little pressure. Remove from the heat and drain in a mesh strainer; let drain for 5 minutes to remove excess moisture. Wash the saucepan.

3. **Combine the beans** and the white and brown sugars in a food processor. Puree into a smooth chocolate-brown mixture, pausing to scrape down the sides if necessary.

4. **Combine the oil** and pureed beans in the saucepan and heat over medium heat. Stir frequently for about 5 minutes, or until the beans have pulled away from the sides of the pan and thickened into a soft paste. The paste will darken as it cooks and dries out.

5. **Transfer the paste** to a bowl and set aside at room temperature to cool completely. To prevent drying and promote even cooling, occasionally stir the paste as it sits and thickens. Use the paste after cooling. Refrigerate it for up to a week or freeze for up to a month.

Sweetened Mung Bean Paste

Nhân Đậu Xanh Ngọt

Makes 1¹/3 cups

Mung beans are a staple legume in many Asian kitchens, where their delicate, buttery flavor lends richness to both savory and sweet treats. Like red beans, mung beans can be made into a lightly sweet paste to be stuffed inside a baked or steamed bun or dumpling. In fact, the two bean pastes are practically interchangeable. Whereas sweetened red bean paste is vaguely chocolate-like, sweetened mung bean paste resembles marzipan, both in texture and nuanced flavor. This is a Vietnamese version of the paste, with vanilla to round out the flavor and salt to inject a little oomph.

Mung beans are sold at many Asian markets and health food stores. Look for the yellow ones that have been hulled and split. The green ones still have their tough skins.

²/3 cup dried, hulled, and split yellow mung beans

¹/2 cup sugar

¹/4 teaspoon salt

¹/4 teaspoon vanilla extract

3 tablespoons canola oil

1. **Rinse the mung beans,** put them in a bowl, and add water to cover by 1 inch. Let soak for 2 hours, or up to 6 hours.

2. **Line a steamer tray** with parchment paper. Drain the beans well in a mesh strainer and transfer to the prepared steamer tray. Spread the beans out evenly. Steam the beans (see page 17 for guidance) over boiling water for 8 to 15 minutes (the shorter time is for the metal steamer and the longer time is for a bamboo steamer), until the mung beans are tender. Remove the steamer tray and set aside to cool for 3 minutes.

3. **Transfer the warm beans** to a food processor and add the sugar, salt, vanilla, and oil. Process for about 90 seconds, pausing at the beginning to scrape down the sides. At first the mixture will seem too loose, but keep the machine going and eventually the texture will firm up and smooth out. When the paste is medium-soft in texture, resembling marzipan, it is done. Transfer to a plastic container and cool at room temperature before using. The paste can be refrigerated for up to 2 weeks or frozen for a month.

Sweet Rice Dumplings with Palm Sugar and Coconut
Onde Onde

Makes 24 dumplings, serving 6 to 8

Like an American "popper" snack, this diminutive sweet enjoyed in Indonesia, Malaysia, and Singapore should be eaten whole: when you bite into it, the dumpling squirts lovely melted palm sugar into your mouth. The lightly smoky, caramel-like sugar then blends with the chewy rice dough and rich grated coconut in your mouth.

These dumplings, also called *klepon*, are typically celadon green, since the dough features *pandan* (screwpine) leaves, a beloved ingredient in many parts of tropical Asia (see the Note below on buying the leaves). I like to amplify their herbal essence with vanilla. If *pandan* leaves are unavailable, just the vanilla and water are fine. Many cooks add food coloring for a cheery mint-green note; I prefer not to.

Seek out Malaysian and Indonesian palm sugar (called *gula melaka* and *gula jawa*, respectively) for the best results. It is sold at Chinese and Southeast Asian markets, usually as thick cylinders wrapped in paper or plastic. The reddish-brown sugar is solid but moist. Shave off thin pieces with a knife to measure it out easily. If palm sugar is unavailable, combine 1/4 cup firmly packed dark brown sugar and enough molasses (a good tablespoon) to moisten the sugar well enough to roll it into balls.

1/4 cup packed palm sugar

1 cup finely shredded fresh or frozen, thawed coconut (see page 225)

Scant 1/8 teaspoon salt

4 to 6 large fresh or frozen, thawed pandan leaves (optional)

1/2 cup water

1/2 teaspoon vanilla extract

1 drop green food coloring mixed with 1 teaspoon water (optional)

4 1/2 ounces (1 cup) glutinous (sweet) rice flour (any Thai brand, such as Erawan)

1. To make the balls of palm sugar for the filling, measure it out in rounded 1/4 teaspoons, dislodging the sugar balls from the spoon with a push of a finger. You want 24 balls total, so after measuring the sugar, distribute any leftover among the balls.

Press and roll each ball between your hands into a smooth, compacted sphere, a scant 1/2 inch in diameter. Put the balls on

a plate, cover with plastic wrap, and set aside. The sugar will develop a sheen as it sits.

2. If you are using fresh coconut, put it in a bowl and toss with the salt. If the thawed coconut feels noticeably damp, put it in a paper towel and gently squeeze out some of moisture; then transfer it to a bowl and toss with the salt. Set aside near the stove.

3. Cut the pandan leaves into 1-inch-long pieces. Put into a blender or electric mini-chopper and add the water. Run the machine to pulverize the *pandan* and create a fragrant green liquid resembling wheat grass. The *pandan* will get torn into thin, fibrous pieces.

Position a mesh strainer over a bowl and line it with a paper towel. Pour the *pandan* liquid through to strain it. Pick up the paper towel

continued

and squeeze out as much liquid as possible. You need 1/2 cup, so add water or remove some of the liquid as needed. Add the vanilla and, if you want more color in the *pandan* liquid, add the food coloring, too. If you are not using the *pandan* leaves, simply stir together the water with the vanilla and food coloring. Or just combine the water and vanilla. Set the liquid aside.

4. Fill a medium saucepan with water and bring to a boil. Lower the heat and cover to keep hot.

5. Put the glutinous rice flour in a bowl and make a well in the center. Pour in the flavored water and use a wooden spoon to combine the ingredients, working from the center to the rim of the bowl. When the dough becomes hard to stir, switch to using one hand to knead it in the bowl. The resulting dough will have a slight sheen and feel soft but somewhat stiff; at this stage it is not fully malleable. If the dough doesn't hold together, it is dry so add water by the 1/2 teaspoon to moisten. If the dough sticks to your hand, work in additional flour, 1 teaspoon at a time.

Now use the "Glutinous Rice Dough: Mother Dough Method" instructions on page 211 to create a malleable, elastic dough. Cut the finished dough into 4 pieces.

6. Before assembling the dumplings, return the water to a gentle boil. Because the dumplings can leak if they sit uncooked, assemble and cook them in small batches. For each batch, use one piece of dough. Roll the dough into a 6-inch-long log, then cut it into 6 even-size pieces.

To make a dumpling, hold a piece of dough, with one of the cut ends up, near your fingertips. Use the thumb or an index finger to

make a shallow well in the dough. Put a ball of palm sugar in the well, gently pressing it down to sink it into the dough. Push and press the dough to fully enclose the sugar and seal well. Roll the ball between your hands to even out the surface. Repeat with the remaining dough pieces to make five more dumplings.

When the batch is assembled, add the dumplings, one at a time, to the boiling water. To make sure the dumplings do not stick, jiggle the saucepan or gently stir with a spoon. After about 2 minutes, the dumplings should float to the surface. When this happens, let them cook for 1 more minute. Then use a slotted spoon to lift the dumplings, either individually or in pairs, from the water, pausing above the pan to shake off excess water.

Deposit the dumplings in the coconut. Dredge each one in coconut, then transfer to a plate. Repeat with the remaining dumplings before assembling the next batch.

7. If you are not serving them right away, cover the dumplings with plastic wrap to prevent them from drying. They are best on the day they are prepared. However, leftover dumplings should be kept at room temperature for no more than 2 days. They will harden and become inedible if chilled.

Note: Resembling gladiola leaves, spear-shaped *pandan* leaves are sold at Southeast Asian and some Chinese markets. Fresh leaves are usually bound by rubber bands and look like a rolled-up green belt. Frozen leaves are typically folded in half and sold in long Cryovac packages, usually shelved near other frozen tropical items, such as banana leaves and grated coconut. Frozen *pandan* comes from Thailand or Vietnam and is labeled *bai toey* or *lá dứa* in Thai or Vietnamese, respectively.

Sticky Rice and Mung Bean Dumplings in Ginger Broth

Chè Trôi Nước

Makes 12 dumplings, serving 4 to 6

Soft and chewy sticky rice dumplings have a nuanced natural sweetness that is savored by fans of East and Southeast Asian cuisines. As the recipes in this book show, they lend themselves to many occasions, cooking techniques, and fillings. Regardless of type, sticky rice dumplings never fail to please.

Old-fashioned cooks pound just-cooked sticky rice to create their dough. Modern cooks like me reach for convenient glutinous (sweet) rice flour for our favorite sticky rice dumplings. Preparations involving poaching the dumplings and serving them in broth (like a sweet soup) are common in Asia. I grew up with this classic Vietnamese rendition, not realizing that fried shallots contributed to their richness until my mother revealed it to me one day. The intersection between sweet and savory contributes to these dumplings' allure.

1/3 cup dried, hulled, and split yellow mung beans

GINGER BROTH

3 cups water

1/2 cup lightly packed light brown sugar

Scant 1/2 cup white sugar

Chubby 2-inch section fresh ginger, peeled, halved lengthwise, and bruised with the side of a knife

3 tablespoons canola oil

1 shallot, chopped (1/4 cup total)

1/8 teaspoon salt

6³/4 ounces (1¹/2 cups) glutinous (sweet) rice flour (any Thai brand such as Erawan)

3/4 cup water

1¹/4 cups Coconut Dessert Sauce (page 221) (optional)

1¹/2 tablespoons hulled raw (white) sesame seeds, toasted

1. Rinse the mung beans, put them in a bowl, and add water to cover by about 1 inch. Let soak for 2 hours, or up to 6 hours.

2. Meanwhile, make the broth, use a pot at least 8 inches wide so that the dumplings will later sit in one layer. Combine the water, brown and white sugars, and ginger in the pot. Bring to a boil, then lower the heat to a simmer for 5 minutes. Turn off the heat, cover, and let steep for at least 45 minutes, or until the broth is gingery enough for your liking. It is fine to steep for hours. When you are satisfied, remove the ginger, cover, and set aside.

3. Line a steamer tray with parchment paper. Drain the beans and then transfer them to the steamer tray. Evenly spread out the beans. Steam the beans (see page 17 for guidance) over boiling water for 8 to 15 minutes (the shorter time is for the metal steamer and the longer time is for the bamboo steamer), or until the mung beans are tender. Remove the steamer tray and set aside to cool. Or, transfer the beans to a bowl and occasionally stir them to hasten the cooling.

Process the cooled beans in a food processor to a fluffy consistency. It should look like fine cornmeal but hold together when a small amount is pinched between your fingers. You should have about 1 cup.

continued

4. To prepare the filling, combine the oil and shallot in a small saucepan. Heat over medium heat until the shallot sizzles. Continue to fry for 4 to 5 minutes, frequently swirling the pan to evenly cook, until most of the shallot is golden brown. Remove from the heat and stir in the mung beans and salt. If the filling feels stiff, add water by the teaspoon. Aim for a texture like that of dry mashed potatoes: if you press some between your fingers, it should stick together and leave your fingers slightly oily.

Let the filling cool for about 5 minutes. To shape the filling, measure out 1 scant, lightly packed tablespoon of filling and use one hand to press it into a 1-inch ball. Gently roll the ball between both hands to smooth the surface. Repeat to make 12 balls. Place the balls on a plate as you work and cover them with plastic wrap when done. Set aside.

5. To prepare the dough, fill a medium saucepan with water and bring to a boil. Lower the heat and cover to keep hot.

6. Put the glutinous rice flour in a bowl and make a well in the center. Pour in the water and use a wooden spoon to combine the ingredients, working from the center to the rim of the bowl. When the dough becomes hard to stir, switch to using one hand to knead it in the bowl. The resulting dough will have a slight sheen and feel soft but somewhat stiff; at this stage it is not fully malleable. If the dough doesn't hold together, it is dry so add water by the $1/2$ teaspoon to moisten. If the dough sticks to your hand, work in glutinous rice flour, 1 teaspoon at a time.

Now, use the "Glutinous Rice Dough: Mother Dough Method" instructions on page 211 to create malleable, elastic dough. Cut the finished dough into 2 pieces.

7. Before making the dumplings, return the water to a boil and have a bowl of water handy. Then, assemble and poach the dumplings in batches. Roll one of the dough pieces into a 6-inch-long log. Cut it into 6 even-size pieces, taking care to make the tapered end pieces a little longer than the others.

For each dumpling, use your fingers to gently press on a piece of dough from the center toward the rim to create a 3-inch round that is slightly thinner at the middle than at the rim. (It's like shaping a tiny pizza.) Place the dough in the palm of one hand and use your other hand to center a ball of filling in the dough. Bring up the sides of the dough, then push and pinch the dough together to completely enclose the filling. Pinch and twist off excess dough.

Roll the dumpling between your hands to create a smooth ball. Rest it in the palm of your hand, then press down with the base of your thumb to flatten the ball into a fat disk about 1 inch thick and $13/4$ inches wide. Set on your work surface and repeat with the remaining pieces of dough and filling.

8. Once a batch of dumplings is assembled, add it to the boiling water. Gently shake the pan or nudge the dumplings to prevent them from sticking. When a dumpling floats to the surface, after about 3 minutes, use a slotted spoon to transfer it to the bowl of cold water to cool and set; the dumplings will lose their fuzzy appearance once they are in the water. While the first batch poaches, assemble the second batch and then repeat the cooking. (With the dough left over from pinching off the excess, you can make $1/4$-inch balls and poach those as an unfilled addition, if you like.)

9. Return the broth to a simmer. Remove the dumplings from the water and add to the ginger broth. Let the dumplings sit in the broth for 5 to 7 minutes, turning them midway, to reheat and allow the dumplings to absorb the flavors. Avoid boiling, as that forms little bubbles on the dough surface. Turn off the heat and set aside for about 10 minutes to cool.

Serve the dumplings warm in rice bowls with plenty of broth. Top with coconut sauce and finish with a sprinkling of sesame seeds. Eat with a spoon to blend some of the broth with the dumpling in each bite. Sip on extra gingery broth like soup. Refrigerate leftovers in the ginger broth and reheat broth and dumplings together over medium-low heat.

GLUTINOUS RICE DOUGH: MOTHER DOUGH METHOD

Doughs made from glutinous (sweet) rice flour are notoriously hard to manage because they can be dry, fall apart, and sag. They do not yield easily to your will. I have tried a number of techniques over the years, including combining flours and using just-boiled water, but this one, which I call the "mother dough method," works very well for dumplings that are poached. This method calls for precooking a small portion of dough and then kneading it back into the raw dough to introduce enough elasticity to tame the dough.

The instructions below take off from where you have made the dough from combining the rice flour and water. Remember to return the saucepan of water to a boil before proceeding.

1. To make the "mother dough," pinch off a bit of the prepared dough, about 3/4 inch in diameter. Roll it into a ball, then flatten it into a 1/4-inch-thick disk. Drop the disk into the boiling water. After the dough rises to the top and floats horizontally, 1 to 2 minutes, let the dough cook for a further 15 seconds.

2. Meanwhile, dust your work surface with 1 tablespoon of glutinous rice flour. Take the raw dough and flatten it into a 4-inch disk, about 3/4 inch thick. When the mother dough is done, use a slotted spoon to lift the dough from the water, giving it a gentle shake to remove excess water. Set the spoon aside for about 15 seconds to slightly cool the dough.

3. Center the small cooked mother dough atop the big raw disk. Fold in the sides of the dough to enclose and start kneading, using the heel of your hand to push the raw and cooked dough together. Add extra glutinous rice flour as needed to prevent sticking; use a dough scraper if the dough is unwieldy. After kneading for about 2 minutes, both doughs should be well combined. What was initially stiff dough should now be supple, malleable, and slightly tacky like Play-Doh. Cut the finished dough into the number of pieces required by the recipe and cover with plastic wrap to prevent drying. The dough may sit at room temperature for up to 2 hours.

If you are assembling the dumplings soon, lower the heat on the boiling water and cover to keep hot. Otherwise, turn off the heat on the water.

Banana and Coconut Sticky Rice Packets

Kao Tom Padt

Makes 12 packets

If you enjoy rice pudding, you'll love these Thai packets of soft sticky rice flavored by coconut cream. Steaming in banana leaves lends an alluring fragrance to the rich rice, which encases soft banana and cooked black beans. The beans offer interesting texture and color contrast in these popular street snacks.

According to legend, *kao tom padt* (also called *kao tom madt*) was all that some religious pilgrims had on their journey to visit the Lord Buddha. They presented their precious food to the Lord Buddha upon arriving, and that gesture continues today as these packets are still an offering at religious ceremonies.

Thai cooks typically make these packets in large quantities and thus soak and boil a fair amount of black beans. For small homemade batches, canned black beans, drained and rinsed of their canning liquid, work fine. Omit the beans for *nom n'sahm chaek*, a Cambodian New Year must-have. You can also grill the steamed packets and serve them with the Coconut Dessert Sauce (page 221).

1 1/2 cups sticky rice (long-grain or short-grain variety)

2 1/4 cups coconut cream (see Note below)

Scant 3/4 cup sugar

1/2 teaspoon plus 1/8 teaspoon salt

3 ripe but firm bananas, each about 7 inches long

1/2 cup canned black beans, rinsed (optional)

12 (9 by 12-inch) pieces fresh or frozen, thawed banana leaf, trimmed of brown edges, rinsed, and wiped dry

1. **Put the rice** in a bowl and add water to cover by 1 inch. Let stand for at least 5 and up to 12 hours. (The cooking technique below requires a longer soaking than normal.)

2. **Drain the rice** in a mesh strainer and rinse. Let sit a minute, then shake to expel excess water.

3. **Combine the coconut** cream, sugar, and salt in a large nonstick skillet. Heat over medium-high heat for about 2 minutes, or until the mixture begins bubbling. Add the rice and stir to mix well. Cook for about 6 minutes, stirring

often. Slightly decrease the heat if the mixture sputters so much that it feels out of control. This stage of cooking is complete when most of the liquid has been absorbed and the thickened mixture resembles a slightly soupy rice pudding or risotto; the rice grains will be translucent and cling together as a slippery mass in the glossy liquid. Expect the rice to be chewy-firm and not fully cooked. Remove from the heat and set aside to cool for about 20 minutes, or until cool enough to touch. The rice will absorb more of the liquid.

4. **Meanwhile,** peel the bananas, removing any strings as you work. Cut each in half crosswise, then halve each lengthwise. You should have 12 quarters total. Set aside on a plate. Have the beans nearby. If the banana leaves feel stiff, soften them by passing each over the flame of a gas stove or a hot electric burner.

5. **Before assembling** the packets, use a rubber spatula to divide the rice into 12 wedges like a pie.

6. **Use one piece** of banana leaf for each packet. Put it on your work surface, smoother side up and one of the shorter sides closest to you. Tear or use scissors to cut off a long, narrow strip, about 1/3 inch wide, and set aside to use later to secure the packet. Put a portion of soft rice on the center of the leaf and use the spatula to press it into a 5-inch-diameter circle. Sprinkle a scant 2 teaspoons of beans on the rice. Then vertically center a piece of banana on top and gently press down to secure in place.

Pull up the long sides of the leaf so that they meet in the center, pressing gently so the rice covers the top of the banana; pick up the packet and mold it into cylindrical shape, if you like. To close, fold the long side of the leaf over twice; for less bulk, reopen the packet, fold one of the sides of the leaf down to cover the rice, then roll it up cigar style. The result will be a long, open-ended tube. Now, fold the ends of the leaf in to close (they will partially overlap, as they would if you were wrapping a gift), and tie the ends down with the reserved leaf strip. (You can use kitchen string instead.) Repeat to make the rest.

7. **Place the packets,** seam side down, in steamer trays in one layer. Steam over boiling water (see steaming guidelines on page 17) for 20 to 25 minutes, until the rice is tender; the banana leaf will turn dark olive green.

8. **Serve warm** or at room temperature, unwrapped on an open leaf, and with a fork; the leaf is inedible. Refrigerate leftovers and steam for about 10 minutes to refresh. To freeze for up to 1 month, wrap each packet in plastic wrap and then put them all in a zip-top plastic bag; thaw and steam to reheat.

Note: For coconut cream, spoon off the thick creamy plug from the top of an *unshaken* can of coconut milk. If you've just purchased the can, and it was jostled in transport home, let it sit for a day to separate. The Mae Ploy brand of coconut milk contains proportionately more cream than most other brands; use the leftover "skim" milk to prepare other rice dishes. To get the 2 1/4 cups of coconut cream you'll need for this recipe, 2 (19-ounce) or 3 (13 1/2-ounce) cans of coconut milk should suffice. Pure coconut cream is sometimes available at Chinese and Southeast Asian markets; Aroy-D and Kara brand, packaged in aseptic boxes like juice, are excellent.

9 Sauces, Seasonings, Stocks, and Other Basics

Tangy Soy Dipping Sauce

Makes about 2/3 cup

Great on their own, Chinese *jiǎozi* get a fantastic flavor boost when dipped in a zippy sauce like this one. The tart-salty-spicy combination adds a complex edge to the dumplings.

There's no such thing as a definitive dipping sauce, since cooks and diners mix up their own according to personal taste. At the least, your sauce should be tangy and savory. But add some nutty, hot chile oil, and your eating experience will enter a different orbit. Chinese dumplings are wonderful with an extra kick of ginger or garlic in the sauce, too. I prepare the sauce in advance, but you can set out the ingredients and invite guests to do it themselves.

1/3 cup light (regular) soy sauce

2 1/2 tablespoons unseasoned rice, Chinkiang, or balsamic vinegar

1/8 teaspoon sugar (optional)

1 to 3 teaspoons Chile Oil (page 216) (optional)

1 tablespoon finely shredded fresh ginger, or 2 teaspoons finely minced garlic (optional)

Combine the soy sauce, vinegar, and sugar in a bowl. Stir to dissolve the sugar. Taste and adjust the flavors to your liking for a tart-savory balance. Add as much chile oil as you like for some heat. The sauce can be prepared several hours in advance up to this point. Right before serving, add the ginger or garlic for a fresh layer of punch.

Korean Dipping Sauce

Makes about 2/3 cup

There are many ways to tweak a dipping sauce for Korean *mandu* (pages 44 and 46). The base is on the light side and great on its own, but you can add a variety of extras for more complexity and body.

1/4 cup Korean, Japanese, or light (regular) soy sauce

3 tablespoons unseasoned rice vinegar

2 tablespoons water

1 teaspoon sugar

1 teaspoon sesame oil

OPTIONAL ADDITIONS

2 teaspoons garlic, minced and crushed into a paste

1 teaspoon toasted white (hulled) sesame seeds

1 small scallion (white and green parts), thinly sliced

1/2 medium-hot chile, such as Fresno, Holland, or jalapeño, thinly sliced

In a small bowl, combine the soy sauce, vinegar, water, and sugar. Stir to dissolve the sugar and then taste. Adjust the flavor to suit your palate to arrive at a tart-savory balance. Add the sesame oil. For extra oomph and a thicker sauce, add the garlic, sesame seeds, scallion, and/or chile. Set aside for a good hour to allow the flavors to bloom.

Chile Oil

Makes 1¹/4 cups

Used in Chinese, Japanese, and Southeast Asian cooking, chile oil is easy to prepare at home, and it's infinitely better than store-bought. Its intense heat enlivens many foods, especially dumplings, which benefit when chile oil is part of the dipping sauce or used as a garnish.

Some cooks add aromatics, such as ginger, star anise, and Sichuan peppercorns, to the oil, but I like to keep the chile flavor pure. While you may use other cooking oils, such as canola oil, my preference is for the kind of peanut oil often sold at Chinese markets, which is cold pressed and filled with the aroma of roasted peanuts. It is texturally light, has a high smoking point, and offers a wonderful nuttiness that pairs well with the intense chile heat. Lion & Globe peanut oil from Hong Kong is terrific. Use just the infused oil or include the chile flakes for an extra brow-wiping experience.

¹/4 cup dried red chile flakes or coarsely ground dried chiles
1 cup peanut oil

1. Put the chile flakes in a dry glass jar.

2. Attach a deep-fry thermometer to a small saucepan and add the oil. Heat over medium-high heat until smoking hot (the temperature will top 400°F) and remove from the heat. Wait 5 to 7 minutes for the temperature to decrease to 325° to 350°F (drop a chile flake in and it should gently sizzle), and then pour the oil into the glass jar. The chile flakes will sizzle and swirl and then settle down.

Cool completely before covering and storing. Give it a couple days to mature before using. Chile oil keeps for months in the cupboard.

Chile Garlic Sauce

Makes ²/3 cup

This ubiquitous Asian condiment does not need to be purchased. In fact, it has a wonderful, bright flavor when made at home. In the late summer, when chiles are at their peak red color and spicy-fruity flavor, I buy a bunch at the farmers' market and make a batch or two of this sauce.

Keep the sauce uncooked if you enjoy a wild, robust flavor. Or, cook the sauce for a more mellow finish. I often blend different kinds of chiles so as to not create too much of a burn.

6 ounces hot or medium-hot red chiles, such as cayenne, Fresno, habañero, Holland, jalapeño, serrano, or Thai, chopped
3 or 4 cloves garlic, chopped (use less for the raw version)
¹/2 teaspoon salt
1¹/2 tablespoons sugar
1¹/2 tablespoons distilled white vinegar

1. Put the chiles, garlic, salt, sugar, and vinegar in an electric mini-chopper or food processor. Grind to a coarse texture. Take a whiff; it should make you sweat a bit. Taste and adjust the flavor with extra salt for depth or sugar to mitigate the heat.

2. For an uncooked sauce, simply transfer the sauce to a jar and let it stand for at least 30 minutes to blend the flavors before using.

For the cooked version, transfer the chile mixture to a small saucepan. Bring to a vigorous simmer over medium heat, then lower the heat to gently simmer for about 5 minutes, or until the sauce no longer smells raw. Remove from the heat and set aside to cool. Transfer to a jar. Refrigerated, the sauces keep well for a good 6 months.

Sweet Soy Sauce

Makes a scant 1/2 cup

Sweet, salty, and rich, this delicately flavored condiment unites and enhances the flavors of Cantonese steamed rice rolls (pages 156 to 160). It comes together quickly and tastes great, especially if flavorful cold-pressed peanut oil, the kind sold at Chinese markets, is used. If you use canola oil, add a dash of sesame oil for nuttiness.

1 tablespoon sugar

1 1/2 tablespoons light (regular) soy sauce

1 1/2 teaspoons dark soy sauce

1/4 cup water

1 tablespoon peanut oil or canola

Dash of sesame oil (optional)

Combine the sugar, light and dark soy sauces, water, and oil in a small saucepan. If using canola oil, add a dash of sesame oil. Bring to a boil over medium heat, stir to make sure the sugar has dissolved, then remove from the heat. Transfer to a heatproof bowl and set aside to cool completely before using. The sauce can be prepared up to 2 days in advance, covered, and left at room temperature.

Note: It is customary to liberally drizzle this sauce onto the rice rolls to flavor them. Expect the sauce to pool at the bottom of the plate when you do so. If you want to hold back, pour some onto the plated rolls, serve the rest on the side, and invite guests to help themselves.

Sweet and Sour Sauce

Makes 1 cup

A rich, dark honey color, this tart-sweet-savory sauce does not resemble the cloying, sticky, bright red sauce that's often served at Chinese restaurants. You can whip it up quickly to enjoy with snacks such as fried wontons. For spicy tropical flair, use unsweetened pineapple juice instead of water and include 2 teaspoons of minced ginger and a chopped Thai chile with the other seasoning at the beginning.

1/4 cup sugar or lightly packed light brown sugar

1/4 teaspoon salt

1 tablespoon ketchup

1 tablespoon light (regular) soy sauce

3 tablespoons unseasoned rice vinegar or cider vinegar

1/2 cup water

2 teaspoons cornstarch dissolved in 2 tablespoons water

1. Combine the sugar, salt, ketchup, soy sauce, vinegar, and water in a small saucepan. Bring to a near boil over medium heat, stirring occasionally to dissolve the sugar. Give the cornstarch a stir and then add it to the pan. Continue cooking, stirring, for about 15 seconds, or until the sauce comes to full boil and thickens.

2. Remove from the heat, transfer to a serving bowl, and set aside for 10 minutes to cool and concentrate in flavor. Taste and add extra salt, if needed. Serve warm or at room temperature. Feel free to prepare this sauce a day in advance.

Spicy Roasted Tomato Sauce

Makes 1 1/2 cups

When you present dumplings with this sauce, the combination may recall an Italian pasta dish, but the sauce's zesty qualities resemble the Latin flavors of Mexico more than of Europe. But on closer analysis, the combination of chile, ginger, herbs, and spices is definitely Asian, specifically Nepal's Himalayan cuisine, which blends Chinese, Indian, and Tibetan traditions. In the Nepalese repertoire, this sauce is a type of *achar* (a moniker for chutneys and pickles) and is what typically accompanies *momo*; it's great with Tibetan *momo*, too.

With a tangy edge, moderate heat, and spiced depth, the sauce has a multilayered punch that begins seemingly subtle but finishes with a certain feistiness. Sometimes ground toasted sesame seeds are added for richness, but I find that they mute the other flavors too much.

3/4 pound ripe tomatoes

1 medium-hot red chile, such as cayenne, Fresno, Holland, or jalapeño

1 clove garlic, chopped

2 teaspoons chopped fresh ginger

1/4 teaspoon salt

3 tablespoons water

1 teaspoon fresh lime or lemon juice (optional)

2 1/2 tablespoons finely chopped fresh cilantro or mint leaves

1/4 teaspoon ground, toasted cumin seed or Sichuan peppercorn (optional)

1. Position an oven rack about 4 inches away from the broiler. Put the tomato and chile atop a piece of aluminum foil on a baking sheet and broil for about 6 minutes, or until the skins have pulled away and are a bit charred. Turn over and broil the other side for another 2 minutes. Continue, if necessary, to roast and char all over. Remove from the oven and set aside to cool.

2. Remove and discard the skins from the tomatoes and chile. Cut away the stems and, if you like less heat, scrape out and discard the chile seeds. Coarsely chop and set aside.

3. Combine the garlic, ginger, and salt in a mortar and pound with the pestle into a fragrant paste. Add the chile and pound to a rough texture. Add the tomatoes and gently mix to break the tomato apart. It will remain chunky. Transfer to a bowl, then stir in the water, lime juice, cilantro, and cumin. (For a fine texture, use an electric mini-chopper and process in stages to ensure a smooth consistency. Blend the water and lime juice with the tomato. Stir in the cilantro and cumin to finish.)

4. Set the sauce aside for 30 minutes to blend the flavors. Taste and add extra salt for depth, lime juice to cut the heat, or water to thin out the sauce. Aim for a medium-hot tang. This sauce is best enjoyed the day you prepare it, but it can be refrigerated overnight and returned to room temperature before serving.

SEEDING CHILES

I do not seed chiles, as their extra heat contributes wonderful excitement to foods. However, if you want to lessen the burn, remove both the seeds and the pithy membrane from chiles before using them.

Garam Masala

Makes 1/4 cup

Making your own garam masala spice blend for Indian foods is easy and inexpensive, and the results will be superior to store-bought. Toasting and grinding the spices in small batches ensures freshness.

The blend varies among cooks, and there is the subtle traditional blend of cardamom, cinnamon, cloves, and black pepper. I prefer a slightly bolder approach that includes cumin and coriander, too. Whole spices are available at reasonable prices from Asian markets and the bulk section of many health food stores.

1/2 teaspoon cardamom seeds (taken from about 12 green cardamom pods)

11/2-inch cinnamon stick, broken into small pieces

1/2 teaspoon whole cloves

2 teaspoons black peppercorns

1 tablespoon plus 1 teaspoon cumin seeds

1 tablespoon plus 1 teaspoon coriander seeds

Combine the cardamom seeds, cinnamon stick, cloves, peppercorns, cumin seeds, and coriander seeds in a dry skillet and toast over medium heat, shaking frequently, for 2 to 3 minutes, until there is a heady, sweet fragrance. Remove from the heat and cool slightly for a few minutes. In batches, grind to a powder in a spice grinder or clean, dry electric coffee grinder dedicated to grinding spices. Store in an airtight container.

Fresh Mint Chutney

Makes 2/3 cup

While this relish boldly says, "I am mint!," it also has a bite from chile, ginger, and raw onion. Lime juice and sugar tame and unite the ingredients. This, along with the Tamarind and Date Chutney (page 220), provides just the right bright accents to Indian Samosas (page 115).

3 tablespoons finely chopped yellow onion

1 or 2 hot green chiles, such as Thai or Serrano, chopped

1 teaspoon minced fresh ginger

Generous 1/4 teaspoon salt

1 teaspoon sugar

11/2 tablespoons fresh lime juice

3 tablespoons water

2 cups lightly packed fresh mint leaves, coarsely chopped (1 large bunch)

1. Put the onion in a mesh strainer and rinse for about 5 seconds under cold running water. Transfer to an electric mini-chopper and add the chile, ginger, salt, and sugar. Grind to a coarse texture, stopping the machine to scrape down the sides several times. Add the lime juice, water, and mint. Process to a fine texture; it should resemble a thick pesto. Occasionally stop the machine and scrape down the sides to facilitate an even puree.

2. Transfer to a serving bowl and set aside for 5 to 10 minutes to allow the flavors to bloom. Taste and adjust the flavors. Add water by the teaspoon if the relish is too thick; however, it should not be liquid. Set aside for at least 30 minutes for the flavors to meld and for the texture to slightly thicken. The initial bright green color will dull, but the flavor will remain robust. This relish tastes best fresh but can be refrigerated for up to 2 days.

Tamarind and Date Chutney

Makes 1¹/₄ cups

This tart-sweet relish is thick enough for you to plop some into the crevices of a samosa for a wonderful, classic Indian food taste treat. Tamarind is known as the "date of India," and the delectable marriage of the two kinds of dates in this chutney is a natural. Both ingredients lend body, their flavors perfectly complementing each other. I've eaten this chutney off a spoon.

If available, use *jaggery* (unrefined Indian sugar) or Southeast Asian palm sugar instead of the brown sugar. Sticky dark brown slabs of tamarind pulp are sold at Chinese, Indian, and Southeast Asian markets in a double layer of plastic packaging. Soft dates, such as Medjools, work best. Otherwise, soak chewy, hard dates in just-boiled water for about an hour to soften them, then drain and proceed.

3¹/₄ to 4 ounces seedless tamarind pulp (a lump the size of a small lemon), broken into 3 or 4 pieces

1¹/₃ cups warm water

³/₄ cup coarsely chopped pitted dates (about 5 ounces)

¹/₄ cup lightly packed light brown sugar

¹/₂ teaspoon salt

¹/₂ teaspoon cayenne

¹/₂ teaspoon pounded, toasted cumin seeds or ground cumin

1. In a small saucepan, combine the tamarind and 1 cup of the water over medium heat. Bring to a simmer and cook, uncovered, for 5 minutes. Occasionally stir with a fork to break up the pulp. Remove from the heat, cover, and set aside to steep and further soften for 5 minutes, or until the tamarind solids have expanded. When you stir the mixture, the pulp should easily combine with the water.

2. Position a coarse-mesh sieve over a bowl and pour in the tamarind mixture. Using a rubber spatula or metal spoon, vigorously stir and press the solids against the mesh to force as much of the pulp through as possible. If necessary, return the pulp to the saucepan, add some of the already-strained liquid, stir to loosen up more of the pulp, and then work it through the sieve again. When the pulp is spent, discard the fibrous leftovers. The resulting liquid will resemble chocolate cake batter. You should have ²/₃ to ³/₄ cup.

3. Combine the tamarind liquid, dates, the remaining ¹/₃ cup water, the brown sugar, salt, and cayenne in a food processor. Process to a smooth, thick texture. Occasionally pause the machine and scrape down the sides. The ideal texture is thick enough to mound on a spoon, but you can add extra water for a thinner sauce.

Transfer to a bowl and stir in the cumin for a pungent finish. Taste and adjust the flavors, as necessary, especially if you thinned the chutney. Set aside for a few hours for the flavors to blend and bloom. Serve, refrigerate for up to 2 weeks, or freeze for a month.

Green Chutney

Makes 2/3 cup

A simple, everyday relish from India, this condiment adds a wallop of fresh spiciness to food. Each cook has a different take on green chutney, and many add chopped onion and grated coconut. The straightforward approach here keeps the flavors bright. Green chutney is purposely hot, but feel free to seed the chiles or use a less-alarming chile, such as jalapeño, for less dramatic results.

1 or 2 hot green chiles, such as Thai or serrano, chopped
1 clove garlic, chopped
1/2 teaspoon salt
1 teaspoon sugar
1 1/2 cups packed coarsely chopped fresh cilantro stems and leaves
1/4 cup packed fresh mint leaves
2 tablespoons fresh lime juice
Water (optional)

1. **Put the chile,** garlic, salt, and sugar in an electric mini-chopper. Grind to a finely chopped texture, stopping the machine to scrape down the sides several times. Add the cilantro, mint, and lime juice. Process to a fine texture like that of a thick pesto. It should mound on a spoon.

2. **Transfer to a** serving bowl and set aside for 5 to 10 minutes to allow the flavors to bloom a bit. Taste and adjust the flavors. Lime and sugar will cut the heat, but you do want a nice salty, sweet, sour, hot, pungent finish. Add water by the teaspoon if the chutney is too thick; however, it should not be liquid. Set it aside for at least 30 minutes to mellow. This chutney is at its zippy best when freshly made, but it can be refrigerated for up to 2 days.

Coconut Dessert Sauce

Makes 1 1/4 cups

Vietnamese cooks, particularly those from the southern region, love to add creamy richness to their sweets by drizzling on a little of this sauce (called *nước cốt dừa ngọt*) right before serving. I don't limit my uses to Viet preparations; this simple sauce can grace many Southeast Asian foods. Somewhat thick like yogurt, the sauce can be prepared days in advance for you to use cold, warm, or at room temperature.

1 cup coconut milk
2 pinches of salt
1 tablespoon sugar
3 tablespoons water
1 1/2 teaspoons cornstarch dissolved in 2 teaspoons water

1. **In a small saucepan,** whisk together the coconut milk, salt, sugar, and water. Place over medium heat and bring to a near-simmer, lowering the heat if the coconut milk spits or pops. Give the cornstarch mixture a good stir and add it to the sauce, mixing well. Cook, stirring, for about 30 seconds, or until the sauce thickens; then remove from the heat.

2. **Let the sauce cool,** uncovered, to concentrate the flavors before serving. It will keep in a tightly closed container in the refrigerator for up to 3 days. If you are serving it warm, reheat gently over low heat.

Chicken Stock

Makes about 12 cups

This is my standard, multipurpose Asian chicken stock. Good-quality chickens are a premium ingredient, so make the most of your investment. Save and freeze chicken parts as you prepare other dishes. Every once in a while, especially when the freezer gets full, brew some stock. It freezes beautifully. And in a pinch, make the shortcut version from canned broth (see the Variation, below).

4 1/2 to 5 pounds chicken parts or bones with some meat on them

4 quarts water

1 large yellow onion, quartered

Chubby 3-inch piece fresh ginger, unpeeled and smashed with the flat side of a knife

2 1/2 teaspoons salt

1. Rinse the chicken under cool water to remove any bloody residue. Remove and discard any loose pieces of fat. Wielding a heavy cleaver designed for chopping bones, whack the bones to break them partway or all the way through, making the cuts at 1 to 2-inch intervals, depending on the size of the bone. This exposes the marrow, which enriches the stock.

2. Put the bones in a stockpot, add the water, and place over high heat. Bring almost to a boil and then lower the heat to a simmer. For the next few minutes, use a ladle or large, shallow spoon to skim off and discard the scum that rises to the top. Add the onion, ginger, and salt and adjust the heat to maintain a simmer. You should have a constant stream of small bubbles breaking lightly on the surface. Let the stock cook, uncovered, for 2 1/2 hours.

3. Remove the pot from the heat and let stand undisturbed for 30 minutes, to allow the impurities to settle and congeal. Position a fine-mesh sieve (or a coarse-mesh sieve lined with cheesecloth or paper towel) over a large saucepan. Gently ladle the stock through the sieve. Remove and discard the bones as they get in your way. Tilt the stockpot to ladle out as much clear stock as possible, then discard the sediment-laden liquid and any remaining bits at the bottom of the pot.

4. Taste the stock. If it is not as flavorful as you would like, simmer it to reduce the liquid and concentrate the flavors. Once you are satisfied with the flavor, let the stock cool completely, cover, and refrigerate for at least 8 hours, or until the fat solidifies on the surface. Remove and discard the fat. The stock is now ready to use. Or, refrigerate for up to 1 week or freeze for up to 3 months.

VARIATION: SHORTCUT STOCK

Homemade stock has inimitable depth and flavor, but in an emergency, you can closely mimic homemade by doctoring up canned broth with some Asian flavor. (Choose a brand that tastes like chicken and not much else.) In a saucepan, dilute the canned broth (use the full-sodium kind) with water in a ratio of 2 parts broth to 1 part water. Start with between 5 and 10 percent more liquid than what you will actually need because there will be some evaporation during the short simmering.

For every 4 cups of liquid, you will need 2 quarter-size slices of ginger and 1 scallion, cut into 3-inch lengths. Lightly smash these ingredients with the broad side of a cleaver or chef's knife. Bring the broth and water to a simmer, add the ginger and scallion, and simmer gently, uncovered, for 20 minutes. Discard the ginger and scallion. The stock is now ready to use.

Korean Beef Stock

Makes about 10 cups

Take a page from Korean cooks who gently simmer lean beef with lots of scallions, onion, and garlic for a light, flavorful stock. The black peppercorns impart a golden hue as well as a spicy undercurrent. I prefer shank because there's a little marrow bone for flavor, the gelatinous meat imparts richness, and the leftovers can be used for an old-fashioned Chinese treat (see Note below). You can opt for oxtail, rump, brisket, or other stewing meat but know that a little bone, meat, and fat together make for good stock flavor.

2 to 2 1/2 pounds beef shank

14 cups water

5 cloves garlic, bruised

Chubby 2-inch piece fresh ginger, unpeeled, halved lengthwise, and smashed with the flat side of a knife

1 medium yellow onion, quartered

4 large scallions (white and pale green parts), cut into 3-inch lengths and bruised

2 1/2 teaspoons salt

1/2 generous teaspoon black peppercorns

1. **Put the beef** in a stockpot and add the water. Bring to a boil over high heat, skim the scum that rises, and then add the garlic, ginger, onion, scallions, salt, and peppercorns. Lower the heat to gently simmer for about 2 hours, or until the stock has reduced by about a quarter. Throughout the simmering time, skim off the scum and fat as they gather on the surface.

2. **Remove from the heat.** Use tongs to remove the beef from the pot, reserving it for another use (see the Note below). There are usually few impurities in this stock so there is no need to let it stand undisturbed before straining.

Position a fine-mesh sieve (or a coarse-mesh sieve lined with cheesecloth or paper towel) over a large saucepan. Gently ladle the stock through the sieve. Tilt the stockpot to ladle out as much clear stock as possible, discarding any sediment-laden liquid and any remaining bits at the bottom of the pot.

3. **Taste the stock.** If it is not as flavorful as you would like, simmer it to reduce the liquid and concentrate the flavors. Once you are satisfied with the flavor, let the stock cool completely, cover, and refrigerate for at least 8 hours, or until the fat solidifies on the surface. Remove and discard the fat. The stock is now ready to use. Or, store in a tightly closed container in the refrigerator for up to 1 week or in the freezer for up to 3 months.

Note: The leftover meat is not fully tender by the time the stock is done, so you'll need to repurpose it. I often use it for a homey Chinese dish called 1-2-3-4-5 beef.

In a saucepan, combine 1 tablespoon Shaoxing rice wine or dry sherry, 2 tablespoons unseasoned rice vinegar, 3 tablespoons sugar, 4 tablespoons soy sauce, and 5 tablespoons water. Stir to dissolve and adjust the flavors for a tangy-sweet-savory balance. Add the meat and additional water to cover. Simmer for about 30 minutes, or until the beef is tender. Then raise the heat to vigorously simmer for about 15 minutes to reduce the liquid by about half. Remove from the heat and serve with rice. Scallion, ginger, and star anise can be added during simmering for extra flavor notes.

Char Siu Pork

Makes about 1 1/2 pounds

Garlicky and savory-sweet, this roasted pork is a mainstay of Cantonese barbecue shops and dim sum houses. Aside from eating it straight, which is hard to resist, there are countless uses for it, including as a filling for steamed buns (page 100) and garnish for wontons in soup (page 70). Make a batch of roast pork, and you'll have enough for a number of different applications.

To make the pork look appetizing, char siu (*chǎshāo* in Mandarin) is often prepared with food coloring. But chemical coloring isn't needed here, as the marinade employs dark soy sauce to impart an appealing reddish brown color to the meat. Select a well-balanced and fragrant Chinese five-spice blend that is not too medicinal or too sweet. For an unusual smoky edge, roast the pork over a wood fire, as the pros do in Kuala Lumpur.

2 1/3 pounds boneless pork shoulder, well trimmed (2 pounds after trimming)

MARINADE

3 cloves garlic, minced

3 tablespoons sugar

3/4 teaspoon Chinese five-spice powder

4 1/2 tablespoons hoisin sauce

3 tablespoons honey

2 tablespoons plus 1 teaspoon Shaoxing rice wine or dry sherry

3 tablespoons light (regular) soy sauce

1 1/2 tablespoons dark (black) soy sauce

1 tablespoon sesame oil

1. **Quarter the pork** lengthwise into strips about 6 inches long and 1 1/2 inches thick. If there are odd-size pieces, they should be of the same thickness.

2. **To make the marinade,** in a large bowl, whisk together the garlic, sugar, five-spice powder, hoisin sauce, honey, rice wine, light and dark soy sauces, and sesame oil. Set aside 1/3 of the marinade, cover, and refrigerate to later baste the meat. Add the pork to the remainder and use a spatula or tongs to coat evenly. Cover with plastic wrap and refrigerate for 6 to 8 hours, or even overnight, turning the pork 2 or 3 times.

3. **Remove the pork** and reserved marinade from the refrigerator 45 minutes before cooking. Position a rack in the upper third of the oven and preheat to 475°F. Line a baking sheet with aluminum foil and place a flat roasting rack on the baking sheet. Put the pork on the rack, spacing the pieces 1 inch apart to promote heat circulation. Discard the used marinade, wash and dry the bowl, and put the reserved marinade in it.

4. **Roast, basting with** the marinade every 10 minutes, for 30 to 35 minutes. To baste, use tongs to pick up each piece and roll it in the marinade before returning it to the rack, turning the pork over each time. The pork is done when it looks glazed, is slightly charred, and, most important, registers about 145°F on an instant-read meat thermometer. Remove from the oven.

5. **Let the meat rest** for 10 minutes to finish cooking and seal in the juices before using. Or, let it cool completely, wrap tightly, and freeze for up to 3 months.

South and Southeast Asian cooks have ready access to freshly grated and shredded coconut. They either do it themselves or buy it at the market. Abroad, our options include frozen grated coconut, sold at Chinese and Southeast Asian markets. It is fine for fillings and okay for garnishing. But if you would like to send a dumpling like the Malay Sweet Rice Dumplings with Palm Sugar and Coconut (page 205) over the top, start with a mature, hairy, brown coconut. (The green or pale ones are immature and lack the requisite rich flesh.) Select one that is heavy for its size—the sign of lots of meat—and shake it to make sure there's liquid inside, an indication of freshness.

At home, crack it open by heating it in the oven. This expands the shell, making the flesh easier to pry away in large pieces that are perfect for grating or shredding. Cracking a coconut without heating it is great if you have an Asian-style grater or shredder to dig into the concave flesh while it is still attached to the shell. Here is the oven method.

1. Position a rack in the middle of the oven and preheat to 400°F. Locate the 3 black spots, or "eyes," at the top of coconut. Using a Phillips screwdriver or a hammer and large nail, pierce holes in 2 of the eyes and pour out the liquid, capturing it and reserving it to drink or discarding it. (Make sure the holes are a good size, or the water will dribble out very slowly.) Put the coconut on a baking sheet and bake for 15 minutes. The heat will loosen the meat from the shell. The coconut may crack in the oven, which is fine.

2. Remove the coconut from the oven. Holding it with a kitchen towel, firmly tap it around the equator with a hammer until it has cracked around the entire circumference and broken apart. Try to keep the pieces as large as possible. Use a dinner knife to pry the coconut meat from the shell. Discard the shell.

3. Using a vegetable peeler, shave off the papery brown skin from the white coconut meat. Rinse the meat to remove any excess bits of brown skin. You can refrigerate the coconut pieces for up to 3 days before shredding the meat.

4. There are many options for grating and shredding coconut. The best tools I have found are a box grater and a single-plane grater. In fact, my cheap plastic-and-metal grater works like a champ. The smallest holes yield a fine grated texture as well as fluffy, narrow shreds. Whatever your tool, rotate the pieces of coconut as you work to protect your fingers. A rasper or hand-held rotary grater work well, too, but the old-fashioned box grater has a larger work surface area so you can grate more efficiently. For the best flavor, use the coconut the day you grate or shred it.

Note: If frozen or fresh coconut is totally unavailable, resort to sweetened flaked coconut. Measure out the quantity needed and then soak it in hot water to cover for 5 minutes. Drain well, and gently squeeze in a paper towel to get rid of excess moisture. The coconut is ready to use.

Resources

In keeping with the homey, easy-going nature of dumplings, I have tried to minimize the use of hard-to-find ingredients and equipment. Some items, however, require a trip to an ethnic market or specialty store. Here are some tips to help you source what you need.

- Locate an Asian enclave near your home. If there are no designated areas, such as Little India, Chinatown, or Koreatown, check the yellow pages for ethnic grocers and shops, and try to find a common neighborhood or street where there are a number of them. Then mine the businesses and restaurants.

- Query people in the know, such as restaurant chefs, owners, and wait staff, about their favorite shops.

- Do not limit yourself to specific ethnic markets for specific ingredients. Many markets nowadays cater to a pan-Asian clientele, and their inventory is often well stocked for East, Southeast, and South Asian cuisines.

- Go beyond Asian markets. Visit Latin, Middle Eastern, and Caribbean grocers. Peruse health food stores and the international or Asian food aisle at mainstream supermarkets, too.

- Surf the Internet and pose questions at culinary message boards, such as egullet.com and Asian food blogs.

- Purchase from online retailers, if local sources are limited. Suggestions include:

  Gourmetsleuth (Los Gatos, CA)
  Gourmetsleuth.com
  Tortilla press, woks, steamers, coconut graters, and coconut scrapers

  Grocery Thai (Los Angeles, CA)
  Grocerythai.com
  Thai rice flour, tapioca starch, frozen *pandan* leaves

  Indomart (Loma Linda, CA)
  Indomart.us
  Search, using foreign terms, for Indonesian ingredients, such as *gula jawa* palm sugar, and *kemiri* candlenuts

  Kalustyan's (New York, NY)
  Kalustyans.com
  Spices, fresh curry leaves, and many kinds of flours and starches

  Temple of Thai (Carroll, IA)
  Templeofthai.com
  Southeast Asian ingredients, equipment, and cookbooks

  Wok Shop (San Francisco, CA)
  Wokshop.com
  Woks, steamers, and many other kinds of cooking equipment

For additional resources, check Asiandumplingtips.com.

Selected Bibliography

The works listed here helped me to explore Asian food culture, research ingredients, and crystallize my own dumpling-making techniques. Their authors provided insights that shaped the contents of this book, and I am grateful for those contributions.

Anderson, E. N. *The Food of China.* New Haven: Yale University Press, 1988.

Andoh, Elizabeth. *Washoku: Recipes from the Japanese Home Kitchen.* Berkeley: Ten Speed Press, 2005.

Association of Nepalis in the Americas. *The Nepal Cookbook.* Ithaca, NY: Snow Lion Publications, 1996.

Blonder, Ellen Leong. *Dim Sum: The Art of Chinese Tea Lunch.* New York: Clarkson Potter, 2002.

Chan, Chen Hei. *Dim Sum: Traditional Favourites and Innovative Creations.* Singapore: Marshall Cavendish Cuisine, 2005.

Chang, K. C., ed. *Food in Chinese Culture: Anthropological and Historical Perspectives.* New Haven: Yale University Press, 1977.

Choi, Kitty. *Foundation Dim Sum Making.* Hong Kong: Food Paradise Publishing Co., 2004.

Cooks Illustrated. *The New Best Recipe.* Brookline, MA: America's Test Kitchen, 2004.

Cost, Bruce. *Asian Ingredients.* New York: Quill, 2000.

Davidson, Alan. *The Oxford Companion to Food.* Oxford: Oxford University Press, 1999.

Hiremath, Laxmi. *The Dance of Spices: Classic Indian Cooking for Today's Home Kitchen.* Hoboken, NJ: John Wiley & Sons, Inc., 2005.

Huang, Su-Huei. *Chinese Snacks, Revised.* Monterey Park, CA: Wei-Chuan Publishing, 1985.

Iyer, Raghavan. *Betty Crocker's Indian Home Cooking.* Hoboken, NJ: Wiley Publishing, Inc., 2001.

Jaffrey, Madhur. *An Invitation to Indian Cooking.* New York: Vintage Books, 1975.

Jelani, Rohani. *Malaysian Cakes & Desserts.* Singapore: Periplus Editions, 2001.

King, Niloufer Ichaporia. *My Bombay Kitchen: Traditional and Modern Parsi Home Cooking.* Berkeley: University of California Press, 2007.

Knechtges, David R. "A Literary Feast: Food in Early Chinese Literature." *Journal of the American Oriental Society* 106, no.1 (1986): 49–63.

Kongpan, Sisamon. *The Best of Thai Cuisine.* Bangkok: Sangdad Publishing, 2004.

Kuo, Irene. *The Key to Chinese Cooking.* New York: Alfred A. Knopf, 1977.

Lee, Cecilia Hae-Jin. *Eating Korean: From Barbecue to Kimchi, Recipes from My Home.* Hoboken, NJ: John Wiley & Sons, 2005.

Lee, Hwa Lin. *Chinese Dim Sum*. Monterey Park, CA: Wei-Chuan Publishing, 1990.

Lin, Florence. *Florence Lin's Complete Book of Chinese Noodles, Dumplings and Breads*. New York: William Morrow and Company, Inc., 1986.

Lo, Eileen Yin-Fei. *The Dim Sum Book: Classic Recipes from the Chinese Teahouse*. New York: Crown Publishers, Inc., 1982.

McGee, Harold. *On Food and Cooking: The Science and Lore of the Kitchen*. New York: Scribner, 1984, 2004.

Nguyen, Andrea. *Into the Vietnamese Kitchen: Treasured Foodways, Modern Flavors*. Berkeley: Ten Speed Press, 2006.

Nordin, Norsailina. *Malay Kuih*. Singapore: Marshall Cavendish Cuisine, 2008.

Ong, Pichet, and Genevieve Ko. *The Sweet Spot: Asian-Inspired Desserts*. New York: William Morrow, 2007.

Oseland, James. *Cradle of Flavor: Home Cooking from the Spice Islands of Indonesia, Malaysia, and Singapore*. New York: W. W. Norton & Company, 2006.

Polushkin, Maria. *The Dumpling Cookbook*. New York: Workman, 1977.

Sahni, Julie. *Classic Indian Cooking*. New York: William A. Morrow, 1980.

Shimbo, Hiroko. *The Japanese Kitchen: 250 Recipes in a Traditional Spirit*. Cambridge: Harvard Common Press, 2000.

Simonds, Nina. *Classic Chinese Cuisine*. Shelburne, VT: Chapters Publishing, Ltd., 1994.

Tan, Terry, and Christopher Tan. *Shiok! Exciting Tropical Asian Flavors*. Singapore: Periplus, 2003.

Teoh, Debbie. *Underwraps! Recipes for Juicy Rolls, Tasty Parcels and Delicate Dumplings*. Singapore: Marshall Cavendish Cuisine, 2005.

Trang, Corinne. *Essentials of Asian Cuisine: Fundamentals and Favorite Recipes*. New York: Simon & Schuster, 2003.

Tropp, Barbara. *The Modern Art of Chinese Cooking*. New York: Hearst Books, 1982.

Wangmo, Tsering, and Zara Houshmand. *The Lhasa Moon Tibetan Cookbook*. Ithaca, NY: Snow Lion Publications, 1999.

Young, Grace. *The Wisdom of the Chinese Kitchen: Classic Family Recipes for Celebration and Healing*. New York: Simon & Schuster Editions, 1999.

Acknowledgments

Dumplings are one of my all-time favorite foods, and I am delighted to have the opportunity to write this book. Many thanks to Lorena Jones for championing the concept at Ten Speed Press, and for passing the project on to Aaron Wehner and Clancy Drake. Clancy, you're an exceptional editor, and I'm grateful for your guidance and instincts.

Publishing is a team effort and this work greatly benefited from the expertise of copyeditor Andrea Chesman, proofreader Leslie Evans, creative director Nancy Austin, designer Betsy Stromberg, illustrator Ann Miya, indexer Ken Della Penta, and publicist Kristin Casemore. Many others at Ten Speed Press contributed their time and energy, and I very much appreciate their support.

The engaging photos represent the hard work of three talented people, photographer Penny De Los Santos, food stylist Karen Shinto, and prop stylist Natalie Hoelen. It was a pleasure to collaborate and eat the sets with you!

While writing the manuscript, I was amazed by the number of friends and colleagues who shared my enthusiasm for Asian dumplings. Recipe testers Mare Anderson, Lillian Chou, Alex Ciepley, Victor Fong, Georgia Freedman, Sue Holt, Doug Jeffery, Susan McCombs, Al Meyers, Candace Moyer, Susan Pi, Karen Shinto, Makiko Tsuzuki, and Lea Yancey volunteered to refine the instructions and flavors.

Many others generously lent their culinary knowledge and contacts, took me on dumpling crawls, and steered me toward the right direction. I'm especially indebted to James Oseland, Christopher Tan, Elizabeth Andoh, Cherie Barkey, Carl Chu, Todd Coleman, Jay Dautcher, Robyn Eckhardt, Divinia Esperanza, David Hagerman, Joel Hung, Joyce Jue, Ruta Kahate, Niloufer King, Nancie McDermott, and Jarrett Wrisley.

My mother, Tuyet Thi Nguyen, instilled in me a love of food and cooking. She taught me to be observant, disciplined, and curious in the kitchen. As I polished the recipes, she was the happy beneficiary of any dumpling that I could freeze and transport to her home in Southern California (a seven-hour drive from mine).

Finally, I am most thankful to my husband, Rory O'Brien, for his unending patience as I obsessed about dough texture, cooking techniques, fillings, and shapes. Thank you for indulging me and being the best life partner.

Index